Competency-Based Education for Professional Psychology

Competency-Based Education for Professional Psychology

Edited by Mary Beth Kenkel and Roger L. Peterson

American Psychological Association
Washington, DC

Published by
American Psychological Association
750 First Street, NE
Washington, DC 20002
www.apa.org

To order
APA Order Department
P.O. Box 92984
Washington, DC 20090-2984
Tel: (800) 374-2721; Direct: (202) 336-5510
Fax: (202) 336-5502; TDD/TTY: (202) 336-6123
Online: www.apa.org/books/
E-mail: order@apa.org

In the U.K., Europe, Africa, and the Middle East, copies may be ordered from
American Psychological Association
3 Henrietta Street
Covent Garden, London
WC2E 8LU England

Typeset in Goudy by Stephen McDougal, Mechanicsville, MD

Printer: Maple-Vail Books, York, PA
Cover Designer: Watermark Design, Alexandria, VA
Technical/Production Editor: Kathryn Funk

Library of Congress Cataloging-in-Publication Data

Competency-based education for professional psychology / edited by Mary Beth Kenkel and Roger L. Peterson.
    p. cm.
  Includes bibliographical references and index.
  ISBN-13: 978-1-4338-0458-8
  ISBN-10: 1-4338-0458-1
  1. Psychology—Study and teaching (Graduate)—United States. 2. Competency-based education—United States. I. Kenkel, Mary Beth. II. Peterson, Roger L., 1944- III. American Psychological Association.

  BF80.7.U6C66 2010
  150.71'173—dc22
                                       2009004650

British Library Cataloguing-in-Publication Data
A CIP record is available from the British Library.

Printed in the United States of America
First Edition

CONTENTS

CONTRIBUTORS

Jules C. Abrams, PhD, ABPP, Widener University, Chester, PA

Tamara L. Anderson, PhD, Biola University, La Mirada, CA

Jeffrey E. Barnett, PsyD, ABPP, independent practice, Arnold, MD, and Loyola College in Maryland, Baltimore

Jeffrey L. Binder, PhD, ABPP, Argosy University, Atlanta, GA

Kathi A. Borden, PhD, Antioch University New England, Keene, NH

Clark D. Campbell, PhD, George Fox University, Newburg, OR

Raymond E. Crossman, PhD, The Adler School, Chicago, IL

James E. Dobbins, PhD, Wright State University, Dayton, OH

Kelly Ducheny, PsyD, Howard Brown Health Center, Chicago, IL

Michael Horowitz, PhD, The Chicago School of Professional Psychology, Chicago, IL

Mary Beth Kenkel, PhD, Florida Institute of Technology, Melbourne

Robert A. King II, PsyD, Forest Institute, Springfield, MO

Marcie Kirkup, Forest Institute, Springfield, MO

Radhika Krishnamurthy, PsyD, Florida Institute of Technology, Melbourne

Jeffrey M. Lating, PhD, Loyola College in Maryland, Baltimore

Kathleen A. Malloy, PhD, ABPP, Wright State University, Dayton, OH

Lorraine Mangione, PhD, Antioch University New England, Keene, NH

E. John McIlvried, PhD, University of Indianapolis, Indianapolis, IN

Lavita Nadkarni, PhD, University of Denver, Denver, CO

Donald R. Peterson, PhD, Rutgers University, New Brunswick, NJ

Roger L. Peterson, PhD, ABPP, Antioch University New England, Keene, NH

Gargi Roysircar, PhD, Antioch University New England, Keene, NH

Christine N. Runyan, PhD, Forest Institute, Springfield, MO

Mark E. Skrade, PsyD, Forest Institute, Springfield, MO

Mark Stanton, PhD, ABPP, Azusa Pacific University, Azusa, CA

George Stricker, PhD, Argosy University—Washington, DC, Arlington, VA

Steven J. Trierweiler, PhD, University of Michigan and independent practice, Ann Arbor

Fredrick S. Wechsler, PhD, PsyD, ABPP, Argosy University, Phoenix, AZ

LaPearl Logan Winfrey, PhD, Wright State University, Dayton, OH

Stephanie C. Wood, PhD, MHA, Forest Institute, Springfield, MO

Jed A. Yalof, PsyD, ABPP, Immaculata University, Immaculata, PA

Competency-Based Education for Professional Psychology

Competency-Based Education for Professional Psychology

Edited by Mary Beth Kenkel and Roger L. Peterson

American Psychological Association
Washington, DC

INTRODUCTION

MARY BETH KENKEL AND ROGER L. PETERSON

This book presents a model of professional psychology doctoral education and training that has been developed, augmented, and refined by the National Council of Schools and Programs of Professional Psychology (NCSPP) over more than 30 years. Whereas the model has particular relevance to the 81 professional schools/programs of NCSPP, its components and methods have applicability in many settings and organizations committed to the education, training, professional development, and regulation of professional psychologists. By presenting the model and engaging in the critically important conversations about the education of professional psychologists that occur in all types of settings across the country, we believe the book will be of value to all those interested in professional psychology education.

An examination and evaluation of professional psychology education is very timely. Over half of the clinical psychologists graduating each year come from professionally oriented doctoral programs in psychology. Therefore, the type of training those students receive has a tremendous impact. A professional psychology training model must prepare students for the dramatic changes in health care in the 21st century and the concurrent changes in the roles of professional psychologists. At the same time, the model has relevance for psychologists already in practice who are attempting to update their skills and knowledge for today's challenges.

Furthermore, the explication of the professional psychology educational model is particularly relevant given the American Psychological Association's (APA's) Commission on Accreditation's commitment to model-based accreditation. In this accreditation process, each doctoral, postdoctoral, and internship program is evaluated with reference to the training model that it has adopted. The training model may be one that has been developed and promulgated by a national professional psychology organization. This allows some diversity in educational models and practice while guaranteeing high standards that come with the development and scrutiny of a model by a national community of educators. This book provides a valuable service by presenting a coherent and reasoned explication of the professional psychology model and by presenting methods for implementing the model or some of its elements in different training settings. No other book is devoted to such a thorough articulation and in-depth discussion of a psychology doctoral training model.

The book is addressed to the community of psychologists involved with professional education, both within and beyond the boundaries of NCSPP. In addition to doctoral training programs, many predoctoral internships and postdoctoral programs, both those accredited and those seeking accreditation, use some form of the professional psychology training model and engage in training for many of the same competencies described in this book. The "local clinical scientist" as described in chapter 7 of this volume is among the most common training models cited and used by predoctoral clinical internships. In addition, those involved with the assessment, regulation, and professional development of psychologist practitioners will find within this volume the expected knowledge, skills, and attitudes (KSAs) of competent psychologists and ways to teach and evaluate them.

WHAT IS NCSPP?

Founded in 1976, NCSPP is an organization of professional schools and programs dedicated to the improvement and advancement of doctoral education and training in professional psychology. As of February 2009, NCSPP has 64 full members (i.e., those with accreditation by the APA) and 17 associate members (i.e., those with regional accreditation but not yet APA accredited). NCSPP has developed a tradition of holding focused annual conferences with presentations, discussion groups, and informal conversations with colleagues in structured groups and in less formal and more relaxed venues. It is through these meetings that the training model was developed and refined over the past 30 years.

NCSPP has taken the lead in developing a series of books on training. The first major national conference sponsored by NCSPP was Quality in

Professional Psychology Training (1981), and it resulted in the initial NCSPP volume (Callan, Peterson, & Stricker, 1986). The pivotal Standards and Evaluation in the Education and Training of Professional Psychologists Conference, the Mission Bay Conference, as it came to be known, took place in 1986. It was the first conference systematically designed to articulate a blueprint for professional psychology education and training models and resulted in the second NCSPP volume (Bourg et al., 1987) and an article in *American Psychologist* (Bourg, Bent, McHolland, & Stricker, 1989). The conference on Ethnic Diversification in Psychology Education and Training (1989) in Puerto Rico raised awareness of the need for ethnic diversification in all aspects of professional psychology education, training, and practice. From this conference came the third book in the NCSPP series (Stricker et al., 1990). A conference on women followed 2 years later. The conference on The Core Curriculum in Professional Psychology (1990) in San Antonio continued the work of articulating professional psychology models of education and training begun at Mission Bay and led to the fourth book in the NCSPP series (Peterson et al., 1992). This present volume builds upon that work and augments it with the further development of the model occurring in the conferences since 1990 (Peterson, 2008).

INTRODUCTION TO THE PROFESSIONAL PSYCHOLOGY EDUCATIONAL MODEL

The educational model developed by NCSPP uses a competency-based core curriculum, including seven competencies seen as essential for psychological practice. Each competency has major domains and consists of a set of KSAs that should be covered in the training program. Through a series of courses and other educational experiences that meet APA's Commission on Accreditation and licensing standards, the model stresses preparation for actual roles as practitioners in a variety of service delivery settings and encompasses a broadened view of psychology with a flexible epistemology and multiple ways of knowing. Perhaps one of the most unique components of the model is the delineation of how practitioners doing practice remain local clinical scientists doing disciplined inquiry. The model emphasizes many elements of practice, including the multiple roles of psychologists, the importance of attention to self as a professional psychologist and reflective practice, the centrality of practicum and internship training, and the necessity of systematic evaluation of student learning and program outcomes. The model acknowledges the social nature of professional psychology and the public responsibility of the profession to serve the larger society and gives special consideration to issues of ethnic, racial, gender, and other forms of diversity.

ORGANIZATION OF THE BOOK

The book is divided into four parts. Part I describes the professional psychology educational model in detail, spells out the professional core competencies, and discusses the philosophical underpinnings of the training model (chap. 1). Two aspects of the model are discussed further in separate chapters. Chapter 2 describes the origin of the competency model in professional psychology programs and how competency training is now being used to guide training and evaluation in other realms of professional psychology. Chapter 3 addresses the centrality of quality in professional psychology training and examines its meaning and potential threats to it.

Part II contains seven chapters, one on each of the competencies: relationship, assessment, intervention, research and evaluation, consultation and education, management and supervision, and diversity (chaps. 4–10, respectively). Each chapter contains a table summarizing the learning goals for different training levels, or developmental achievement levels (DALs). The three DALS are prepracticum level, preinternship level, and graduation level, and the learning goals include KSAs for each domain of the competency at each DAL. In addition, the chapters in Part II describe methods for teaching the competencies at different steps in the educational process.

Part III describes how to obtain, manage, enhance, and evaluate the resources needed to effectively implement the professional training model. Resources for providing quality psychological training are a result of effective advocacy, be it at the school/university level or with external agencies or funders. The advocacy chapter (chap. 11) provides information on how to enlist the support of others in the training mission as well as on the importance of teaching future psychologist practitioners (i.e., students) how to advocate for better funding of psychological services. Clinical training opportunities at external placements as well as at the program's psychological service center are critical proving grounds for students' emerging clinical skills and important program resources. Chapters 12 and 13 describe how to build these experiences so that they are of high quality and integral to the teaching and evaluation of professional psychology competencies. Other key resources are the faculty and administrators in professional psychology programs. Chapter 14 describes one of their critically important roles—the mentoring of students into professional activities; chapter 15 describes the characteristics, activities, and values of faculty and administrators that are vital to the success of the training mission.

Part IV, which consists of the concluding chapter (chap. 16), looks to the future and how the professional psychology educational model will need to evolve in response to emerging societal needs, changing client demographics, and new opportunities for practicing psychologists. The ability of the model and programs to be responsive to these changes and the process for making changes are described.

We want to acknowledge the work of all who have participated in the conferences and deliberations of the NCSPP over the past 30 years. It is through their commitment, thoughtful discussions, and intense efforts that the professional psychology education model was developed and refined. We also thank the chapter authors for consolidating, interpreting, and expanding on the NCSPP work and model and explaining how the model comes to life in the day-to-day work of educators and practitioners. We feel honored to have a role in bringing this work to a broader audience and know that by our doing so the field of psychology and the clients we serve will be better for it.

REFERENCES

Bourg, E. F., Bent, R. J., Callan, J. E., Jones, N. F., McHolland, J. D., & Stricker, G. (1987). *Standards and evaluation in the education and training of professional psychologists: Knowledge, attitudes, and skills.* Norman, OK: Transcript Press.

Bourg, E. F., Bent, R. J., McHolland, J. D., & Stricker, G. (1989). Standards and evaluation in the education and training of professional psychologists: The National Council of Schools of Professional Psychology Mission Bay Conference. *American Psychologist, 44,* 66–72.

Callan, J. E., Peterson, D. R., & Stricker, G. (1986). *Quality in professional psychology training: A national conference and self-study.* Norman, OK: Transcript Press.

Peterson, R. L. (Ed.). (2008). National Council of Schools and Programs of Professional Psychology integrated resolutions through 1996. Retrieved February 20, 2009, from http://www.ncspp.info/NCSPPResolutionsthrough1996.pdf

Peterson, R. L., McHolland, J., Bent, R. J., Davis-Russell, E., Edwall, G. E., Magidson, E., et al. (Eds.). (1992). *The core curriculum in professional psychology.* Washington, DC: American Psychological Association and National Council of Schools of Professional Psychology.

Stricker, G., Davis-Russell, E., Bourg, E., Duran, E., Hammond, W. R., McHolland, J., et al. (1990). *Toward ethnic diversification in psychology education and training.* Washington, DC: American Psychological Association.

I

OVERVIEW

1

THE NATIONAL COUNCIL OF SCHOOLS AND PROGRAMS OF PROFESSIONAL PSYCHOLOGY EDUCATIONAL MODEL 2009

ROGER L. PETERSON, DONALD R. PETERSON, JULES C. ABRAMS, GEORGE STRICKER, AND KELLY DUCHENY

Since 1976 the National Council of Schools and Programs of Professional Psychology (NCSPP) has devoted itself to the deliberate, systematic, reflective examination of standards for the education and training of professional psychologists by means of a series of annual conferences. Each of the conferences has had a particular focus, and each is responding to changes in the profession and in society. In a process initiated in 1989 (e.g., R. L. Peterson et al., 1992), NCSPP produced a statement on education and training in professional psychology (R. L. Peterson, D. R. Peterson, Abrams, & Stricker, 1997) that would greatly influence NCSPP's understanding of its own educational model and help launch the profession into the 21st century. That paper, to a substantial degree, was based on a series of integrated resolutions from the organization that were brought together in crafting its educational model as well as the rationale and conceptualization of NCSPP's competencies and a description of the five central components of the model.

Drawn from a number of of the NCSPP conferences, the resolutions on education and training have been edited and presented in a coherent fashion. The integrated resolutions as a whole, previously unpublished, now appear on the NCSPP Web site (R. L. Peterson, 2008). The original 1997 paper has become known as the "NCSPP model paper" (R. L. Peterson et al., 1997). It has been systematically updated and provides the basis for this chapter.

Founded in 1976, NCSPP is an organization of professional schools and programs in psychology whose central mission is the progressive improvement, enhancement, and enrichment of professional psychology education and training. This chapter summarizes NCSPP's philosophy, or model of education in professional psychology, as distilled from the integrated resolutions (R. L. Peterson, 2008). Some of the history of NCSPP also appears in the NCSPP model paper (R. L. Peterson et al., 1997) and is summarized to an earlier point in time by Stricker and Cummings (1992) and by D. R. Peterson (1968, 1976, 1997). The definition of NCSPP's model is consistent with the requirement by the American Psychological Association's (APA's) Committee on Accreditation (APA Office of Program Consultation and Accreditation, 2007) that programs identify an educational model that has a "clearly specified philosophy of education and training . . . appropriate to the science and practice of psychology" (p. 5); and that the chosen model "may be one identified through a national conference of psychologists, from which guidelines for professional education and training have been approved by the delegates" (p. 6; cf. Belar & Perry, 1991; Korman, 1976).

EDUCATIONAL MODEL

In elaborating on the educational paradigm described by NCSPP in the integrated resolutions, the following five central components are addressed: (a) a broadened view of psychology, with a flexible epistemology, multiple ways of knowing, and a delineation of how practitioners *doing practice* remain *local clinical scientists* doing *disciplined inquiry*; (b) a description of the pedagogy of integrative experiences; (c) the professional core competencies and the requirements of a competency-based core curriculum in which practical and scientific knowledge, skills, and attitudes (KSAs) are integrated; (d) elements of practice—including multiple roles, the self of the professional psychologist and reflective practice, practicum and internship training, and systematic evaluation; and (e) the social nature of professional psychology and the public responsibility of the profession to serve the larger society, with special consideration of issues related to diversity in all its manifestations. We also discuss the model's implications for professional psychology.

Psychological Science and Education for Professional Psychology

Over the years, the most serious controversies and misunderstandings surrounding the NCSPP model have concerned the role of science in the education of professional psychologists (e.g., Bieshke, Fouad, Collins, & Halonen, 2004; Dawes, 1994; Hays, 1986; Hoshmand & Polkinghorne, 1992; McFall, 1991, 1996; Messer, 2004; D. R. Peterson, 1985, 1991, 1996a, 1996b; Stricker, 1992, 1997; Stricker & Trierweiler, 1995; Trierweiler, 1987; Trierweiler & Stricker, 1998). All professional psychologists, whether PhD or PsyD, are to be scientifically educated and trained in all aspects of their education, not just when they are conducting research or evaluation. NCSPP itself may have contributed to this misunderstanding by including much of its thinking about science, which in fact referred to a "metaperspective" on scientific training, primarily in discussions and text addressing the research and evaluation competency. In light of the enormous importance and widespread discussion of the science-practice issues throughout the psychological community, the NCSPP perspective merits detailed presentation.

Rigorous professional activity has traditionally been conceived as the application of scientific knowledge developed through laboratory experiments or controlled field research to the understanding and solution of human problems. In NCSPP's educational model, practitioners engage the challenge of the human condition directly. Starting with the needs of each client, the NCSPP educational model requires that practitioners bring the best available theoretical conceptions, the most useful available research, and their individual and collective professional experience to bear in studying and improving the functional condition of the client. Professional activity is not the application of knowledge derived from a separate scientific research process; it is a form of science and, indeed, a form of research in and of itself. The process of professional work has been described as "reflection-in-action" by Schön (1983, 1987) and as "disciplined inquiry" by D. R. Peterson (1991, 1995, 1996b). The role of the professional psychologist is that of the "local clinical scientist" (Stricker & Trierweiler, 1995; Trierweiler & Stricker, 1992, 1998). The properly trained professional psychologist is a scientist in the same sense that the skilled physician is a local clinical, biological scientist, and the skilled engineer a local physical scientist. This vision has much in common with that of Bieshke et al.'s (2004) view of the "scientifically minded psychologist."

Of course, as the integrated resolutions say, the education for professional psychologists continues to include the following KSAs:

(a) designing and critiquing approaches to systematic inquiry, using qualitative and quantitative methods; (b) analyzing data, using statistics, both descriptive and inferential, univariate and multivariate, as well as methods appropriate to qualitative data; (c) conducting a scholarly project on

a meaningful problem, typically associated with professional practice in psychology, with a strategy of disciplined inquiry appropriate to the problem. (R. L. Peterson, 2008, p. 16)

Nevertheless, the shift in viewpoint toward the local clinical scientist model endorsed by the NCSPP educational model carries profound implications for the education of professional psychologists. Instead of mandating nomothetic dissertation research that contributes to general scientific knowledge as the central requirement of scientific education and training for all practitioners, the local clinical scientist model allows for situations and issues encountered by practicing professional psychologists to be examined in the course of graduate study as exercises in disciplined inquiry.

An exercise in disciplined inquiry might focus on the following situation: A small group of psychologists observe that parenting training has been underdeveloped in their semirural community and that such training could coordinate well with the therapy of a number of clients and with other community programs. The psychologists then pose several questions. What is in the literature about such training?—What are programs like, are they effective, and do they apply to our situation? What populations will this training serve? Will it serve lower-middle, middle, upper-middle class? What ethnicities? Which kinds of programs should be directed to which groups? How do subgroup expectations and outcomes differ? Which current clients could attend? Would attendance be in addition to or instead of therapy? Who can or will pay—insurance, hospitals, big HMOs, clients, community funds? What will the potential psychoeducational group leaders need to do to prepare themselves? How can the program get the support of different, often competing agencies, practitioners, and professions? Have there been particular events in the community that make these services appropriate now (e.g., a suicide in the high school, crimes by juveniles)?

Of the necessary information, what is not available and therefore must be collected in a disciplined, though inexpensive, way? What are the relevant outcome variables, and how can relevant data be collected? In a way that parallels what professional psychologists do in such situations, students would be trained to engage in conversations over time that cycle through presenting, discussing, reading, and analyzing the available literature, creating a plan to capture needed data, speaking with important stakeholders in the community, receiving feedback, and creating and evaluating potential solutions.

Within NCSPP, programs have taken an array of positions regarding the type of scholarly products integral to scientific education, ranging from requiring relatively small, clinically oriented doctoral projects to requiring dissertations of the level and quality that might be found in traditional PhD programs. Those programs that require dissertations usually emphasize an applied focus that embodies a broader array of investigative approaches and a wider range of dissertation topics—all of which demonstrate an omnipresent

emphasis on disciplined inquiry as basic to clinical education. Types of dissertations may include the following: (a) theoretical analyses; (b) surveys; (c) analyses of archival data; (d) outcome research, including program development and evaluation; (e) systematic qualitative investigations; (f) public policy and legislative analysis; (g) case studies; and (h) group-based nomothetic investigations. (See also R. L. Peterson & Trierweiler, 1999.)

Following graduation and throughout their careers, all practitioners are expected to retain a pervasive, deeply ingrained scientific outlook. A substantial number of graduates will take on the sorts of applied research listed. Some will conduct professionally relevant, generalizable, applied research, and a few will devote themselves to the traditional forms of research that preoccupy the faculties of most research universities. In a general way, these outcomes are not substantially different from those produced by traditional training models. The difference is that career expectations and educational experiences in the NCSPP model are designed to match the realities of professional work in communities—as closely as these realities are now known and as clearly as they can be foreseen for the years ahead. These realities only rarely arise from traditional versions of the disciplinary core or from preparation for careers in academic research—careers that are unlikely to be available to the great majority of graduates, regardless of the program type.

The Practitioner as Local Clinical Scientist

The integrated resolutions (R. L. Peterson, 2008) articulate the ways in which practitioners doing practice remain scientific:

> Professional psychologists systematically acquire and organize information about psychological phenomena and often engage in the general practice of science. This requires selection, modification, and construction of the most rigorous attainable methods for investigating the local conditions with which each inquiry is concerned. Nonetheless, it is recognized that, because of the particular conditions that frequently limit inquiry in the local contexts of professional psychological practice (e.g., nonrepeatability of phenomena in time, privacy), the scientific goals of consensual verifiability, replicability, and universal communicability are attainable more in principle than in practice. (p. 15)

NCSPP adopted Trierweiler and Stricker's (1992; Stricker & Trierweiler, 1995; Trierweiler & Stricker, 1998) vision of local clinical scientists who are

> critical investigators of local (as opposed to universal) realities (a) who are knowledgeable of research, scholarship, personal experience, and scientific methodology; and (b) who are able to develop plausible, communicable formulations for understanding essentially local phenomena using theory, general world knowledge including scientific research, and most important, their own abilities as skeptical scientific observers. (Trierweiler & Stricker, 1992, p. 104)

"Therefore, research training in professional psychology should be viewed as essential for developing and enhancing critical thinking in students, and it should be integrated throughout the curriculum" (R. L. Peterson, 2008, pp. 15–16). "Skills in local investigation and in problem solving (thinking on one's feet) assume unusual importance" (Trierweiler, 1992, p. 10). According to Trierweiler (1992),

> The guiding metaphor becomes a Sherlock Holmes or a Jane Marple standing in direct confrontation with the constraints, mysteries, banalities, and surprises of unique realities, rather than the distant, conservative, skeptical, and abstractly speculative university-based scientist most of us have struggled with in our professional identities. (pp. 10–11)

The clinical supervision of the local clinical scientist should be marked by the repeated use of two questions. The first question is: How do you know? This question directs the student to examine assumptions, to think beyond absolute received truths, and to seek evidence. The second question is: Does it apply? This question emphasizes the need to apply generalizations to the local situation in a thoughtful and discriminating way. Both questions emphasize the tension between aggregate findings and individual exemplars. The careful weighing of evidence from various sources and the considerations inherent in applying the general to the unique are the hallmarks of the local clinical scientist. Though the goals and forms of scientific training in professional programs differ from those in traditional programs, rigorous scientific training is equally important in both models of education.

Following is a composite clinical vignette that, for brevity, reports little of the usual inquiry about personal and family history and the length, depth, and breadth of the concerns and symptoms that brought the client to the psychologist. This portrayal emphasizes diversity as well as economic and local concerns in clinical work.

> Marie is a 48-year-old divorced woman of French-Canadian ethnicity experiencing depression and anxiety across many areas of her life. "Worrying, worrying, always worrying," she says. She gets angry at small things and physically "doesn't feel right." Everything seems to have some sort of problem connected with it. Marie manages a small family-owned grocery store in semirural New Hampshire, taken over from and for her partially retired parents, who still call her Marie-Claire. Her parents don't have much for retirement beyond their house, the store, and Social Security. Her dad has type 2 diabetes and seems to have some serious symptoms, though Marie does not yet understand their potential consequences. Both parents "drink more wine than they should." She is worried for the store's future because a huge, big-city chain grocery store is coming to town within a few miles. Divorced for a decade, Marie is beginning to "date" her ex-husband, Jacques, who at 56 has said that he is now too old for the "wandering ways I used to have." He runs a small sawmill that Marie thinks "does OK." His old friends and coworkers call him Frenchy not

because he has an accent, but because his dad had a bit of one and they called him Frenchy. Recently, Marie has found herself going back to the Catholic church, the same parish she left when she "threw Jacques out" a few years before the divorce. Their 19-year-old son, John (only the family calls him Jack) is a sophomore attending the local state college and living at home. Marie thinks he, too, is depressed and is just barely staying above academic disaster. Referred after being convinced by an acquaintance, Marie has no one in her family or among her close friends who has ever seen a psychologist. She's not quite clear about what she and the clinician are supposed to do. Questions about her current psychological state and how she functioned over the past 10 years indicate that Marie seems to be dealing with things reasonably well, although she worries that she is nearing her "breaking point."

No doubt, any scientifically trained clinician would immediately think about the evidence-based cognitive and interpersonal treatments for depression, along with those for anxiety. In addition, possible issues surrounding menopause merit further discussion. If Marie had a family doctor she trusted, there probably should be an immediate referral to this doctor for examination (if a gynecologist were not available) and perhaps for antidepressant medication. Yet, what should the clinician do when Marie says, "But I don't like him, he doesn't listen, spends almost no time with me, and has to remind himself of my name by looking at the chart. I don't have any other doctors. My HMO is awful"?

Already in the vignette are manifestations of the Holmes–Marple metaphor. The clinician's general knowledge (and perhaps intuition or orientation?) supplies the initial leads that move toward the world rather than intrapsychic material: From the local newspapers, the clinician knows that many big, new grocery stores have come into southern New Hampshire, and the result has been to force out of business small family markets that have been located for years in tiny New England villages. Does this information apply? If so, Marie's economic worries are likely to be real, perhaps even more serious than she thinks. From the clinician's knowledge of local history comes information about the French-Canadian immigrants' movement to New Hampshire. Some came to work in the then thriving New Hampshire mills, as a result of the economic situation in Canada about the time when Marie's grandparents were young adults. Given that history, does the potential economic failure of the store have special family meaning, given that such a business was likely to have been the essence of security earlier in the century? Or is this inappropriately applying a stereotype?

What needs to be known about Catholicism, particularly Marie's version, and the meaning of her divorce in this context and, again in the context, apparently, of Jacques' affairs, and what does it mean to her to be going back to her church? What about the possibility of her renewing the relationship with Jacques?—Is this a beneficial reconciliation, loneliness, wishful

thinking? Are gender issues relevant? What is happening to John? Is he experiencing a minor identity crisis, only a sophomore slump, or something more serious? How much of this is Marie's depressed point of view? What is it like for students like John who live at home to attend this particular college, which is 25 miles away? What psychological resources for referrals for John are available in the community or at the college?

What about the health of Marie's parents: Is her dad in medical danger from the complications of diabetes?; Are her parents alcoholics?; What health care resources are available to them? What role regarding her parents' health does Marie feel she wants to play or feel obliged to play? Is this really a family or couples case? If so, who among the many possibilities are the people who should meet with one another? If an adult development perspective is applied, how does it change the clinician's conclusions? There are the usual practical concerns as well: What will her health insurance pay for? Given her financial situation, what can she afford? What other supportive or psychoeducational community resources are available? Given her lack of experience with psychotherapy, what does Marie expect? Does she imagine a five- to eight-session treatment, typical across the country, and who is supposed to say what to whom?

Of course, this list of issues and concerns to be addressed by the local clinical scientist would be much longer and clearer if an actual report of the initial conversation about symptoms, diagnosis, treatment, and relevant data had been portrayed here. This broadened line of inquiry not only helps psychologists understand Marie more deeply and richly, it also strongly encourages a treatment plan that includes a greater emphasis on a stress-coping approach and that literature. To conduct even this initial interview in a meaningful fashion, the local clinical scientist needs to know and systematically include a substantial amount of relevant local knowledge, in addition to that associated primarily with professional psychology.

Multiple Ways of Knowing

To paraphrase the integrated resolutions (R. L. Peterson, 2008), the broadened educational domain of professional psychology (e.g., its theories, research methods, and applications) is characterized by scholarly, disciplined thought that is grounded in science, the humanities, and personal and professional experience and is enhanced by interdisciplinary perspectives and a broad-based array of continually developing methods. Reflexive professional psychology requires critical analysis of the theories that guide disciplined inquiry and the methods through which investigations are conducted. Study of the philosophical foundations of inquiry, including, for example, epistemological and theoretical assumptions and implicit values (e.g., D. R. Peterson & Peterson, 1997) and the associated ethical issues, are therefore important in the education of professional psychologists.

The epistemological basis of disciplined inquiry in psychology must be comprehensive; responsive to wide-ranging, diverse, and fluid social contexts; and cognizant of invariably embedded values. This condition requires multiple ways of knowing that inform and enrich each other and that are appropriate and sensitive to the diverse populations to which they are applied. These ways of knowing include an enhanced array of methods drawn from related fields of inquiry—quantitative and qualitative, objective and subjective. Methods and formulations that increase understanding of women's issues and of diversity are stressed more strongly than they have been in the past.

As shown in the vignette, to get a more complete clinical view of Marie, the necessary multiple ways of knowing require integrating material from the traditional scientific psychology knowledge base (including psychopathology, treatment approaches and outcomes, development, gender issues) with some basic medical information about menopause and diabetes; a knowledge of the local economic circumstances and available resources (as drawn from regional newspapers as well as general conversations and experiences); some history and relevant local historical narratives; knowledge about a local ethnic culture; a reasonably sophisticated understanding of a particular religion; and, of course, the economic and service delivery issues surrounding managed care—all working together in the context of a psychologist–client relationship. Though any particular list differs from situation to situation and from client to client, the work of professional psychologists inevitably requires multiple sources of data, collected in ways consistent with a variety of epistemologies (cf. D. R. Peterson & Peterson, 1997).

In their roles as researchers, professional psychologists need explicit educational experiences to become self-critical with respect to the methodological, sociopolitical, and philosophical implications of inquiry. The integrative, reflective, educational experiences, described next as a central element of the NCSPP pedagogy, are just as relevant for the role of researcher as they are for the role of clinician. Conclusions should be carefully consistent with the limits of research designs, and particular consideration should be given to the likelihood of negative impact on underserved populations.

These positions, which may seem on the surface to be no more than bland ecumenical clichés, have general as well as clinical consequences. The areas of knowledge seen as relevant to professional psychology are greatly expanded. There is a strong movement away from narrow and doctrinaire conceptualizations of psychological science toward perspectives that oblige methodological multiplicity (e.g., R. L. Peterson & Trierweiler, 1999). Epistemology and critical thinking become more central to professional psychology training. An appropriate scientific basis for professional psychology demands an openness to the other groups and disciplines who share psychologists' concerns in a manner that emerges as an enlarged argument for ecological

relevance. See also D. R. Peterson and Peterson (1997) for much greater detail.

Integrative Pedagogy

Even at this point in the portrayal of the NCSPP model, it is clear that the model necessitates a pedagogy of integrative experiences that are designed to educate students as local clinical scientists. To be more explicit, in this section we characterize the educational experiences and the contexts in which a conversation about a case like Marie's becomes part of a student's learning. Though not a focus of the integrated resolutions, pedagogical commonalties are implicit in many of NCSPP's writings, in conversations at meetings over the years, and in examples initially collected for this chapter. The integrative pedagogy of the NCSPP model can be seen as having the following seven aspects.

- *Academic–scientific materials, both research and theory, including general, relevant information.* Academic–scientific materials are used in combination with concepts and a process that facilitates local application (Stricker & Trierweiler, 1995; Trierweiler & Stricker, 1998). In a single learning experience, for example, materials might include critical discussions of information on a certain disorder, on possible treatments, on multiproblem clients and families, on ethical issues, on relevant issues of diversity, and on the economic realities of treatment, including the differences and contradictions that regularly appear in the literature.
- *Real examples and real experiences.* These include the instructor's cases, cases seen under supervision, and live demonstrations and videos of students, instructors, and other practitioners. Students have the opportunity to engage in the real phenomena of professional psychology practice, so that disciplined inquiry can arise initially out of attention to the phenomena, not to a research problem.
- *The development of each individual student as a professional psychologist, his or her professional self, in a reflective process.* This is described later in detail under "The Self of the Professional Psychologist and Reflection Practice."
- *Explicit discussion of relevant social issues, marginalization, power, and authority.* This is described later in detail in the section on "Social Responsibility, Diversity, and Gender."
- *The local, unique elements relevant to a particular client or professional situation.* This is exemplified in the case of Marie (e.g., D. R. Peterson & Peterson, 1997; Trierweiler and Stricker, 1998).

- *Faculty and supervisory role models.* Role models enthusiastically engage in those professional activities that mirror the experiences students will encounter in clinical training and in postgraduate practice.
- *Appropriate attitudes, including explicit ways of thinking like a psychologist.* Thinking like a psychologist is integrated such that it will permeate all professional work.

To take an example typical of many professional programs, an advanced student in a small group situation might present a diagnostic, conceptual, therapeutic, or ethical issue in a practicum case in light of the psychological literature for the feedback of the faculty leader and student colleagues. In such situations, the faculty person, and ultimately the students, should continually ask, What have you observed? Why did you do that? What were the client's reactions? What is it like for you to sit with this client? How are these issues viewed by people of the same gender, ethnicity, and culture as the client? What, therefore, does this mean? What are your assumptions? How does this fit with your deeply held beliefs? and, of course, What is the evidence for your position? or How do you know that? As a presented case unfolds over time, different psychological literature may become relevant along with an evolving focus on the practice dilemmas that arise when a client's situation goes beyond the available readings. In this way, participants become attuned to reflection and disciplined inquiry.

These integrative pedagogies have developed in an interesting variety of ways. All are designed to provide the best attainable professional service for each individual, group, or organizational case with which the students and faculty are concerned. Also, all are designed to be firmly embedded in the relevant scholarly knowledge, to reflexively educate the professional psychology graduate student, and to open doors that should lead to improved technologies and generalizable knowledge of relevance to the profession.

Core Curriculum and the Professional Core Competency Areas

NCSPP members developed an innovative way of thinking about the professional psychology core curriculum, which emphasizes competency over particular disciplinary content.

Brief History of the Core Competencies

Work leading to the development of the core competencies began when NCSPP took on an important sequence of new tasks in the early 1980s. The organization shifted away from its initial major concern, almost preoccupation, with accreditation issues, organizational issues (freestanding vs. university-based schools), and type of degree (PsyD vs. PhD) culminating in the 1980s with a self-study and moved toward creative and proactive work de-

signed to enhance the quality of practicing psychologists educated in professional programs (Stricker & Cummings, 1992). This new direction led to the development of the NCSPP vision of core competencies for curriculum design and ultimately to a way of conceptualizing activities in professional psychology (Bent & Peterson, 1998).

Around 1981, NCSPP embarked on the empirical survey of existing professional school programs. Seven major areas, seen as characterizing professional programs, including initial, tentative work on a core curriculum, were explored in a complex process that continued over 4 years. This self-study gave rise to the first major national conference sponsored by NCSPP as well as the first major publication of NCSPP, *Quality in Professional Psychology Training: A National Conference and Self-Study* (Callan, Peterson, & Stricker, 1986). One conclusion drawn by consensus from this work was that professional schools had much in common with the scientist-professional PhD programs, perhaps surprisingly much if they truly had different education and training objectives. It seemed clear that studying the differences between professional programs (in university-based and freestanding schools) was only a first step. Many thought it would be more productive to work toward developing a professional psychology education and training vision with common core KSAs (values) that had the outcome of producing competent practicing psychologists. This aspiration became a major focus of NCSPP over the next decades.

Bent (1986) created a basic conceptual structure for curriculum design that employed a quality assurance and program development format, stressing the importance of operational definitions with a focus upon the integration of a matrix of KSAs. This design served as a guideline for the organization of the 1986 NCSPP Conference, which resulted in the book *Standards and Evaluation in the Education and Training of Professional Psychologists: Knowledge, Attitudes, and Skills* (Bourg, Bent, McHolland, & Sticker, 1987). The pivotal Mission Bay Conference, as it came to be known, was the first conference systematically designed to articulate a blueprint for professional psychology education and training models (Bourg et al., 1989) and resulted in the second NCSPP volume (Bourg et al., 1987). The focus of the conference process was to delineate the KSAs that should characterize the practicing psychologist in the near future and the elements of the related NCSPP education and training programs that were to bring them to fruition. The concept of competencies emerged when a number of conference subgroups, separately dealing with particular aspects of KSAs, concluded that knowledge and skills could not be conceptually separated when enacted in practice. Furthermore, attitudes generally pervaded all professional activity and were a central influence in just about everything that characterizes professional psychologists. NCSPP members recognized that specific, identifiable KSAs are conceptually and pragmatically joined in the competencies. Once this integrating concept of competency combining KSAs was agreed on, a key con-

ference resolution specified that there should be a single, generic core curriculum in all professional programs and that core curriculum should be organized around core competency areas that represent key, related clusters of activities derived from and organized around an analysis of the social circumstances, needs, and demands of psychological practice—characteristics of what professional psychologists actually do. Scientific discipline-based and science-based knowledge was seen as an element of all the competencies rather than conceived as forming separate competencies or a separate scientific core. Bent and Jones (1987) and Bent and Cannon (1987) proposed the six competency areas that emerged as central to the current and future practice of psychology. Competency areas would be defined as functional expressions in practice of the coherent, distinguishable, though overlapping areas of KSAs characteristic of the practicing psychologist.

Several years later, the 1990 national conference in San Antonio, The Core Curriculum in Professional Psychology, continued the work of articulating the professional psychology model of education and training begun at Mission Bay and led to the fourth book in the NCSPP series (R. L. Peterson et al., 1992). The competency-based curriculum was a central focus (Weiss, 1992), and the six professional core curriculum areas were discussed in detail and defined. To bring these ideas together, evolving curricula were to be designed to combine practical and scientific knowledge with professional skills and attitudes to produce the outcome goal of a particular competency. The edited volume by R. L. Peterson et al. (1992) in its entirety provided the first, comprehensive, in-depth presentation of the competency-based approach to the core curriculum in practitioner programs that is at the heart of this chapter.

Logic for the Competency Approach

As has been said, specific, identifiable KSAs can be conceptually and pragmatically joined in the concept of competencies. They directly represent key, related clusters of activities derived from and organized around an analysis of the social circumstances, needs, and demands of psychological practice—characteristics of what professional psychologists actually do. Competencies can then be seen as the building blocks for more complex professional roles and for the vision of training for multiple roles. As was clear from the beginning, competencies can be operationally defined at various levels. In the beginning of the 21st century, the efforts involved in the Benchmarks conference and with the developmental achievement levels (DALs) build on this aspect of the conceptualization.

In the early 1990s, a number of groups and programs had thought about professional psychology in terms of competencies, either explicitly or implicitly. These groups and programs included the Joint Council on Professional Education in Psychology (JCPEP, 1990), the APA Office of Program Consultation and Accreditation (1996), Wright State School of Professional Psychology at both the basic and advanced level, and the

American Board of Professional Psychology (ABPP, 1993) at the specialty level. The APA Office of Program Consultation and Accreditation (1996) incorporated a version of the NCSPP core competencies as part of the required doctoral curriculum in the new version of the accreditation guidelines developed at that time, and it continues in the current *Guidelines and Principles* (APA Office of Program Consultation and Accreditation, 2007).

Contrasts With Traditional Approach to Curricula

The competency approach is in direct contrast to the traditional curricular emphasis on the accumulation of knowledge in particular disciplinary content areas (R. L. Peterson, 1992a, 1992b; Weiss, 1992). As is appropriate to the world of practice in contrast to the world of academia, the goal of professional education should be that competencies are available for practice and should go beyond the accumulation of knowledge. This is a major philosophical change from the historical approach to the core curriculum that was supposed to reflect the traditional areas in the discipline. In this older perspective, the research findings of university psychological science were thought to be narrowly applied by professional psychologists (R. L. Peterson, 1992a, 1992b). This view now seems outdated, oversimplified, and in several important ways, inaccurate (D. R. Peterson, 1991, 1995, 1996b; D. R. Peterson & Peterson, 1997). Schön (1983) argued convincingly that this concept of professional activity as applied science does not accurately represent the way experts in any of the fields he examined (architecture, engineering, business management, and town planning as well as psychotherapy) actually function in practice. For this reason, he replaced the idea of applied science with his concept of reflection-in-action—something NCSPP sees as an element of all competencies and an aspect of its pedagogy.

Professional Core Competency Areas

A comprehensive statement about the competencies was made in the original NCSPP model paper (R. L. Peterson et al., 1997) that is the foundation for the current chapter. The new versions detailed in the following subsections were created as parts of the developmental achievment levels (DALs), work products of the NCSPP January 2007 Developing Our Competencies in Clinical Training Conference. They include the original six competency areas plus diversity. These descriptions were developed as a part of a complex, multistep process of review and revision, which continued via the Internet long after the original meeting. They were finally approved as an element of the NCSPP model on August 15, 2007.

Relationship

Relationship is the capacity to develop and maintain a constructive working alliance with peers, colleagues, supervisors, members of other disci-

plines, consumers of services, and community organizations. The relationship competency is foundational to, and supportive of, all other competencies (Polite & Bourg, 1992) and is greatly impacted by students' "awareness and connection to their self-identity" (R. L. Peterson, 2008, p. 12). "It involves the whole person and thus may include intellectual, emotional, cognitive, physical, cultural, and spiritual aspects, as well as the context or environment surrounding the person" (NCSPP, 2007, p. 8). Attitudes essential for the relationship competency include, but are not limited to, (a) intellectual curiosity and flexibility, (b) open-mindedness, (c) belief in the capacity for change, (d) appreciation of individual and cultural difference, (e) personal integrity and honesty, and (f) belief in the value of self-awareness (R. L. Peterson, 2008). These attitudes can be seen as embedded in the pedagogy of integrative experiences described earlier.

The six domains of the relationship competency are (a) professional demeanor, (b) self–other, (c) interpersonal connection, (d) cultural adaptability, and (e) ethics.

> Professional demeanor includes issues of boundaries, role comfort and courtesy. The self domain concerns issues of self-awareness and self-understanding, which is extended in the domain of other to an understanding and appreciation of varied individuals. Interpersonal connection deals with relational facets such as perspective taking, communication, and negotiation. Cultural adaptability addresses the importance of appreciating individual and cultural differences and acquiring the relevant knowledge, skills, and attitudes in training. Ethics involves respect and care, but also legal and ethical standards. (NCSPP, 2007, p. 9)

Assessment

Psychological assessment is a complex, integrative, and conceptual activity (Krishnamurthy et al., 2004) that involves making inferences from multiple sources of information to achieve a comprehensive understanding of a client or client system. It involves the ability to "measure and formulate degree of need and mental status, develop psychological profiles in response to particular referral problems, and evaluate outcome with tests" (NCSPP, 2007, pp. 3–4), measures, and diagnostic interviewing across a range of client populations (Turchik, Karpenko, Hammers, & McNamara, 2007). The assessment competency requires students to integrate data from multiple sources, to effectively answer referral questions, and to communicate their inferences and recommendations clearly (NCSPP, 2007).

The assessment competency is composed of four domains:

> (a) interviewing and relationships, (b) case formulation, (c) psychological testing, and (d) ethics and professionalism. . . . The interviewing and relationships domain addresses a student's ability to gather appropriate information through clinical interview and to create and maintain an empathic and flexible interpersonal stance. The domain of case formula-

tion relates to a student's ability to understand a client's presenting problem, diagnose and conceptualize psychopathology and clearly communicate that conceptualization to a range of audiences. The domain of psychological testing relates to the choice, use, scoring and interpretation of assessment tools. The fourth domain of ethics and professionalism addresses the integration of ethical and professional decision making in all assessment activities." (NCSPP, 2007, p. 4)

Intervention

Intervention includes "activities that promote, restore, sustain, and/or enhance positive functioning and a sense of well-being in clients through preventive, developmental, and/or remedial services" (R. L. Peterson et al., 1997, p. 380). "Development of competence in intervention requires understanding of theory and its application in personality, psychopathology, change processes, and the interactions and influences of social, environmental, cultural, and physiological factors . . . " (NCSPP, 2007, p. 16). The intervention competency has four domains: (a) planning, (b) implementation, (c) evaluation, and (d) ethics (de la Fuentes, Willmuth, & Yarrow, 2005).

> Planning is comprised of the assessment of therapeutic needs, case formulation, selection of the best strategy to match the client's needs, such as evidenced based practice rationale for strategies (APA Presidential Task Force on Evidence-Based Practice, 2006), influence of individual, cultural and contextual differences, knowledge base of possible interventions and ability to integrate and think critically. Implementation is comprised of flexibility to adapt/modify strategies, utilizing consultation and adjunctive/alternative sources, ability to manage the therapeutic relationship/process and termination. Evaluation is comprised of performance appraisal/self-evaluation, use of supervision and consultation, knowledge of methods of evaluation, and attitude, e.g., operating as a local clinical scientist. The ethics domain is comprised of practice management, life-long learning, self-awareness and self-care, ethical, legal and professional practice issues, licensure and specialization and management of special situations (e.g., danger to self or others and abuse). (NCSPP, 2007, p. 16)

Research and Evaluation

To give particular emphasis to the NCSPP position on science and practice issues, the authors discussed the majority of the material on the research and evaluation competency in the previous section Psychological Science and Education for Professional Psychology. The DALs identified three specific domains in this competency:

> (a) critical evaluation of research, (b) conducting and using research in applied settings, and (c) ethics and professional competence. . . . The first domain of critical evaluation of research addresses the ability to locate, evaluate, and titrate professional literature, and to determine the

applicability of that literature to specific clinical questions. It requires an openness to multiple ways of knowing and an understanding of the strengths and weakness of different forms of research. The second domain addresses the ability to design, implement and interpret research and to use research in applied settings. It includes efforts to identify and minimize personal biases that can impact the design, implementation and application of clinical research results, and the use of clinical research in local clinical settings. The third domain of ethics and professional competence addresses compliance with ethical guidelines and students' identity as a local clinical scientist. (NCSPP, 2007, p. 31)

Consultation and Education

Consultation and education is the fifth NCSPP competency.

Consultation refers to the planned collaborative interaction between the professional psychologist and one or more clients or colleagues, in relation to an identified problem area or program. Psychological consultation is an explicit intervention process that is based on principles and procedures found within psychology and related disciplines, in which the professional psychologist has no *direct* control of the actual change process. . . . Education is the directed facilitation by the professional psychologist of the growth of knowledge, skills, and attitudes in the learner. (McHolland, 1992, p. 165)

"Competency in education involves knowledge about models of learning and pedagogy, as well as the foundations of, and innovations in, instructional design and evaluation. It also involves skill building in facilitating student knowledge acquisition and scholarly and personal development . . . " (NCSPP, 2007, p. 41).

Five domains have been identified in the consultation-education competency: (a) knowledge of evidence-based theories, models, and interventions; (b) integration of research and evaluation; (c) building consultation and education relationships; (d) problem-solving and implementation; and (e) ethical and professional practice (NCSPP, 2007). The first domain refers to "a developing understanding and application of the concepts, theories, and principles underlying the practice of consultation and education, including emerging evidence-based theories and practices." The second domain "includes the ability to evaluate critically the existing literature and its application, and to conduct research." The third domain "refers to an understanding of the *roles* of consultant and educator and the cultivation of an effective and sensitive *relationship* with clients." The fourth domain "refers to an evolving understanding of the indications and contraindications for specific educational and consultative approaches, as well as the development of skills and attitudes for implementing them." The fifth domain "refers to familiarity with the ethical principles and legal standards underlying the prac-

tice of consultation and education and operating according to those laws and standards" (NCSPP, 2007, pp. 41–42).

Management and Supervision

Management includes activities that organize, direct or control services offered to the public (Bent et al.,1992). These activities require effective functioning within organizations, an understanding of financial management and strategic planning, and the ability to influence public and organizational policy (Dyer, 1999; NCSPP, 2007; Swift, 1996).

According to Bernard and Goodyear (2004),

> Supervision is a form of management and represents an intervention pro-vided by a more senior member of a profession to a more junior member or members of the same profession. The relationship is evaluative, ex-tends over time, and has the simultaneous purposes of enhancing the professional functioning of the more junior person, monitoring the qual-ity of professional services offered to the client, and serving as a gatekeeper of those who are to enter the particular profession. (p. 8)

The DALs identify five domains of this competency:

> (a) assuring the well being of the client or organization . . . ; (b) training and mentoring of supervisees and those being managed, which refers to the educative/facilitative dimensions of the supervisor/manager role; (c) evaluation/gatekeeping, which refers to the responsibilities associated with formative and summative feedback to supervisees and communicating evaluative messages to external groups such as academic programs, ad-ministrative personnel, and licensing boards; (d) ethics, functioning within the standards of the profession which cuts across all aspects of the competency; and (e) health care leadership and advocacy, which refers to the roles and functions associated with managing programs or organi-zations as well as influencing organizational, governmental and societal values and policies in the health care arena. . . . " (NCSPP, 2007, p. 35)

Because the majority of graduates of professional psychology programs are ultimately employed in positions requiring management and supervisory skills, NCSPP is convinced that this competency should occupy an enhanced status in the core curriculum. Going further, professional psychology pro-grams should support advanced preparation for leadership, advocacy, and public and social policy planning roles. Many programs have required courses in supervision, with appropriate readings. Some programs have a second level of experience that may include a practicum in supervision or the experience of supervising beginning graduate students—all, of course, under faculty su-pervision. Some programs have required courses that explicitly include cov-erage of topics, such as management, public policy, health care delivery sys-tems, and administration. A few have joint degrees with management departments, have executive tracks, or offer a small sequence of courses in

this area. Elective practicum experiences in these areas are beginning to emerge.

Diversity

"The diversity competency requires the ability to identify and understand issues of individual and cultural difference (ICD), and issues of power, privilege and oppression. This understanding informs and influences all professional functions and activities. . . ." (NCSPP, 2007, p. 24). Although this is newly listed as a competency, it is a longstanding concern for NCSPP. Previously, it was the topic of an entire conference and resulted in the publication of NCSPP's third volume, *Toward Ethnic Diversification in Psychology Education and Training* (Stricker et al., 1990). Competency in diversity requires an affirmation of the richness of human differences, ideas, and beliefs. Important dimensions of diversity include (but are not limited to) age, disability and health, ethnicity, gender, language, national origin, race, religion and spirituality, sexual orientation, and social economic status as well as the intersection of these multiple identities and multiple statuses. Exploration of power differentials, power dynamics, and privilege is at the core of understanding diversity issues and their impact on social structures and oppression (Kupers, 1997).

> The diversity competency is composed of five main domains . . . : (a) multiple identities; (b) issues of power, oppression and privilege; (c) ICD specific knowledge base; (d) culturally competent service provision; and (e) ethics. . . . The first domain includes an understanding of how students identify and understand themselves and others as having multiple identities, and how they use that knowledge in their professional activities. The second domain includes an understanding of the constructs of power, oppression and privilege, their impact and psychology's role in social justice. The third domain includes the ability to understand and critique the scientific, theoretical and applied ICD knowledge base, including an understanding of evidence-based scholarship and its appropriate application to diverse populations. The fourth domain includes students' ability to provide culturally competent services in all of their professional roles. The fifth domain includes students' ability to integrate an awareness of ICD into ethical decision making. (NCSPP, 2007, pp. 24–25)

Other Required Knowledge

From the competency perspective, professional education is more inclusive but is, in fact, no less scientific. The integrated resolutions indicate that professional competencies continue to be related to an evolving and developing knowledge base that should include the following areas: (a) biological bases of behavior, (b) cognitive-affective bases of behavior, (c) cultural bases of behavior, (d) dysfunctional behavior and psychopathology, (e)

the historical and philosophical context of psychology, (f) life span development, (g) professional ethics and standards, (h) psychological measurement,
(i) social bases of behavior, and (j) theories of individual and systems functioning and change.

Elements of Practice

In a context that reflects (a) the core competencies, (b) the wide range
of activities in which professional psychologists are currently engaged and
will be in the future, and (c) the likelihood of an expanded scope of practice
in the future, NCSPP has long emphasized the need to prepare psychologists
for multiple roles. The educational process is not seen as one in which the
student is pumped full of knowledge and skills that are then dispensed to the
public for a price but as an experience through which the personal and professional self of each student is systematically developed, consistent with
Schön's (1983) ideas of reflective practice. In keeping with these conceptions, NCSPP supports a wide variety of practicum and internship models
along with a strong emphasis on systematic evaluation of students, programs,
and NCSPP member programs as a group.

Multiple and Expanding Roles

The integrated resolutions put forward that the primary task of education in professional psychology is preparation for effective functioning in the
multiple roles graduates will fill during the course of their careers (R. L.
Peterson, 2008). Conceptually, the idea of competencies is closely related to
the idea of professional roles. Preparation for the wide array of roles evident
in professional life is dependent on an education with a very broad understanding of each of the professional competencies. Though the need was stated
in 1997, professional training programs still need to greatly enhance, not
ignore or minimize, education for the competencies of (a) consultation and
education and (b) management and supervision. Many programs have
struggled with and ultimately expanded their offerings in these areas. For the
future, the expansion of psychology's scope of practice is critical. Education,
training, and credentialing should be sufficiently flexible to prepare for, per-
mit, and promote new and expanding roles in new settings so as to be responsive to emerging social issues. This flexibility has led to an increasing number of interdisciplinary training programs, joint degree programs, and
partnerships in service delivery.

The Self of the Professional Psychologist and Reflective Practice

"Preparation in professional psychology involves the education of the
personal and professional selves of students" (R. L. Peterson, 2008, p. 3) so as
to develop the habits of reflective practice and lifelong learning. Awareness
of self and self–other relatedness is central.

As educators, the creation and nurturance of respectful, collegial, and empowering relationships with students are of central importance. . . . Professional socialization experiences should be designed to foster student awareness of how students' personal and professional selves affect and are affected by their professional relationships, their profession, their training, the culture of their programs, and their clinical work. The knowledge of how inequalities of power and authority determine the nature of relationships, and the promotion of responsible use of power and authority, are critical elements of this experience. (R. L. Peterson, 2008, p. 4)

Both academic and interpersonal material relevant to inequalities of power and authority appear in a variety of educational topics. These issues occur academically in the study of ethics and the roles and responsibilities of professional psychologists, in the study of racism and diversity, in some interpretations of gender issues, and in critiques of traditional epistemologies. All of these issues underscore the importance of training in both reflective practice and person-focused (i.e., social and interpersonal) sorts of educational experiences that provide a context in which such conversations can occur (D. R. Peterson, 1985, 1995; Singer, Peterson, & Magidson, 1992). Different aspects of self and different ethical principles become relevant as professional psychologists move through multiple roles. Programs that educate professional psychologists carry an obligation to systematically attend to, develop, and evaluate the personal and interpersonal fitness of graduates.

Practicum and Internship Training

Recognizing that, for supervised practice in psychology, there is no one correct training model, NCSPP strongly supported a diversity of practicum and internship models within professional psychology. The desirability of integrative service, inquiry, and teaching models in clinical training was reaffirmed. A strong relationship between educational coursework and field training is particularly valued.

Systematic Evaluation

NCSPP professional psychology educators have committed themselves to outcome and evaluation research to assess traditional and alternative models of training and service. There continues to be general affirmation of the need for systematic evaluation of students, programs (including faculty and supervisors), and services. Evaluation of professional competence in field experiences is to be based on a three-way learning contract among the student, the practicum or internship center staff, and the program faculty. Critical aspects of the evaluation process involve supervision; direct observation; and instruments and procedures incorporating self-evaluation, student peer evaluation, and program field faculty evaluation. Critical to an institution's ability to vouch for the quality of its graduates, competency-based clinical examinations were endorsed by NCSPP delegates. Such examinations should assess

competence relevant to professional practice using multimethod evaluation techniques (that might include live evaluation or other direct scrutiny of students' work by means of audiotapes and videotapes, written case presentations, examinations by faculty, and presentations to peers) as generally exemplified in the ABPP exam. Professional psychology programs should attend not only to academic progress but also to evaluating students with regard to those personal attitudes, aptitudes, and values that appear likely to predict future professional competence.

Social Responsibility, Diversity, and Gender

NCSPP has taken leadership in emphasizing the social nature of professional psychology and the social responsibilities of both programs and graduates. Against the backdrop of the history of education and training in psychology, NCSPP has believed that issues related to diversity and gender needed additional, particular attention (Stricker et al., 1990). In this context, the authors are especially pleased that NCSPP chose to endorse its seventh competency of diversity (as discussed earlier). Important dimensions of diversity—including gender, physical status, spirituality and religion, sexual orientation, race and ethnicity, socioeconomic status, ability and disability, and age—are fundamental elements of human experience and should be integrated throughout the education and training of professional psychologists, the science itself, and the organizations in which the education and training occur. Diversity is now a key part of accreditation. Issues relevant to ethnic and racial diversity (Davis-Russell, Forbes, Bascuas, & Duran, 1992; Stricker et al., 1990) and to women (Edwall, 1992; Edwall & Newton, 1992; Magidson, Edwall, Kenkel, & Jackson, 1994) demand systematic focus and attention, as in the case of Marie. Inherent in these concerns is the necessity of the responsible use of and education about power, oppression, authority, and sociopolitical structures. "Professional psychology values the sharing of power, equal access to opportunity, social justice, affirmation of differences and the prevention of marginalization as primary goals" (R. L. Peterson, 2008, p. 2).

By 2009, most (if not all) psychological organizations have mission resolutions espousing values regarding diversity and gender. The work of NCSPP in the area of diversity has gone far deeper. One measure is, of course, that the 1989 NCSPP conference (Stricker et al., 1990) was devoted to ethnic and racial diversity. The 1990 NCSPP conference was focused on gender diversity. In both meetings, detailed resolutions were developed, and important themes were critiques of American psychology as overly influenced by the perspectives of White men. Many believe that professional psychology education and practice has been changed forever as a result of these conferences. Further work on diversity was also done in the 2008 conference titled Advancing the Multicultural Agenda: From Aspiration to Actualization.

Social Nature of Professional Psychology

Education must be socially responsive and responsible. A profession of psychology can be justified only if it meets the fundamental needs of the larger society (D. R. Peterson, 1996a, 1996b; R. L. Peterson, 2005). Professional practice in psychology and the education for that practice are fundamentally social, not private or individual. This social vision and understanding are apparent in a number of areas: (a) an examination of the importance of the socially situated role of psychologists, (b) the basic and underlying aspect of the relationship competency, (c) historical analyses of the social influences on the core curriculum in professional psychology (R. L. Peterson, 1992a, 1992b; Weiss, 1992), (d) the development of the competency areas, (e) the necessity of directing explicit attention to the organizational contexts and cultures in which education occurs, (f) the interpersonal nature of reflective education, and (g) the development of a broad-based definition of social responsibility.

IMPLICATIONS FOR PROFESSIONAL PSYCHOLOGY

A decade following the original NCSPP model paper, this work continues to have a number of implications for the training and practice of professional psychologists:

1. The seven competencies and the competency model can be seen as a heuristic for the field. For those who think in terms of learning theory, the competencies suggest a much clearer way of thinking about educational goals. The overall model has and will continue to help those in the field of psychology understand the growth of competencies from the beginning student to the graduate pursuing ABPP certification. In pragmatic formulations that can be developed and enhanced over the years, the competency model organizes conversations about both current and expanded roles for the future, educational experiences leading to those roles, and credentialing for them. The seed of this thinking has born fruit in the Competencies conference, the Benchmarks conference, and in the creation of the DALs.

2. Students are being educated in the broadest sense to be professional psychologists, not—to mention some stereotypes—psychotherapists with a few science courses or researchers with a few clinical courses. With a broad education perhaps we psychologists can hope for better and more respectful professional communication among us.

3. Graduates explicitly educated to become practitioners are likely to be better prepared to do what they will actually do after graduation, that is, educated as clearly as the realities can be known or the future foreseen. Practitioners who trained in earlier times with narrower models often had much

to learn on their own about the professional world after receiving their doctorates.

4. Students who seek a career in psychology as a helping profession are educated in a model that is committed to service delivery as a primary value. Graduates are less likely to feel that they have become second-class citizens by entering practice or by not living up to their program's espoused but often unrealistic research goals. Practitioners, specifically trained to serve in that capacity, may be more likely to retain connections with their programs and institutions in a way that will facilitate continuing education, enhance graduates' pride and acknowledgement of value in the work they are doing, and enhance mutual respect among differently trained psychologists.

5. Beyond the problems of individuals, the NCSPP model provides education with the focus and background for dealing with social issues and diversity with sensitivity. Though attention to these areas has certainly been an important part of NCSPP's vision, NCSPP recognizes that people in other parts of psychology, other disciplines, and in other walks of life have also addressed these issues.

6. Expanded curricular attention still needs to be given to consultation and education and to supervision and management to reinforce that these activities are critical aspects of professional psychology practice. If it can be said that some of psychology was asleep, or at least napping, as the changes in health care of the past several years developed, we are still dozing. This training should help prepare graduates with the versatility and the flexibility to adjust to the future and take a leadership role in the challenges that lie ahead.

7. This model values attention to attitudes as a critical aspect of professional development and systematically articulates how the self of the student professional psychologist should be involved in reflective professional education and practice. Without substituting self for science, this reflexive model is consistent with, not divergent from, mainstream professional values.

8. This model places a strong emphasis on professional psychology pedagogy.

9. Over the long term, on the basis of concepts like the local clinical scientist and disciplined inquiry, the most significant impact of this model may be to focus attention on how science is actually—and could be more effectively—implemented in psychological practice. All too frequently, psychology is dichotomized along many dimensions: science versus practice, empirical versus clinical, American Psychological Society versus APA, cognitive–behavioral versus psychodynamic, clinical versus actuarial, scientist–practitioner versus professional, and so forth. Though some of these conceptual pairs do denote bona fide and important differences, the practice of psychology as characterized in the concepts and examples of the local clinical scientist may bring these groups together because they identify common, desirable processes for practice that are based on disciplined inquiry and are in a language that is familiar across subcultures. We, the authors, think it is

more productive to think of these pairs as dialectic processes awaiting syntheses rather than as dichotomies. Though there are ways in which solutions to this problem of dichotomies seem straightforward, it is also evident that this problem is much more complex than meets the eye, and answers are not obvious, easy, or fully developed (e.g., D. R. Peterson, 1991; D. R. Peterson & Peterson, 1997; Schön, 1983, 1987; Trierweiler & Stricker, 1992, 1998).

In many ways, there is a great degree of overlap between the NCSPP practitioner–scholar model and the scientist–practitioner model. In best examples of each, there might be little disagreement—if there were agreement on which are the best examples. Still, practitioner-model advocates still might say that the Boulder model includes too much emphasis on the examination and production of career-irrelevant research, whereas the scientist–practitioner advocates might say that the science disappears in the focus on clinical work. At bottom, though, there is a common interest: Psychological science is an integrative, disciplined, reflexive way of thinking that helps all psychologists to work together to solve great and important human problems.

REFERENCES

American Board of Professional Psychology (1993). *Application manual for specialty recognition and affiliation.* Columbia, MO: Author.

American Psychological Association Office of Program Consultation and Accreditation (1996). *Book 1: Guidelines and principles for accreditation of programs in professional psychology.* Washington, DC: Author.

American Psychological Association Office of Program Consultation and Accreditation (2007). *Book 2: Accreditation operating procedures.* Washington, DC: Author.

American Psychological Association, Presidential Task Force on Evidence-Based Practice (2006). Evidence-based practice in psychology. *American Psychologist, 61*, 271–285.

Belar, C. D., & Perry, N. W. (1991). *Proceedings: National conference on scientist-practitioner education and training for the professional practice of psychology,* Sarasota, FL: Professional Resource Press.

Bent, R. J. (1986). Toward quality assurance in the education of practicing psychologists. In J. E. Callan, D. R. Peterson, & G. Stricker (Eds.), *Quality in professional psychology training: A national conference and self-study* (pp. 27–36). Norman, OK: Transcript Press.

Bent, R. J., & Cannon, W. G. (1987). Key functional skills of a professional psychologist. In E. F. Bourg, R. J. Bent, J. E. Callan, N. F. Jones, J. McHolland, & G. Stricker (Eds.), *Standards and evaluation in the education and training of professional psychologists: Knowledge, attitudes, and skills* (pp. 87–97). Norman, OK: Transcript Press.

Bent, R. J., & Jones, N. F. (1987). Knowledge and skills in professional psychology programs. In E. F. Bourg, R. J. Bent, J. E. Callan, N. F. Jones, J. McHolland, & G. Stricker (Eds.), *Standards and evaluation in the education and training of professional psychologists: Knowledge, attitudes, and skills* (pp. 35–44). Norman, OK: Transcript Press.

Bent, R. J., & Peterson, R. L. (1998). *The core competency curriculum for the professional psychology model: Implication and implementation*. Unpublished manuscript.

Bent, R., Schindler, N., Dobbins, J., Davis-Russell, E., Edwall, G., Polite, K., et al. (1992). Management and supervision competency. In R. Peterson, J. McHolland, & R. Bent (Eds.), *The core curriculum in professional psychology* (pp. 121–126). Washington, DC: American Psychological Association.

Bernard, J., & Goodyear, R. (2004). *Fundamentals of clinical supervision* (3rd ed.). Boston: Allyn & Bacon.

Bieschke, K. J., Fouad, N., Collins, F., & Halonen, J. (2004). The scientifically-minded psychologist. *Journal of Clinical Psychology, 60,* 713–724.

Bourg, E. F., Bent, R. J., Callan, J. E., Jones, N. F., McHolland, J. D., & Stricker, G. (1987). *Standards and evaluation in the education and training of professional psychologists: Knowledge, attitudes, and skills*. Norman, OK: Transcript Press.

Bourg, E. F., Bent, R. J., McHolland, J. D., & Stricker, G. (1989). Standards and evaluation in the education and training of professional psychologists: The National Council of Schools of Professional Psychology Mission Bay Conference. *American Psychologist, 44,* 66–72.

Callan, J. E., Peterson, D. R., & Stricker, G. (1986). *Quality in professional psychology training: A national conference and self-study*. Norman, OK: Transcript Press.

Davis-Russell, E., Forbes, W. T., Bascuas, J., & Duran, E. (1992). Ethnic diversity and the core curriculum. In R. L. Peterson, J. D. McHolland, R. J. Bent, E. Davis-Russell, G. E. Edwall, E. Magidson, et al. (Eds.), *The core curriculum in professional psychology* (pp. 147–151). Washington, DC: American Psychological Association and National Council of Schools of Professional Psychology.

Dawes, R. M. (1994). *House of cards: The collapse of modern psychotherapy*. New York: Free Press.

de la Fuentes, C., Willmuth, M., & Yarrow., C. (2005). Competency training in ethics education and practice. *Professional Psychology: Research and Practice, 36,* 362–366.

Dyer, R. L. (1999). Public policy administration and the psychologist. In W. O'Donohue & J.E. Fisher (Eds.), *Management and administration skills for the mental health professional* (pp. 261–274). San Diego, CA: Academic Press.

Edwall, G. E. (1992). Broadening the core curriculum. In R. L. Peterson, J. D. McHolland, R. J. Bent, E. Davis-Russell, G. E. Edwall, E. Magidson, et al. (Eds.), *The core curriculum in professional psychology* (pp. 129–132). Washington, DC: American Psychological Association and National Council of Schools of Professional Psychology.

Edwall, G. E., & Newton, N. (1992). Women and the core curriculum. In R. L. Peterson, J. D. McHolland, R. J. Bent, E. Davis-Russell, G. E. Edwall, E. Magidson,

et al. (Eds.), *The core curriculum in professional psychology* (pp. 141–146). Washington, DC: American Psychological Association and National Council of Schools of Professional Psychology.

Hays, S. C. (1986). A training model in search of a rationale. *American Psychologist, 41,* 593–594.

Hoshmand, L. T., & Polkinghorne, D. E. (1992). Redefining the science–practice relationship in professional training. *American Psychologist, 47,* 55–66.

Joint Council on Professional Education in Psychology (JCPEP). (1990). *Report of the JCPEP.* Baton Rouge, LA: Author.

Korman, M. (1976). *Levels and patterns of professional training in psychology.* Washington, DC: American Psychological Association.

Krishnamurthy, R., VandeCreek, L., Kaslow, N. J., Tazeau, Y. N., Miville, M. L., Kerns, R., et al. (2004). Achieving competency in psychological assessment: Directions for education and training. *Journal of Clinical Psychology, 60,* 725–739.

Kupers, T. A. (1997). The politics of psychiatry: Gender and sexual preference in *DSM–IV.* In M. R. Walsh (Ed.), *Women, men, and gender: Ongoing debates* (pp. 340–347). New Haven, CT: Yale University Press.

Magidson, E., Edwall, G. E., Kenkel, M. B., & Jackson, J. (1994, January). *Women's issues in professional psychology: The National Council of Schools and Programs of Professional Psychology Tucson conference, 1991.* Paper presented at the National Council of Schools and Programs of Professional Psychology Midwinter Conference on Standards for Education in Professional Psychology: Reflection and Integration, Cancun, Mexico.

McFall, R. M. (1991). Manifesto for a science of clinical psychology. *The Clinical Psychologist, 44,* 75–88.

McFall, R. M. (1996). Making psychology incorruptible. *Applied and Preventive Psychology, 5,* 9–16.

McHolland, J. (1992). National Council of Schools of Professional Psychology Core Curriculum Conference Resolutions. In R. L. Peterson, J. D. McHolland, R. J. Bent, E. Davis-Russell, G. E. Edwall, K. Polite, et al. (Eds.), *The core curriculum in professional psychology* (pp. 153–176). Washington, DC: American Psychological Association.

Messer, S. B. (2004). Evidence-based practice: Beyond empirically supported treatments. *Professional Psychology: Research and Practice, 35,* 580–588.

National Council of Schools and Programs in Professional Psychology. (2002). Diversity Competency Statement. Retrieved August 6, 2007, from http://www.ncspp.info/div.htm

National Council of Schools and Programs in Professional Psychology. (2007). NCSPP Competency Developmental Achievement Levels. Retrieved December 1, 2007, from http://www.ncspp.info/pubs.htm

Peterson, D. R. (1968). The doctor of psychology program at the University of Illinois. *American Psychologist, 23,* 511–516.

Peterson, D. R. (1976). Need for the doctor of psychology degree in professional psychology. *American Psychologist, 31*, 792–798.

Peterson, D. R. (1985). Twenty years of practitioner training in psychology. *American Psychologist, 40*, 441–451.

Peterson, D. R. (1991). Connection and disconnection of research and practice in the education of professional psychologists. *American Psychologist, 46*, 422–429.

Peterson, D. R. (1995). The reflective educator. *American Psychologist, 50*, 975–983.

Peterson, D. R. (1996a). Making conversation possible. *Applied and Preventive Psychology, 5*, 17–18.

Peterson, D. R. (1996b). Making psychology indispensable. *Applied and Preventive Psychology, 5*, 1–8.

Peterson, D. R. (1997). *Educating professional psychologists: History and guiding conception.* Washington, DC: American Psychological Association.

Peterson, D. R., & Peterson, R. L. (1997). Ways of knowing in a profession: Toward an epistemology for the education of professional psychologists. In D. R. Peterson, *Educating professional psychologists: History and guiding conception* (pp. 191–228). Washington, DC: American Psychological Association.

Peterson, R. L. (1992a). Social construction of the core curriculum in professional psychology. In R. L. Peterson, J. D. McHolland, R. J. Bent, E. Davis-Russell, G. E. Edwall, E. Magidson, et al., (Eds.), *The core curriculum in professional psychology* (pp. 23–36). Washington, DC: American Psychological Association and National Council of Schools of Professional Psychology.

Peterson, R. L. (1992b). The social, relational, and intellectual context of the core curriculum and the San Antonio conference. In R. L. Peterson, J. D. McHolland, R. J. Bent, E. Davis-Russell, G. E. Edwall, E. Magidson, et al. (Eds.), *The core curriculum in professional psychology* (pp. 3–12). Washington, DC: American Psychological Association and National Council of Schools of Professional Psychology.

Peterson, R. L. (2005). 21st century education: Toward greater emphasis on context—Social, economic, and educational. *Journal of Clinical Psychology, 61*, 1121–1126.

Peterson, R. L. (Ed.). (2008). *National Council of Schools and Programs of Professional Psychology integrated resolutions through 1996.* Retrieved February 25, 2009, from http://www.ncspp.info/NCSPPResolutionsthrough1996.pdf

Peterson, R. L., McHolland, J., Bent, R. J., Davis-Russell, E., Edwall, G. E., Magidson, E., et al. (Eds.). (1992). *The core curriculum in professional psychology.* Washington, DC: American Psychological Association and National Council of Schools of Professional Psychology.

Peterson, R. L., Peterson, D. R., Abrams, J. C., & Stricker, G. (1997). The National Council of Schools and Programs of Professional Psychology educational model. *Professional Psychology: Research and Practice, 28*, 373–386.

Peterson, R. L., & Trierweiler, S. J. (1999). Scholarship in psychology: The advantages of an expanded vision. *American Psychologist, 54*, 350–355.

Polite, K., & Bourg, E. (1992). Relationship competency. In R. L. Peterson, J. D. McHolland, R. J. Bent, E. Davis-Russell, G. E. Edwall, K. Polite, et al. (Eds.), *The core curriculum in professional psychology* (pp. 83–88). Washington, DC: American Psychological Association and National Council of Schools of Professional Psychology.

Schön, D. A. (1983). *The reflective practitioner: How professionals think in action.* New York: Basic Books.

Schön, D. A. (1987). *Educating the reflective practitioner: Towards a new design for teaching and learning in the professions.* San Francisco: Jossey-Bass.

Singer, D. L., Peterson, R. L., & Magidson, E. (1992). The self, the student, and the core curriculum: Learning from the inside out. In R. L. Peterson, J. D. McHolland, R. J. Bent, E. Davis-Russell, G. E. Edwall, E. Magidson, et al. (Eds.), *The core curriculum in professional psychology* (pp. 133–140). Washington, DC: American Psychological Association and National Council of Schools of Professional Psychology.

Stricker, G. (1992). The relationship of research to clinical practice. *American Psychologist, 47,* 543–549.

Stricker, G. (1997). Are science and practice commensurable? *American Psychologist, 52,* 442–448.

Stricker, G., & Cummings, N. A. (1992). The professional school movement. In D. K. Freedheim (Ed.), *History of psychotherapy: A century of change* (pp. 801–828). Washington, DC: American Psychological Association.

Stricker, G., Davis-Russell, E., Bourg, E., Duran, E., Hammond, W. R., McHolland, J., et al. (1990). *Toward ethnic diversification in psychology education and training.* Washington, DC: American Psychological Association.

Stricker, G., & Trierweiler, S. J. (1995). The local clinical scientist: A bridge between science and practice. *American Psychologist, 50,* 995–1002.

Swift, M. (1996). Clinical psychologists and the business of psychology: A training innovation. *Innovations in Professional Psychology Education and Practice: Preparing for the New Millennium.* Paper presented at the National Council of Schools and Programs in Professional Psychology Midwinter Conference, Clearwater, FL.

Trierweiler, S. J. (1987). Practitioner training: A model with rationale intact. *American Psychologist, 42,* 37–45.

Trierweiler, S. J. (1992, August). The local clinical scientist: A model for integrating training in research and practice. In G. Stricker (Chair), *Research training in clinical psychology.* Symposium conducted at the meeting of the 100th Annual Convention of the American Psychological Association, Washington, DC.

Trierweiler, S. J., & Stricker, G. (1992). Research and evaluation competency: Training the local clinical scientist. In R. L. Peterson, J. McHolland, R. J. Bent, E. Davis-Russell, G. E. Edwall, E. Magidson, et al. (Eds.), *The core curriculum in professional psychology* (pp. 103–113). Washington, DC: American Psychological Association and National Council of Schools of Professional Psychology.

Trierweiler, S. J., & Stricker, G. (1998). *The scientific practice of professional psychology.* New York: Plenum.

Turchik, J. A., Karpenko, V., Hammers, D., & McNamara, J. R. (2007). Practical and ethical assessment issues in rural, impoverished, and managed care settings. *Professional Psychology: Research and Practice, 38,* 158–168.

Weiss, B. J. (1992). Toward a competency-based core curriculum in professional psychology: A critical history. In R. L. Peterson, J. D. McHolland, R. J. Bent, E. Davis-Russell, G. E. Edwall, E. Magidson, et al. (Eds.), *The core curriculum in professional psychology* (pp. 13–21). Washington, DC: American Psychological Association and National Council of Schools of Professional Psychology.

2

APPLYING THE COMPETENCY MODEL TO PROFESSIONAL PSYCHOLOGY EDUCATION, TRAINING, AND ASSESSMENT: MISSION BAY AND BEYOND

KATHI A. BORDEN AND E. JOHN McILVRIED

Professional psychology education and training has recently shifted its focus to a competency-based model. Nelson (2007) described many of the historical forces contributing to an increased emphasis on competencies, starting with the advent of professional credentialing and program accreditation in professional psychology in the 1940s. The National Council of Schools and Programs of Professional Psychology (NCSPP) played a major role in igniting the more recent shift in focus to competency-based education, training, and assessment. The original NCSPP competencies list was derived from the "key functional skills" of professional psychologists (Bent & Cannon, 1987) and was delineated at the NCSPP's Mission Bay Conference (Bourg et al., 1987). To a large extent, those competencies still compose the core curriculum in professional psychology, as reflected in licensing and accreditation criteria, as well as the curricula of the majority of professional psychology training programs in the United States.

More recent trends have contributed to the emphasis on competencies. For example, the "internship bottleneck" led to concerns that quality of education and training (i.e., mastery of competencies) was being sacrificed for quantity of practicum hours. In addition, mobility issues in the United States and Canada have emphasized competencies as one way to improve consistency across credentialing jurisdictions (Edwards, 2000; Stigall, 2003). Finally, for the public to understand what psychology is and does, we must describe the competencies we expect of psychology practitioners (Kaslow et al., 2004).

Since the original NCSPP competencies work, professional psychology has focused increasingly on a competency-based model of education and training (Kaslow et al., 2004). Regional accrediting bodies now focus on evaluating outcomes (competency assessment is one type of outcome evaluation) as one criterion for accreditation, and the recognition standards of the Council for Higher Education Accreditation (CHEA), the organization that accredits accrediting organizations, state, "The agency's accreditation standards [must] effectively address . . . success with respect to student achievement in relation to the institution's mission, including, as appropriate, consideration of course completion, state licensing examination, and job placement rates" (CHEA, 2006, p. 30). After Mission Bay, several publications described the NCSPP competency model more fully (Peterson, Peterson, Abrams, & Stricker, 1997; Peterson et al., 1992). Competency-based training models have been espoused by representatives of the other training councils in professional psychology, including school psychology (Farling & Agner, 1979; Kratochwill, 1982), counseling psychology (Murdock, Alcorn, Heesacker, & Stoltenberg, 1998; Stoltenberg et al., 2000), and scientist–practitioner (Belar & Perry, 1992) training councils. Revisions of the *Guidelines and Principles for Accreditation of Programs in Professional Psychology* of the American Psychological Association (APA; Committee on Accreditation, 2005) have reflected an increasing emphasis on competencies and specifically list many of the NCSPP competency areas in their program approval criteria. Now, all accredited programs must include and demonstrate effectiveness of education and training in these areas.

At the broad-based Competencies Conference in 2002 (Kaslow et al., 2004), participants further developed and reorganized the core competencies (e.g., Rodolfa et al., 2005) into a "competency cube," with three dimensions representing functional competencies (common professional activities), foundational competencies (basic to all areas of performance), and stages of professional development. Spawned by the Competencies Conference, the APA's work on benchmarks (Assessment of Competency Benchmarks Work Group, 2007) and the NCSPP's work on developmental achievement levels (DALs; NCSPP, 2007) have advanced the specification of expected competency levels.

The body of literature on the identification, definition, and conceptual organization of competencies essential to professional psychology education

and training has been growing. Unfortunately, there is much less work on how best to teach competencies and how to assess them. The remainder of this chapter focuses on the assessment of competencies as a common thread that intersects our educational efforts, the development of clinicians across their careers, the complexities of practice in the real world, and future efforts at enhancing the competence of professionals in our field.

COMPETENCY AND THE EDUCATION-ASSESSMENT INTERFACE

The knowledge, skills, and attitudes (KSAs) embodied in the seven core competency areas identified by the NCSPP consist of essential components of professional practice and should be included in education and training efforts (McIlvried & Bent, 2003) and in the assessment of students and graduates. One trend that has significant implications for the competency-based approach is evidence-based practice in psychology (EBPP; APA Presidential Task Force on Evidence-Based Practice, 2006). EBPP often takes the form of guidelines for best practice (including empirically supported principles and methods). This same emphasis and rigor should be applied to evidence-based educational and assessment methods to help us identify best practices (e.g., Moran & Malott, 2004). Unlike other health professions, the curriculum in professional psychology is not standardized across programs, and there is no single, mandated model of education or particular set of goals to which programs must adhere. Because of this, practices have varied significantly among programs. Nonetheless, it is possible to develop a general set of criteria to help programs develop best practices for their particular model and goals so that students acquire the KSAs appropriate to crucial competency areas.

Best practices in education suggest that different strategies may be more effective for different purposes. On the one hand, a didactic strategy may be the most economical and effective way of transmitting factual knowledge. On the other hand, observation and practice may be the preferred method for teaching clinical skills. In contrast to these, experiential activities may be much more effective in developing desired attitudes and values. Best practices in educating competent graduate students and future psychologists would involve a combination of methods and experiential components in developing the KSAs deemed important for competent professional practice. These methods may be combined across program elements and within courses to address program goals and objectives. An interesting example of this type of approach can be found in Guth and McDonnell (2004), who applied a similar strategy to the area of group work.

There is a critical connection between educational efforts and attempts to assess the effectiveness of those efforts. Instructional methodologies are informed by and in turn enrich assessment endeavors such that the development and measurement of competence are intertwined as part of an on-

going feedback system. For example, knowledge-based assessment (deriving from didactic instructional methods) may be used to evaluate the acquisition of essential information in both formative (e.g., quizzes, exams, term papers) and summative (e.g., comprehensive exams, portfolios, the EBPP) evaluations.

Skill-based assessment (the corollary to observation and practice instructional methods) may be used to evaluate essential functions of professional psychologists. Instructors frequently use methods such as role plays, observations through a mirror, and feedback on videotaped client sessions in formative assessments of students in their classes. Similarly, we often rely on practicum and internship evaluations from supervisors, participation in research projects, and case presentations as part of qualifying or diplomate examinations as summative assessments of competence with respect to clinical skills.

Attitude-based assessment (related to experiential instructional methods) may be used to assess the development and internalization of attitudes, beliefs, and values deemed critical for professional psychologists. As part of formative assessment, instructors frequently use methods such as in-class discussions, small group exercises, reaction papers, and so on, whereas summative assessment may involve feedback from supervisors and mentors, responses from client surveys about their experience with the clinician, peer evaluations, and similar approaches.

The preceding is certainly not exhaustive, nor is it intended to suggest that any given type of goal can be achieved only through a particular set of instructional methodologies or assessment methods. For example, knowledge can certainly be gained through observation, practice, or experiential methods (not simply via lecture) and can likewise be assessed through methods other than written work products. In addition, a number of instructional and assessment methods, such as problem-based learning noted by Kaslow (2004), involve a complex interplay of didactic, observational, and experiential components that cannot be easily teased apart. From a developmental view, more complex and integrative methodologies such as problem-based learning may be particularly useful later in the educational process, after students have mastered fundamental concepts and skills.

A recommended best practice is for programs to examine their various curricular elements and components and to specify the KSAs that they hope to accomplish through each of these along with the differing pedagogical strategies (didactic, experiential, observation, and practice) and assessment methodologies that they plan to use. The best practice advocated is not for all programs to have the same goals, educational methodologies, assessment procedures, or outcomes. However, it is the authors' view that discussions by faculty and administrators of the use of particular pedagogies and assessment methods to achieve specific goals within a program are far too infrequent.

CHALLENGES AND OPPORTUNITIES IN THE
ASSESSMENT OF COMPETENCE

Evaluating competence is not simple, even for a profession with expertise in assessment. The following sections describe a variety of challenges and opportunities for professional psychology in the development of enhanced methods for the assessment of competence.

Developmental Considerations

Identification and definition of competencies are necessary prerequisites to their assessment. In addition, a requirement for meaningful evaluation is the establishment of criteria relevant for each stage of a professional psychologist's development. The Benchmarks meeting held in September 2006 resulted in a document (Assessment of Competency Benchmarks Work Group, 2007) that specifies levels of performance in each competency area expected at the prepracticum, preinternship, prelicensing, and advanced practice and specialization levels. For each competency at each level, the Benchmarks document provides behavioral anchors and suggested assessment methods. Following the Benchmarks meeting, the NCSPP underwent a similar process of defining DALs (NCSPP, 2007). This resulted in a document summarizing expected KSAs for each competency at the prepracticum, preinternship, and doctoral degree completion levels. One future challenge will be to expand on the developmental aspects of competency assessment and to develop appropriate measurement technologies and instruments for each level.

To fully realize a developmental assessment system, we will need to examine current practices. Some aspects of student assessment do appear to change over the course of graduate programs. For example, in many programs, the emphasis on knowledge acquisition at the beginning of programs (e.g., scientific bases of psychology) is assessed through faculty evaluations of student coursework. As students move forward, supervisor ratings are added. Later in the program, student ability to integrate KSAs across competency areas is assessed in various ways. For example, an abridged version of the American Board of Professional Psychology examination process that requires a clinical work sample and an interview by faculty about the clinical work has been used as a qualifying examination by several NCSPP programs for at least 20 years. In addition, integration skills are assessed through the dissertation, which, in most NCSPP programs, requires extensive integration of research and practice. Finally, the internship requires increased professional independence and integration across domains.

However, assessment methods do not always reflect this developmental pedagogy. For example, annual review forms now used by many programs

often do not change over the course of a student's schooling. Similarly, practicum forms often closely resemble internship evaluation forms and do not adequately evaluate newly introduced competencies or increased competency integration, for example, whether the student increasingly integrates research into clinical work in the spirit of the local clinical scientist. The amount of attention to developmental factors in assessment methods is not adequate if we believe there are qualitative as well as quantitative changes in competence over time.

Another developmental challenge derives from typical career trajectories. Certain competencies may be more central at certain career stages than others. For example, all students might need to have skill in test administration and scoring. Later on, a forensic psychologist may need much more extensive testing skill than will an outpatient therapist.

As professional psychologists progress in their training and in their careers, their idiosyncratic professional niches are likely to become more individualized, specialized, and limited in scope. This will pose a challenge because it is difficult to evaluate the strengths and weaknesses of an assessment method that is relevant for only a small group of individuals. Further, once psychologists have gained the requisite knowledge and skills, difficult-to-measure attitudes (e.g., do no harm, lifelong learning) may become more central to a psychologist's competence. Related to this, the cross-cutting competencies and skills involved with relationship, diversity, ethics, information retrieval and evaluation, communication, and so forth, may grow more important in competency assessment at career stages beyond the basic KSA gates (e.g., credentialing).

A final developmental issue relates to assessment itself. We cannot suddenly spring new methods of assessment on psychology students or graduates without some preparation. Rather, assessment methods should be reasonably consistent or gradually introduced throughout the careers of professional psychologists (Roberts, Borden, Christiansen, & Lopez, 2005). Continuity of assessment methods reduces the portion of method variance that results from lack of familiarity with the assessment format. An often ignored but essential component of this is the need to teach students to do adequate self-evaluations starting early in school and continuing throughout their careers, particularly after the doctoral program when external assessments become infrequent, but the need for evaluation remains. After licensing, psychologists should not be expected to suddenly and automatically be able to evaluate their competence for various tasks if they have not received supervised practice in self-assessment.

Complex and Abstract Constructs

Another set of challenges results from the specificity of the constructs we attempt to assess. As the domain of interest becomes more abstract and

difficult to operationalize, assessment becomes more difficult. Thus, we are pretty good at assessing knowledge and moderately successful at assessing skill. However, the measurement of attitudes is still in its infancy. If we are serious about attitudes being an essential component of the competence of professional psychologists, we will need to be less incidental and more intentional about assessing them. Some program-specific evaluation forms list desirable qualities of professional psychologists (e.g., ethical or have integrity, aware of biases, appreciate diversity, flexible). However, educators and practitioners have been hesitant to delineate essential attitudes, perhaps for fear of imposing their own values on others, and no widely used measure of professional psychology attitudes currently exists. The difficulty of getting psychologists to agree on essential attitudes makes assessment of attitudes difficult at best.

Similarly, we have had greater success at assessing competencies one by one rather than assessing an integrated construct of overall competence. Related to this, Nelson (2007) referred to the concept of "pedagogical signatures" that define specific disciplines. In professional psychology, our signature could be described as a combination of classroom teaching with supervised practice in a clinical setting that typically focuses on discrete competencies. That professional psychology's signature has included little focus on the assessment of clinicians' abilities to integrate complex groupings of KSAs in real-world practice has hampered our ability to teach and measure multiple and integrated competencies. In the authors' experience, students long for the opportunity to interact with clients and with other clinicians in real life, real-time clinical situations (as opposed to, e.g., well-edited movies). Ongoing feedback and evaluation via cotherapy and "in-the-room" observations, such as those done with medical students and residents during grand rounds, are rare in our field. Instead, students, faculty, and supervisors practice privately and rely on one another's reports about what occurs in a professional situation. Audio and videotapes, as well as observation from behind a mirror, are all helpful in approximating in-the-room assessment, but these methods are not equal to it. As psychology moves forward, it will be important to move education, training, and assessment forward to more closely approximate a shared clinical experience in which both student and supervisor become involved as participant observers in the development, practice, and assessment of professional competence.

Innovations and Future Directions

Professional psychology educators have been introducing several innovative methods of assessing competencies and integrated competence. Academic programs have struggled with ways to get practicum supervisors to include more constructive criticism and fewer inflated ratings on evaluation forms. Internship directors have also expressed concerns that programs in-

clude positives and omit negatives when recommending students for internships. The work of the Association of Directors of Psychology Training Clinics (ADPTC) toward defining specific practicum competencies (Hatcher & Lassiter, 2006, 2007) and the ADPTC's development of a model form for competency-based practicum assessment may help by providing anchors for defining adequate performance. Although these efforts are promising, increased reliability and validity of evaluation when using competency-based forms has yet to be demonstrated.

Another innovation, the use of standardized patients (rather than real patients), is becoming more common in both formative and summative assessment, particularly in professional psychology programs affiliated with medical schools. Some have pointed out problems with the reliability and validity of these assessments in medical schools (e.g., Yudkowsky, 2002), and although this technology is promising, it will require further development.

Another method receiving some attention is the 360-degree evaluation in which multiple evaluators with varied roles and relationships with the student or clinician rate that person on a range of competencies. This method has not been tested systematically in professional psychology, but this type of evaluation may be particularly promising in the very challenging area of measuring professional attitudes. Like competency-based rating forms and standardized patient assessments, 360-degree evaluations have yet to be thoroughly tested in professional psychology, but all three of these methods provide promising areas for future research and development.

For purposes of analysis and the future development of assessment technologies, it may be useful to break each block in the competency cube (Rodolfa et al., 2005) into its own "pedagogy and assessment cube" (see Figure 2.1). In this way, each program or the profession as a whole can evaluate the education and training methods that lead to KSAs in a particular competency area and the ways in which those are assessed for students at different points in their careers. This will inform us of gaps that may exist in educational and assessment systems. What will remain to be done then is to evaluate existing means and to develop newer, more effective means of assessing the KSAs associated with specific competencies as well as define a more integrated and holistic construct of competence at each level of professional development. Professional psychology is only beginning to tackle the many challenges associated with this task.

In conclusion, despite major advances in the education, training, and assessment of competencies, we still agree with the conclusion of Roberts et al. (2005) that psychology needs to invest significant resources to develop reliable, valid, useful, culturally relevant, and fair methods of professional competence evaluation. Specifically, we need to develop valid, culturally appropriate measures for the right competencies, applied to the right developing professionals, using the right criteria at each specific point in time. As professional psychology educators, we have our work set out for us. Reminis-

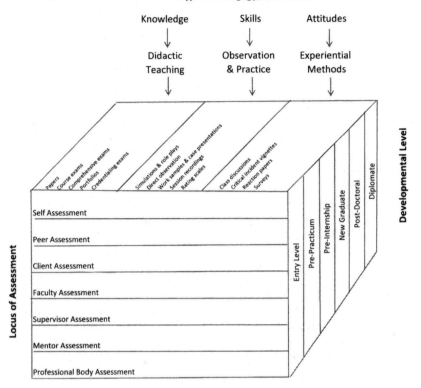

Figure 2.1. Assessment and Pedagogy Cube. Certain types of assessments, such as performance on the dissertation, mini-ABPP qualifying exam, 360-degree evaluation, and so on, are integrative across KSAs and reflect combinations of several assessment methods listed in the cube. Therefore, they are not included separately under a particular pedagogy/assessment category. Adapted from "A Cube Model for Competency Development: Implications for Psychology Educators and Regulators," by E. Rodolfa, R. Bent, E. Eisman, P. Nelson, L. Rehm, & P. Ritchie, 2005, *Professional Psychology: Research and Lractice, 36*, p. 350. Copyright 2005 by the American Psychological Association.

cent of the opening phrase of Rosenhan's (1973) classic study, we might ask, "If competence and incompetence exist [in professional training and practice], how shall we know them?" (p. 250).

REFERENCES

American Psychological Association Committee on Accreditation. (2005). *Guidelines and principles for accreditation of programs in professional psychology.* Washington, DC: American Psychological Association.

American Psychological Association Presidential Task Force on Evidence-Based Practice. (2006). Evidence-based practice in psychology. *American Psychologist, 61*, 271–285.

Assessment of Competency Benchmarks Work Group (2007). *Assessment of competency benchmarks work group: A developmental model for the defining and measuring competence in professional psychology*. Retrieved January 31, 2008, from http://www.apa.org/ed/resources.html

Belar, C. D., & Perry, N. W. (1992). National conference on scientist-practitioner education and training for the professional practice of psychology. *American Psychologist, 47*, 71–75.

Bent, R. J., & Cannon, W. G. (1987). Key functional skills of a professional psychologist. In E. F. Bourg, R. J. Bent, J. E. Callan, N. F. Jones, J. McHolland, & G. Stricker (Eds.), *Standards and evaluation in the education and training of professional psychologists: Knowledge, attitudes, and skills* (pp. 87– 97). Norman, OK: Transcript Press.

Bourg, E. F., Bent, R. J., Callan, J. E., Jones, N. F., McHolland, J. D., & Stricker, G. (Eds.). (1987). *Standards and evaluation in the education and training of professional psychologists*. Norman, OK: Transcript Press.

Council for Higher Education Accreditation. (2006). *Accreditation and recognition in the United States*. Retrieved February 9, 2009, from http://www.chea.org/pdf/Accreditation_and_Recognition_PP_Nov08.pdf

Edwards, H. P. (2000). *A framework for the determination of competencies in relation to mobility for psychology under the AIT*. Retrieved January 31, 2008, from http://www.cpa.ca/cpasite/userfiles/documents/advocacy/PSWAIT/Framework.pdf

Farling, W. H., & Agner, J. (1979). History of the National Association of School Psychologists: The first decade. *School Psychology Review, 8*, 140–152.

Guth, L. J., & McDonnell, K. A. (2004). Designing class activities to meet specific core training competencies: A developmental approach. *Journal for Specialists in Group Work, 29*, 97–111.

Hatcher, R. L., & Lassiter, K. D. (2006). *The practicum competencies outline: Report on practicum competencies*. Retrieved January 31, 2008, from http://www.adptc.org/

Hatcher, R. L. & Lassiter, K. D. (2007). Initial training in professional psychology: The Practicum Competencies Outline. *Training and Education in Professional Psychology, 1*, 49–63.

Kaslow, N. J. (2004). Competencies in professional psychology. *American Psychologist, 59*, 774–781.

Kaslow, N. J., Borden, K. A., Collins, F. L., Forrest, L., Illfelder-Kaye, J., Nelson, P. D., et al. (2004). Competencies conference: Future directions in education and credentialing of professional psychology. *Journal of Clinical Psychology, 60*, 699–712.

Kratochwill, T. R. (1982). School psychology: Dimensions of its dilemmas and future directions. *Professional Psychology: Research and Practice, 13*, 977–989.

McIlvried, E. J., & Bent, R. J. (2003, January). *Core competencies: Current and future perspectives*. Paper presented at the meeting of the National Council of Schools and Programs of Professional Psychology, Scottsdale, AZ.

Moran, D. J., & Malott, R. W. (2004). *Evidence-based educational methods*. San Diego, CA: Elsevier Academic Press.

Murdock, N. L., Alcorn, J., Heesacker, M., & Stoltenberg, C. (1998). Model training program in counseling psychology. *The Counseling Psychologist, 26*, 658–672.

National Council of Schools and Programs of Professional Psychology (2007). *Competency developmental achievement levels (DALs) of the National Council of Schools and Programs of Professional Psychology (NCSPP)*. Retrieved January 31, 2008, from http://www.ncspp.info/pubs.htm

Nelson, P. D. (2007). Striving for competence in the assessment of competence: Psychology's professional education and credentialing journey of public accountability. *Training and Education in Professional Psychology, 1*, 3–12.

Peterson, R. L., McHolland, J. D., Bent, R. J., Davis-Russell, E., Edwall, G. E., Polite, K., et al. (1992). *The core curriculum in professional psychology*. Washington, DC: American Psychological Association.

Peterson, R. L., Peterson, D. R., Abrams, J. C. & Stricker, G. (1997). The National Council of Schools and Programs of Professional Psychology Educational Model. *Professional Psychology: Research and Practice, 28*, 373–386.

Roberts, M. C., Borden, K. A., Christiansen, M. D., & Lopez, S. J. (2005). Fostering a culture shift: Assessment of competence in the education and careers of professional psychologists. *Professional Psychology: Research and Practice, 36*, 355–361.

Rodolfa, E., Bent, R., Eisman, E., Nelson, P., Rehm, L., & Ritchie, P. (2005). A cube model for competency development: Implications for psychology educators and regulators. *Professional Psychology: Research and Practice, 36*, 347–354.

Rosenhan, D. L. (1973). On being sane in insane places. *Science, 179*, 250–258.

Stigall, T. T. (2003). The impact of accreditation on the practice of professional psychology. In E. M. Altmaier (Ed.), *Setting standards in graduate education: Psychology's commitment to excellence in accreditation* (pp. 91–111). Washington, DC: American Psychological Association.

Stoltenberg, C., Pace, T. M., Kashubeck-West, S., Biever, J. L., Patterson, T., & Welch, I. D. (2000). Training models in counseling psychology: Scientist-practitioner versus practitioner-scholar. *The Counseling Psychologist, 28*, 622–640.

Yudkowsky, R. (2002). Should we use standardized patients instead of real patients for high-stakes exams in psychiatry? *Academic Psychiatry, 26*, 187–192.

3

THREATS TO QUALITY IN PROFESSIONAL EDUCATION AND TRAINING: THE POLITICS OF MODELS, OBFUSCATION OF THE CLINICAL, AND CORPORATIZATION

ROGER L. PETERSON

This chapter begins by proposing a different way to think about quality in professional psychology education and training—different from the thumbs up, thumbs down of Nero's coliseum; the 8.9, 9.2, and 7.3 ratings of figure skating; or even the detailed letters of the APA Commission of Accreditation. Specifically, I propose *carrying the question* of quality—that is, accepting that the unresolved issue has no final or complete answer but remaining open to clues all around us (Taylor, 1987a, 1987b). After explaining the concept of carrying the question of quality—acknowledging that complete solutions will remain elusive—I discuss three threats to quality in professional psychology education and training: (a) the politics of models have distracted

The author would like to thank people who have provided feedback on earlier versions of this manuscript: Martin Heesacker, Joyce Illfelder-Kaye, Mary Beth Kenkel, Victor Pantesco, Celiane Rey-Casserly, and George Tremblay.

educators from the bona fide issues of the field; (b) we cannot allow the importance of the key clinical phenomena of our field to be obfuscated; and (c) we cannot be co-opted and undermined by the impact of corporatization on American higher education.

CARRYING THE QUESTION

Let's begin with Taylor's (1987a, 1987b) characterization of "carrying the question" (1987a, p. 6). In the context of adult development, she talked about

> the process of *carrying the question*, simply living with the unresolved situations we're in, and allowing our awareness of the questions we face to serve as a filter for our current life experience. By carrying the question, we focus ourselves to find hints about the answers in the situations that present themselves to us. (1987a, p. 6)

In this sense, everyone carries questions in their lives, questions that should be understood as dilemmas that have no final or complete answers, questions that illuminate an experience in a certain fashion, or questions that direct thought and attention and give meaning. In another paper, Taylor (1987b) described carrying the question as the initial stage in psychological inquiry. It includes such matters as

> the relationship of question to the current state of our knowledge and our life (their personal meaning for us); . . . the nature of the language in which we're willing to frame them (which conversation they're part of), the universe of possibilities to which they allow access, . . . the methods of inquiry implied in the way the question is posed. . . . Once we're carrying a question, we look to our experience for clues from which to construct answers. . . . As scientists, we're responsible for key decisions that determine the kinds of data we'll accept as credible clues. We may scan the entirety of our experience, once we start carrying a question, and find clues at every turn. (p. 3)

If we find ways to carry in our minds questions surrounding the issues of quality in professional psychology education, perhaps we can open our eyes in some fresh way and "find clues at every turn."

POLITICS OF MODELS

Politics surrounding the models of professional psychology education has, at its very best, been difficult, at times vicious and painful, often involving matters of prejudice as much as matters of science or education. Certainly, these differences reflect actual differences in the production of schol-

arly work between models. However, when it comes to the development of clinicians, it is quite clear that excellent professional psychologists have been created by programs from the whole range of models. And each produces psychologists who are not so good.

Of course, the basic positions are well known. As a matter of historical precedent, solidified by the Committee on Accreditation, programs have been obliged to define themselves—their models—in terms of the nature and quantity of the psychological science produced. On the one hand, there is the classic scientist–practitioner model (Belar & Perry, 1992), with its more extreme variant, the clinical scientist model. On the other hand, there is the practitioner–scholar model (R. L. Peterson, Peterson, Abrams, & Stricker, 1997; Peterson et al., this volume) with a number of variants (e.g., practitioner). We are talking not only about the nature and amount of science or practice in a program but also the emphasis in the program culture. Nevertheless, in fact, there is a good deal of overlap in the center of the distribution. The espoused differences are always put forward in terms of model, but almost always there is an evident subtext that one is better than the other. Also, the very things the faculty actually do well themselves may be quite different from those things that they are training others to do.

In the larger scheme of things, of course, arts-and-sciences-based academics whose own contingencies emphasized research productivity over practice have long dominated education in clinical psychology (see D. R. Peterson, 1991, 2003; D. R. Peterson & Peterson, 1997; Stricker, 1997; R. L. Peterson & Trierweiler, 1999), even for those whose primary goal is practice.

The development of the professional psychology education movement and the PsyD was spurred by a vision in which psychologists would be trained for their ultimate primary professional activity, practice, instead of research. This is not a particularly novel idea. The Midwestern cognitive–behavioral tradition so influential in professional psychology directed that the learning processes should be explicitly related to the anticipated outcomes. If you want to train researchers, have them do research. If you want to train practitioners, have them do practice. No one is against research training. It is valuable. But if we want to help people to learn tennis, we don't tell them to spend half their time golfing (Peterson & Ober, 2006).

Of course, there is some relationship because both sports require arm movement, and some people learn both golf and tennis. Though it is possible to do both, one question we should carry is whether academicians ambivalently committed to practice can truly mentor for practice and, conversely, whether faculty ambivalently committed to scholarship can mentor dissertations. People can do some of each; but can they do enough of each to be sufficiently expert, such that they can mentor others?

Certainly, most professional psychology educators are far beyond the idea that traditional research training, especially in its more alienating versions, is the only thing or even the main thing that can provide sufficient

education in critical thinking to be applied to practice. Science must be an aspect of all education and training. Carrying these questions as elements of quality, it is time to examine a number of articulated viewpoints on how science can be applied to practice: D. R. Peterson's (1991) view of disciplined inquiry, Trierweiler and Stricker's vision of the local clinical scientist (Stricker & Trierweiler, 1995; Trierweiler & Stricker, 1992; Trierweiler & Stricker, 1998), and Bieshke et al.'s (2004) description of the "scientifically minded psychologist." Certainly, we are not still fighting about whether all psychologists should be doing research. We know most do not.

Though all models are scientific, there are often underlying epistemological differences, an array of which I have discussed before (e.g., D. R. Peterson, & Peterson, 1997). We are at a point in history in which the discipline of psychology has a number of viable epistemologies, a sampling of which should be included in the curriculum regardless of model. There are also theoretical differences. Though the correlation is far from perfect, there is certainly some tendency for professionally oriented programs to be more psychodynamic and interpersonal while scientist–practitioner programs tilt toward the cognitive–behavioral.

With some selective history, it can be argued that the professional psychology movement both developed in response to a situation in which it seemed close to impossible to educate psychologists primarily for practice in graduate schools of arts and sciences in mainline research universities. Even so, graduates regularly bootlegged in career paths in practice. The contingencies on the faculty were to produce university science, neglect pedagogy, and minimize professional practice as measured in terms of time spent, in terms of importance, and in terms of meaningful involvement in real-world settings. What, then, were the atmospheres and the contingencies within the graduate and professional schools responsible for educating professional psychologists? My point here is that worrying about the differences in models distracts from systematically developing the training of clinicians and makes that training a secondary priority.

Still, from conversations and from the implicit and explicit meanings derived from articles and accreditation materials, there remains a good deal of disagreement and confusion about what the model names actually mean. Like the cognitivists talking to the analysts and vice versa, there is an understandable tendency to expand the relevance of one's own perspective and shrink the relevance of the other's. Proponents of the scientist–practitioner model typically believe that the best way to train both productive scientists and practitioners is to train them equally for both (Belar & Perry, 1992). This grand goal is seldom obtained. It is notable that only a very few in our profession do both well (please add you own favorite example here). Practitioner–scholar advocates believe that training ought to focus on the most likely outcome, being scientifically based practitioners, but with a secondary strength in scholarship. At the same time, *scholarship* was understood to be a

broader term than *science* and inclusive of it when the authors of the NCSPP models appropriated that language (R. L. Peterson et al., 1997). When the word *practitioner* is used alone, practitioner model programs further decrease the emphasis on science and scholarship in training. Certainly some students from PsyD programs are quite well trained in and interested in research. And, of course, many PhD students have preferred clinical career paths to the production of science.

This usage has certainly led to some moderately interesting questions: What about programs staffed by psychologists who were trained in the scientist–practitioner model but in their day-to-day activities produce little or no science themselves? Is it sufficient that their practices are responsive to scientific advances? Or is this like a skier who no longer skis or a writer who doesn't write? Is one still a skier or a writer? Similarly, what credentials should be required of faculty who teach on the practitioner end of the scientist–practitioner model? Ironically, we imagined that the phrase *practitioner–scholar* would help to resolve such dilemmas. But mostly these traditional model labels have led to experiences that look like ethnic clashes—what those scientist–practitioner folks come to think of those professional program psychologists on the other side of the river. These phenomena might be best understood in the words of the anthropological writings on diversity (e.g., Geertz, 2000) or the cultures of practice and of science (D. R. Peterson, 1997) rather than in intellectual debates. Like ethnic clashes, the labels all too often have become flags waved as the raiding parties go out. Further, these labels are not likely to be meaningful indicators of the full array of training events that go on in a particular program. It would be very desirable to make this debate more intellectual, more based on data, and less political than it has been—to be more about carrying these questions.

As suggested, often this seems more to me like enactment of prejudice rather than an intellectual exchange. The social power that provides cohesion to the ingroup serves to vilify the outgroup—something we do to an exquisite degree in the education and training cultures that underlie the different models (R. L. Peterson, 2005). In a classic chapter called "Us and Them," R. D. Laing (1967) described the powerful connections between people that constitute a "we" and an "us": "The invention of Them creates Us, and We may need to invent Them to reinvent Ourselves" (pp. 90–91).

A similar set of ideas occurred in a very interesting exchange between Clifford Geertz (2000) the anthropologist and Richard Rorty (1991) the postmodern pragmatist, on diversity and ethnocentrism. Summarizing the thoughts of Levi-Strauss, Geertz said that loyalty "to a certain set of values inevitably makes people 'partially or totally insensitive to other values' to which other people, equally parochial, are equally loyal" (Geertz, 2000, p. 70). According to Geertz (2000), "in the past, when so-called primitive cultures were only very marginally involved with one another—referring to themselves as 'The True Ones,' 'The Good Ones,' or just 'The Human Beings,'

and dismissing those across the river or over the ridge as 'earth monkeys' or 'louse eggs,' that is, not or not fully human—cultural integrity was readily maintained" (p. 71). That cultural integrity continues to come at a very high price in psychology. There is a kind of ethnocentrism that is inherent in our different education and training cultures. According to Geertz (2000), "the trouble with ethnocentrism is not that it commits us to our own commitments. We are, by definition, so committed. The trouble with ethnocentrism is that it impedes us from discovering at what sort of angle . . . we stand to the world . . . " (p. 75).

We professional psychology educators have to choose to carry the question of the possibility of prejudice. And the outcome cannot be, to borrow another one of Geertz's (2000) wonderful phrases from another context, to make "the world safe for condescension" (p. 77).

The labels of models, at least in internships, may be less relevant than we thought. Research by Rodolfa, Kaslow, Stewart, Keilin, and Baker (2005) supports this contention. They found that training model labels are unrelated to activities at internships. There is the suspicion that there is not much difference in what internships, labeled scientist–practitioner, practitioner–scholar, or practitioner actually do.

THE OBFUSCATION OF PSYCHOLOGICAL PRACTICE

We all have a real daily life—a real relational life. We have a day-to-day life in which we have intense feeling. We have close colleagueships in which we cherish the care we get from others and try to be with them when they are having difficult times with their health or children or relationships. We try to be responsive and helpful; we try to sit with them during times of grave events. We must retain the deep ability to be moved by the experience of others.

Sitting with people who have come to us so we can help them is a central experience in clinical psychology. I am convinced that it is hard to keep quality in mind without retaining this core of experience, because one loses touch. But I also know that many will disagree. It is not that supervision isn't important and closely related or that, say, psychotherapy research isn't virtuous. But they are different kinds of experience. I know every faculty person sees himself or herself as having a fine mix. Too often in the program decisions we make, clinical work does not stay in the center of one's consciousness or focus—it is blurred or perhaps moves to one's metaphorical peripheral vision.

The education of practicing psychologists must be embedded in practice phenomena and anchored in particular contexts, in specific times, places, and narratives. How do we keep this in mind so as to "recontextualize" (Rorty, 1991, pp. 93–110) the abstractions, scientific data, and plans of our disci-

pline, even though they are fascinating and meaningful in themselves? Keeping in mind that the centrality of the clinical experience recontextualizes our education and training.

One reason that the clinical is hard to keep in focus is that it is an interpersonal experience and heavily anchored in ongoing time. A number of times in talks I have tried to connect my life with that of an audience in what I have called "the swirl of experiences, yours and mine." I tell snippets of stories about my life, clinical work, and the disasters we faced as individuals or a nation, no different from what you could tell. They are compelling to a live audience, but in writing they quickly become quaint and oddly historical. It is hard to remember which storm or even which war we were moved by, or even remember which friend's partner was diagnosed with cancer. One time, I talked about reading the entrancing novel *The Famished Road* by Ben Okri (1991), magical realism about modern Nigeria, told from the point of view of a small boy, where the world of spirits mixes with the hopelessness, poverty, oppression, and inevitable violence that has entrapped the people. At another time, I had seen the play *Tuesdays With Morrie* (Albom, 2002), about mentoring, dying, and what is important in life. All of this requires indexing the listeners' experience against mine and creating one's own narrative. Part of this has to do with the different traditions of American psychology as compared with Freud and the Europeans. The Europeans regularly wrote about cases with depth and texture; we provide vignettes. At any one of these larger moments, as at any other moment, around my life as around yours, is all the substance of professional psychology, such as family closeness, gender roles, poverty, AIDS, discrimination, racism, trauma, violence, natural disaster, substance abuse, disease, loss, and deep psychological pain.

Pushed by the force of narrative in my head, I find I want to tell some story here—but that is off the point. Such a descriptive passage would depart from the written tradition of the empirical scientist even though it connects with what pragmatist Richard Rorty (1989, pp. 3–43) called the "strong poet" (following Bloom and Neitzsche). We create truth by deploying a "mobile army of metaphors" (Rorty, 1989, p. 28). This process of coming to see another human being as "one of us" rather than as "them" is a matter of detailed description of what unfamiliar people are like and of redescription of what we ourselves are like (Rorty, 1989). This is how we come to hold our time in thought (Rorty, 1989, p. 55). If we want to carry the question, we psychologist educators have to hold the clinical experiences of our time in thought.

Educators of professional psychologists have had a common experience as we fly home from some supposedly important meeting. As the meeting progressed, our level of background anxiety has increased as something seemed to have fallen off the table. Critical questions like those that make up this same swirl of life I have described as central to professional psychology, seemed to have faded from the context of the meeting's conversations. We regret that we brought up nothing phenomenologically compelling. Perhaps we

wonder whether we really understood the particular group or setting or expected too much. Those of us who feel this way are left with a great responsibility: to find a way that the clinical work is compelling and central—so we can continue to carry the question of quality.

CORPORATIZATION OF PROFESSIONAL EDUCATION

Of the many definitions of *corporatization*, I am referring here to situations in which the goals of selling a product are more important than humane values. Typically, this results in devaluing the voice of disciplinary expertise and increasing the voice of supposed economic expertise, even though there seems to be little evidence that this attitude has produced positive outcomes. There is a tendency toward more hierarchical decision making, espousing transparency like a mantra without enacting it (we are a long way from the double-loop learning of Argyris, e.g., 1999). Faulty processes are papered over.

The corporatization of American higher education is intricately and inextricably entangled with economic and political movements of the past 3 decades (see Gould, 2003). Arguably this is an outgrowth of a cultural movement that began in the Reagan era, was omnipresent during the Bush years, and has resulted in the international economic disaster we are beginning to face in 2009. Top university roles are reframed in corporate language as chief executive officer (CEO) or chief financial officer (CFO). Even at relatively small institutions, the rewards for the top posts have increased at a more rapid rate than faculty salaries. Profit and expansion are the primary definition of success. At this same time, within American culture there are HMOs with obscene profits and overpaid CEOs, the private for-profit forces of Blackwater (who would have been lowly paid regular army in other times), the collapse of Wall Street and elements of the mortgage industry, and omnipresent widespread corporate irresponsibility regarding the environment. Not only is a dominant cultural narrative one of corporatization, but it is one of bad corporatization.

I want to be clear that this is not a critique solely directed at for-profit institutions. Actually, I don't know firsthand whether for-profit institutions have a particularly high dose of corporatization. Universities of all kinds—tuition driven, small and large privates, and state-supported—have corporatized. Although in many circumstances a successful program should pay its own direct and indirect costs, economic gain should not come at the expense of quality. Traditional institutions have accepted that many doctoral programs that are reputation builders may also be money losers (M. Heesacker, personal communication, March 16, 2008). To address another kind of corporatization, accomplished grant-supported researchers are often allowed to buy their way out of teaching. The rush toward online programs is

one more striking effect of this trend. In a variety of forms, the impact of corporatization is broad and deep in higher education.

Within clinical psychology, there seems to be a lack of understanding of the three-party dance: the program, the administration, and external accreditation. Whether spoken or unspoken, the requirements of accreditation are to be outwitted or worked around rather than met. When programs make money, and since institutional enhancements are based on expansion, there is always pressure to increase the number of students and develop new programs. When programs lose money, there is pressure to keep them small. Sometimes the cost of programs is seen to be the costs only of the courses, not the culture that has created and supported them, that is, every element of the program. There is implicit or explicit pressure to take less qualified or unqualified students and pressure for smaller, more junior faculties. Sometimes organizational changes are initiated without the meaningful consultation of internal experts both to obtain particular technical knowledge and for the positive sense of participatory governance.

In the last 15 years, there has been a vast expansion of licensed mental health workers. There are jobs, but reimbursements for psychologists are almost flat in many areas, certainly in my own home state of Hampshire. During this same period, tuitions have gone up, and PsyD graduates have twice the debt levels of PhD graduates (American Psychological Association, Board of Educational Affairs, 2007). As a matter of quality, how can a program conscientiously take into account postgraduate markets? Still, there are not enough mental health services for those in need. How can we expect that graduates will pursue socially virtuous activities with such a big debt?

Though it doesn't have to be this way, corporatization too often suggests that cutting costs comes before the question of quality. Is this mentality appropriate for professional level education? Corporatization leads to the Wal-Martization (e.g., Norman, 2004) of the university and of education. Cheap products are good products; cheap products sell—meaning that the support for and health benefits of the workers, the economic damage to communities in rural America, and the lack of sustainable quality are all unimportant. Isn't a degree in professional psychology more than a commodity? Quality should be something for all of us, not only for a few prestigious places. I have come to think that there are great differences between the best doctoral programs in clinical psychology and the weakest: If we imagine Venn diagrams, they would not have much overlap. If we add a middle circle of average programs, with overlaps on each end, do we each know who we are—and why?

We need to carry the question of quality in professional psychology education and training. We cannot be distracted by the politics of models, lose sight of the clinical amidst the smoke and haze of other activities, or be eroded by corporatization. We have to look our collective selves in the mirror. The stakes are very high.

REFERENCES

Albom, M. (2002). *Tuesdays with Morrie*. New York: Broadway.

American Psychological Association, Board of Educational Affairs. (2007). *A report on the professional psychology internship match imbalance*. Washington, DC: American Psychological Association.

Argyris, C. (1999). *On organizational learning* (2nd ed.). New York: Blackwell.

Belar, C. D., & Perry, N. W. (1992). National conference on scientist–practitioner education and training for the professional practice of psychology. *American Psychologist, 47*, 71–75.

Bieschke, K. J., Fouad, N., Collins, F., & Halonen, J. (2004). The scientifically-minded psychologist. *Journal of Clinical Psychology, 60*, 713–724.

Geertz, C. (2000). *Available light: Anthropological reflections on philosophical topics*. Princeton, NJ: Princeton University Press.

Gould, E. (2003). *The university in a corporate culture*. New Haven, CT: Yale University Press.

Laing, R. D. (1967). *The politics of experience*. New York: Ballantine Books.

Norman, A. (2004). *The case against Wal-Mart*. New York: Raphael Marketing.

Okri, B. (1991). *The famished road*. New York: Anchor.

Peterson, D. R. (1991). Connection and disconnection of research and practice in the education of professional psychologists. *American Psychologist, 46*, 422–429.

Peterson, D. R. (1997). *Educating professional psychologists: History and guiding conception*. Washington, DC: American Psychological Association.

Peterson, D. R. (2003). Unintended consequences: Ventures and misadventures in the education of professional psychologists. *American Psychologist, 58*, 791–800.

Peterson, D. R., & Peterson, R. L. (1997). Ways of knowing in a profession: Toward an epistemology for the education of professional psychologists. In D. R. Peterson, *Educating professional psychologists: History and guiding conception* (pp. 191–228). Washington, DC: American Psychological Association.

Peterson, R. L. (2005, September). Cultures in education and training. In C. Brewer (Moderator), *Epistemological diversity in psychology*. Symposium conducted at the American Psychological Association Educational Leadership Conference, Arlington, VA.

Peterson, R. L., & Ober, M. D. (2006). Reconsidering assumptions: Half-time internships in their historical context. *Professional Psychology: Research and Practice, 37*, 635–642.

Peterson, R. L., Peterson, D. R., Abrams, J. C., & Stricker, G. (1997). The National Council of Schools and Programs of Professional Psychology educational model. *Professional Psychology: Research and Practice, 28*, 373–386.

Peterson, R. L., & Trierweiler, S. J. (1999). Scholarship in psychology: The advantages of an expanded vision. *American Psychologist, 54*, 350–355.

Rodolfa, E., Kaslow, N. J., Stewart, A. E., Keilin, W. G., & Baker, J. (2005). Internship training: Do models really matter? *Professional Psychology: Research and Practice, 36*, 25–31.

Rorty, R. (1989). *Contingency, irony, and solidarity.* Cambridge, England: Cambridge University Press.

Rorty, R. (1991). *Objectivity, relativism, and truth: Philosophical papers* (Vol. 1). Cambridge, England: Cambridge University Press.

Stricker, G. (1997). Are science and practice commensurable? *American Psychologist, 52,* 442–448.

Stricker, G., & Trierweiler, S. J. (1995). The local clinical scientist: A bridge between science and practice. *American Psychologist, 50,* 995–1002.

Taylor, S. (1987a, April). *Transition: Inner work, outer work.* Paper presented at Psychology Department Colloquium, Antioch University, Seattle, WA.

Taylor, S. (1987b, October). *Constructing the knowledge we need: Forays across the received boundaries of scientific inquiry in psychology.* Paper presented at the Faculty College, Antioch University, Yellow Springs, OH.

Trierweiler, S. J., & Stricker, G. (1992). Research and evaluation competency: Training the local clinical scientist. In R. L. Peterson, J. McHolland, R. J. Bent, E. Davis-Russell, G. E. Edwall, E. Magidson, et al. (Eds.), *The core curriculum in professional psychology* (pp. 103–113). Washington, DC: American Psychological Association & National Council of Schools of Professional Psychology.

Trierweiler, S. J., & Stricker, G. (1998). *The scientific practice of professional psychology.* New York: Plenum.

II

THE COMPETENCIES

4

THE RELATIONSHIP COMPETENCY: BROADENING AND DEEPENING

LORRAINE MANGIONE AND LAVITA NADKARNI

The relationship competency occupies a special place, for it is foundational to all other competencies (Polite & Bourg, 1992). Rather than conceptualizing it as one competency in a list, relationship could be envisioned as the substrate, existing under and supporting the other competencies. It is also foundational in that it involves the whole person, including intellectual, emotional, cognitive, physical, cultural, and spiritual aspects as well as involving the context, as it is always relationship with someone. Yet despite its importance, its definition, teaching, and assessment can be vague, difficult to delineate, and even paradoxical.

In this chapter, we offer the National Council of Schools and Programs in Professional Psychology (NCSPP) definition of relationship competency, note its consistency with other definitions, and articulate several dilemmas. To foster curriculum design and implementation, we discuss ideas for teaching, learning, and assessing, including material from NCSPP conferences. We recommend relationship and diversity, and relationship and ethics, as intersects in need of attention and provide ways that they can be infused into the curriculum.

Relationship is the capacity to develop and maintain a constructive working alliance with clients. In the development of relationship skills of professional psychologists, special attention should be given to diversity, including but not limited to gender, race, ethnicity, class, sexual preference, religion, age, physical and mental challenge, culture, and worldview. The relationship competency is the foundation and prerequisite of the other competencies. Therefore, its articulation in the core curriculum is of primary importance. Curriculum design and implementation should include education and training in attitudes essential for the relationship competency, including but not limited to (a) intellectual curiosity and flexibility, (b) open-mindedness, (c) belief in the capacity for change in human attitudes and behavior, (d) appreciation of individual and cultural diversity, (e) personal integrity and honesty, and (f) a value of self-awareness. Curriculum design and implementation should include education and training in the development of interpersonal skills, including empathy, respect for others, and personal relatedness. An essential element of training in this area is experiential learning, with self-reflection and direct observation of behavior and feedback by peers and experts. (McHolland, 1992, pp. 162–163)

The following from Peterson (2007) elaborates on the previous paragraph.

Relationship is the capacity to develop and maintain a constructive working alliance with clients and includes the ability to work in collaboration with others such as peers, colleagues, students, supervisors, members of other disciplines, consumers of services, and community organizations. The relational functioning of professional psychologists is greatly impacted by their awareness and connection to their own self-identity. (p. 11)

Although not articulated as a separate competency at the 2002 Competencies Conference: Future Directions in Education and Credentialing in Professional Psychology, relationship was viewed as a "crosscutting" competency. An individual with strong relationship skills was believed to "convey warmth, empathy, genuineness, and respect for the client" (Spruill et al., 2002, p. 744). Perhaps most illustrative of the central role of relationship was the endorsement of a new core competence, that of "personal suitability or fitness for the profession" (Roberts, Borden, Christiansen, & Lopez, 2005, p. 359). Similarly, the Association of Directors of Psychology Training Clinics delineated relationship as central, developmental, and a competency to develop on practicum.

In this update on relationship competency, we strongly support the above definitions, and we encourage deepening and broadening in these areas: Re-

lationship does indeed apply to all professional relationships; diversity and ethics are key components that need further articulation; and the capacity to take a metaperspective with regard to self and relationships is central to the knowledge, skills, and attitudes (KSAs) to understand, have, and work with relationships.

Table 4.1 describes the developmental achievement levels (DALs) for the relationship competency. The DALs describe the required KSAs across three stages of training: (a) beginning practicum, (b) beginning internship, and (c) completion of degree. Given the unique nature of this competency, in that it is foundational yet also complex and nuanced, and involves the whole of the person as well as the context, the ambiguity and subjectivity of aspects of the relationship competency that are delineated next could invite a spectrum of interpretations.

RELATIONAL DILEMMAS: ISSUES IN LEARNING, TEACHING, AND ASSESSMENT

What constitutes excellence in terms of the relationship competency? What might a relationally adept psychologist look like? Are there defining features and ways to measure them? In this section, we discuss relationship competency dilemmas that frame our thinking.

Nature and Nurture

Can relational capacity and skills be taught, or do students have to arrive already proficient in relationship? Anecdotal evidence seems to point to both possibilities—students need some basic capacity and skill; yet, given that, much can be enhanced and learned. Early screening in admissions and the first year, and early attention to relationship, are necessary. Graduate programs cannot be in the business of changing long-standing character pathology but certainly can support, hone, and challenge students to make changes. A corollary is whether relationship can be taught explicitly or must be absorbed more implicitly. Again we argue that both are necessary, yet too often programs rely on implicit methods. Relationship needs to emerge from the shadows to its rightful place as the foundational competency, foremost in the values of the program as a normal part of the curriculum, not reserved for problematic students.

False Self Juxtaposed to Real Self

The American Psychological Association (APA; 2002) has provided us, given the ethics requirement around self-disclosure and informed consent in graduate school, with the impetus to make relationship more robust and

TABLE 4.1
Knowledge, Skills, and Attitudes and Domains
for the Relationship Competency

Begin practicum	Begin internship	Complete doctoral degree
Professional demeanor domain		
K 1. Understanding of the meaning of professional demeanor 2. Understanding of basic social skills 3. Understanding of the importance of the role of psychologist 4. Understanding of professional boundaries	1. Knowledge of how relationships are central to the multiple roles of professional psychologists 2. Knowledge of norms for professional relationships	1. Understanding of the intersection of diversity and professional demeanor and the significance of context
S 1. Development of basic social skills 2. Ability to be organized, on time, on task, and courteous 3. Demonstration of professional clothing/appearance and good personal hygiene 4. Ability to comfortably converse with others and convey support and acceptance	1. Demonstration of comfort and confidence in role of psychology trainee and recognition of when that comfort and confidence is lacking	1. Ability to interact with others with respect and appropriate assertiveness 2. Ability to reflect on the impact of oneself on others 3. Flexibility in conveyance of professional demeanor based on context and diversity
A 1. Valuation of honesty and integrity 2. Maintenance of a sense of hope and desire to be helpful 3. Maintenance of an attitude of inquiry and openness to experience and ideas	1. Initiation of integration between professional identity and sense of self	1. Respect/manners/ etiquette with those above and below the person in the chain of command
Self domain		
K 1. Knowledge of self-boundaries as they relate to client/therapist roles 3. Understanding of self-based affect, motives, and causes of conflicts	1. Knowledge of theories and models for personal and cultural identity	1. Adequate knowledge of self in role as therapist 2. Knowledge of self and how one responds to specific groups and individuals Knowledge of personal strengths and limits

S 1. Ability to listen and be empathic to others 2. Beginning ability to tolerate affect, conflict, and ambiguity 3. Beginning ability to be aware of own motives, attitudes, behaviors, and effects on others	1. Ability to identify own strengths and weaknesses vis-à-vis relationship 2. Engagement in appropriate self-care especially as it relates to ability for professional relationships 3. Awareness of biases and blind spots with regard to relationships 4. Participation in honest and productive self-reflection 5. Comfort in varying roles, or ability to address its lack 6. Ability to recognize, tolerate, and use one's affect in professional relationships 7. Ability to seek support when needed, including being able to collaborate, do a realistic self-assessment, and recognize relationship ruptures	1. Ability to avoid blind spots and biases in relationships 2. Engagement in regular self-reflection about one's role as therapist and as professional 3. Formation of a positive self-identity about one's professional role 4. Ability to engage in fairly advanced self-evaluation and self-reflection
A 1. Openness to feedback 2. Openness to new ideas or perspectives 3. Desire to help others 4. Inquisitiveness 5. Self-reflectiveness	1. Ability to tolerate ambiguity in relationships, including not knowing and not having the answers 2. Attainment of a strong sense of flexibility within relationships including intervening flexibly 3. Involvement in the development of a sense of professional identity	1. Maintenance of objectivity about self 2. Openness to others' input and views about oneself 3. Commitment to lifelong learning and the fact that professional development will continue to occur

Other domain

K 1. Achievement of beginning level knowledge of other people from the literature in diversity, social psychology, and	1. Knowledge of, and respect for, the complexity of diversity across different cultural groups and perspectives	1. Knowledge of the theoretical interpersonal literature and literature on various models of relationship

continues

TABLE 4.1
Continued

Begin practicum	Begin internship	Complete doctoral degree
therapeutic relationships 2. Knowledge and distinguishing of others as different	2. Understanding of a systems perspective and the contextual nature of relationships 3. Acquisition of a broad fund of knowledge of personality styles and ability to adjust relationships on the basis of those styles 4. Knowledge of norms in a variety of contexts (broadly defined, and relevant to student's specialty and previous work, cultural, professional, by setting) 5. Attainment of a theoretical understanding of how relationships apply to treatment	2. Deeper knowledge of specific others who are different from self
S 1. Ability to engage in perspective taking 2. Ability to articulate aspects of self and other in the therapy relationship	1. Ability to evaluate norms in a variety of contexts (broadly defined, and relevant to student's specialty and previous work, cultural, professional, by setting) 2. Application of contextual information to adjust and enhance professional relationships	1. Ability to step back affectively and cognitively from a relational process 2. Integration of experience with literature to understand relationships 3. Ability to form collegial relationships with others
A 1. Respect for and interest in other cultures and other perspectives	1. Recognition of autonomy and values differences of clients 2. Appreciation of other disciplines and professions	1. Flexibility, tolerance of affect, and curiosity about others

Interpersonal connection domain

Begin practicum	Begin internship	Complete doctoral degree
K 1. Knowledge of basic relationship skills 2. Understanding of the importance of relationship as a foundation for psychologists	1. Knowledge of therapeutic alliance 2. Knowledge of groups and their dynamics 3. Knowledge of the importance and process of metacommunication,	1. Understanding that relationships provide useful data 2. Knowledge of varied population-specific and setting-specific relationships

reflexivity, or processing of relationships

4. Awareness of the possibility of taking a metaperspective on, or stepping back to view, oneself and one's relationships

S 1. Demonstration of basic skills in rapport building, expressing empathy, and listening	1. Ability to form a therapeutic alliance 2. Basic ability to engage others around difficult issues 3. Basic ability to work with others to reflect upon the nature of one's relationship with them 4. Beginning ability to negotiate/accept disagreements 5. Developing ability for metacommunication to repair or learn about relationship ruptures 6. Ability to communicate hope	1. Ability to tolerate affect, stay with others' pain 2. Ability to discuss the relationship with others, to reflect what's happening in the relationship 3. Ability to form a working alliance across contexts and roles 4. Participation in more independent decision making about handling relationships 5. Ability to understand things in the moment, not just upon reflection; can act in the moment sometimes 6. Ability to manage conflict across a variety of professional relationships 7. Ability to begin to relate to others as a professional, not as a student
A 1. Openness to hearing about and understanding the experience of others 2. Valuation of communication 3. Achievement of empathy for others 4. Exhibition of basic compassion toward self and others	1. Attainment of a strong sense of flexibility within relationships including intervening flexibly 2. Commitment to serving the needs of the client (not own needs) 3. Curiosity and openness regarding interpersonal exchange 4. Openness to giving and receiving feedback	1. Internalization of previously described, foundational attitudes 2. Attainment of a greater sense of spontaneity within relationships

continues

TABLE 4.1
Continued

Begin practicum	Begin internship	Complete doctoral degree
Cultural adaptability domain		
K 1. Knowledge of how different worldviews impact relationships 2. Knowledge of helping relationships within a social justice and cultural context	1. Explicit exploration of issues of power and privilege 2. Empathic understanding of marginalization and differences in worldviews	1. Knowledge about working with community healers/leaders 2. Knowledge of different worldviews
S 1. Attainment of flexible verbal skills 2. Ability to express hope of working together given similarities and differences 3. Ability to use the power of the helping role appropriately, given individual and cultural differences (ICDs) 4. Ability to self-reflect	1. Attainment of flexible verbal and nonverbal skills 2. Ability to negotiate expectations for working together given similarities and differences 3. Ability to self-reflect and self-correct with help from others	1. Attainment of flexible, sensitive, and congruent verbal/non-verbal skills 2. Ability to take the other's perspective when working with individuals from diverse groups 3. Integration of different worldviews in the therapeutic relationship 4. Ability to explore ICDs with ease most of the time
A 1. Valuation of exploration of personal history in relation to ICDs 2. Openness to feedback 3. Valuation of ICDs in self and others	1. Valuation of ICDs within the relationship 2. Valuation of nondefensive and honest dialogue regarding ICDs 3. Valuation of self-correction with help from others	1. Celebration of ICDs within the relationship
Ethics domain		
K 1. Basic knowledge of ethics	1. Understanding of legal and ethical requirements of the profession and how they relate to developing professional relationships 2. Knowledge of common ethical dilemmas within populations in their experience	1. Adequate knowledge of recent judicial and legislative decisions regarding complex ethical issues in relationships 2. Understanding of the complexities of ethical guidelines and models of ethical decision making with respect to relationships

S		
1. Ability to identify and discuss some ethical issues surrounding relationships in class exercises 2. Ability to usually self-reflect -under stress -regarding power/privilege -regarding motivation -regarding manipulation -regarding cultural difference -regarding systemic context	1. Ability to articulate some understanding of the legal and ethical requirements of a professional psychologist and see how they relate to developing professional relationships 2. Ability to recognize ethical dilemmas and relational issues involved with them 3. Ability to usually engage in self-correction of inconsistencies in verbal and nonverbal behavior and in use of power	1. Ability to apply ethics across a variety of situations with regard to relationship issues, particularly boundaries 2. Consistent demonstration of appropriate use of power in relationships 3. Appraisal and adoption of one's own ethical decision making model and ability to apply it with personal integrity and cultural competence in all aspects of professional activities 4. Ability to seek and provide consultation around relationships when needed
A 1. Valuation of ethical behavior 2. Valuation of basic self-care 3. Valuation of care of others 4. Valuation of the training role and the profession 5. Respect for self, others, role/profession	1. Recognition of others' autonomy and differences 2. Demonstration of respect for self, others, and the profession both verbally and nonverbally	1. Valuation of social justice as a value 2. Internalization of ethics code and sense of principled judgment, and the ability to apply it in most situations 3. Valuation of lifelong learning about relationships and ethics

Note. K = knowledge; S = skills; A = attitudes. From *Competency Developmental Achievement Levels (DALs) of the National Council of Schools and Programs in Professional Psychology (NCSPP),* (pp. 10–16), by the National Council of Schools and Programs in Professional Psychology, 2007. Available at http://www.ncspp.info/DALof%20NCSPP%209-21-07.pdf. Copyright 2007 by the National Council of Schools and Programs in Professional Psychology. Reprinted with permission.

explicit. Further, the Council of Chairs of Training Councils (2004) provided the policy language, related to informed consent and due process, to assist graduate programs to address relationship and interpersonal difficulties. If we let students know from the beginning, in admissions, that self-disclosure is part of a program, we bring relationship from the margins to the center. Yet, paradoxically, might this have a chilling effect on the openness and naturalness necessary to get to know students and how they function interpersonally? Are we merely teaching some of them to develop more believable "false selfs"? Our perspective is, maybe we are, but we need to protect people's rights to privacy and due process. We are reminded of Yalom's (2005) idea of group therapy as a social microcosm, such that over time, in the group, group members become who they are outside the group. Although a doctoral program differs from a therapy group, the principle remains—people's behav-

ior and character are sufficiently enduring as to be revealed. Yet everyone is forewarned and knows, in a limited way, what they are entering.

Balance of Safety and Judgment

The graduate program must be a large and strong enough container to encompass a plethora of events, feelings, actions, and behaviors over time. Safety is paramount to allowing this to unfold. Yet how do programs provide a safe environment that is also one in which judgments are made about student appropriateness? How does a program encourage self-reflection, self-evaluation, appropriate risk taking, and sharing vulnerabilities without then "entrapping" students? Our perspective is to encourage talking about the dilemma, naming it, and being honest about the power the program holds over the student juxtaposed with the necessity for the student to be open in order to learn (Hawes, 1998). On a programmatic level, safety comes in the form of clarity of process around evaluations and specific criteria to identify problematic students, which also help with liability and faculty consensus.

Combining Individuality With Professionalism

Psychology training is situated within a culture in which promotion of self expression, individualism, and choice seems prominent, even against a backdrop of conformity and consumerism. It is also a changing culture, with mores and values evolving. What, therefore, constitutes a legitimate difference of opinion, personality style, or expression of diversity, and what might be relational and/or ethical problems or deficits in professional behavior? How do politics, broadly construed, and questions of personal choice and freedom, contribute to this issue? For us, clarity resides in the process, not in the content. What is the capacity of the student to take a metaperspective and to understand why something is or is not considered to be professional? Can the student step back and self-reflect and consider where the issue might gather its significance and intensity? Can he or she try on the role of others to imagine the impact? The capacity for self-reflection can clarify the relational ramifications and point to a resolution.

Student, Faculty, and Community Levels

The growth of relationship can only occur in a context in which faculty, supervisors, and administrators are also working toward competence. A psychology program is a community based on relationships, and this communal level may need attention and self-reflection also. As McHolland (1992) described it, "Training should embody the principles inherent in the competency (i.e., constructive working alliances among faculty and students)" (p. 163).

THE TEACHING AND LEARNING OF RELATIONSHIP

Teaching and learning about relationship ought to pervade the graduate program, from admissions to coursework, practicum, supervision, special projects, research, assistantships, dissertation, advising, and independent studies. Each activity can be viewed in terms of subject matter as well as the process. The relationship competency can be taught through the process in any course. This may necessitate a rethinking, particularly in more content-focused courses.

The KSAs relevant to relationship were eloquently defined years ago and appear in the opening definitions of this chapter. Although we generally concur with their articulation, we emphasize ethics and diversity as having grown in importance and therefore requiring more attention. Furthermore, the activity of reflecting on oneself and relationships, described here as taking a metaperspective, bears further discussion, as does conflict management. Relational skills seem to be needed more when things are not going well, when a disagreement arises; therefore, competency in those areas is crucial.

With regard to the methods of teaching relationship, some specific suggestions taken partly from the relationship competency group of NCSPP's pedagogy conference in 2005, the Education and Pedagogy Committee's Task Force on Relationship (Mangione & Campbell, 2005), and conversations on relationship in 2006 are offered in this section, organized developmentally.

For new graduate students, two types of direct learning about relationship seem critical: a class in which to learn basic relational KSAs about work with clients and general professional relationships and a class in which their own emerging or changing identities and their interpersonal processes are clarified and examined. Neither of these should be left to chance or implicit learning alone; a class lets the students know that this is, indeed, foundational. Both classes should be framed within the relational competency, making the values and definition of relationship central. *Issues* should be framed as normal, for it is not in having an issue that renders the student unfit but in how the student addresses the issue. In the first class, experiential types of teaching and learning might take place, such as role playing, role modeling, videotaping with feedback, microskills training, active listening practice, conflict management or resolution, and giving and receiving feedback, in an atmosphere of practice and support. Timely and specific feedback will steer the student in an appropriate direction.

In the second class, which should be limited in size and may be a professional seminar, students would be encouraged to examine (a) self-in-role and how becoming a psychologist affects who they are and is affected by who they are (Singer, Peterson, & Magidson, 1992); (b) identity broadly construed; (c) their way of relating, relating across difference or with diverse populations; (d) their impact on others and others on them; and (e) the

intersect of professional ethics and relationship. This may be done through exercises, a training group type of format, or in conjunction with discussing clinical work. Other experiential learning, such as creating art that represents one's identity or involvement with people in the community who embody a new population for the student, that is then integrated within the class group, could be enlightening. The faculty member must have strong relational skills, an understanding of the group process, and a way to help students sit with difficult feelings, interactions, and ambiguity, without rushing to blame or to fix. Timely and specific feedback on interpersonal processes, and particularly on charged areas that may need attention outside of the classroom, is, again, crucial. In these initial courses students can begin to see the value of an attitude of curiosity about themselves, others, and relational processes, rather than an attitude of judgment or silencing, which is key to the capacity to take a metaperspective.

Relationship as it intersects with ethics and diversity merits explicit inclusion in those courses, addressing the ways in which ethics and diversity involve the whole person and relationships. Ethics in psychology come alive when they are viewed as lived and personal, involving real people and real relationships. Issues of social roles and boundaries involving faculty, students, and clients can be discussed as they are encountered in practice. Diversity can become more meaningful when identity and interpersonal aspects are also taught and felt. There is often a relational component to any dilemmas in diversity or ethics, and that component can be highlighted. For diversity, relational themes of humility and flexibility can be discerned in the DALs, and for ethics, the relational themes of respectfulness and personal autonomy are palpable. An underlying dynamic in both areas is the presence and use of power, and we therefore suggest an analysis of power and its place in psychology as embodied in Hawes (1998).

The student should end the first year with more knowledge and skills about relationship, an attitude of openness and inquiry, and knowing that how he or she forms, maintains, and works within relationships is basic to doing well in psychology.

In the middle years, as students are immersed in clinical training, emphasis within the relational competency could become more sophisticated. For example, Whiston and Coker (2000) discussed spending more time on the development of complex clinical skills, such as experiential confrontation. An important complex skill is the ability to use a metaperspective or take a reflective position within relationships. Taking a metaperspective involves stepping into a cognitive and affective stance one step removed from the situation at hand, which is often a conflict, examining one's own biases, values, affect, and behavior, and finding a larger umbrella under which understanding and acceptance take precedence over explaining and persuading. Others have described a similar process under different names and contexts (Hawes, 1998; Safran & Muran, 2000; Singer et al., 1992; Yalom, 2005).

In a conscious fashion, participants in a relationship are invited to another level of reflection about that relationship.

How can this be taught in graduate school? One way is to practice it, over and over, formally and informally, in all venues of learning. In a contentious class meeting in which students are upset over some action of a faculty member, the meeting facilitator can move to the metaperspective by asking groups to put aside their position, consider their own position and how it was constructed, imagine the other view, and then consider a larger perspective that can see and understand both. One approach often used when teaching diversity is referred to as *fishbowl discussions* (Yeskel & Leondar-Wright, 1997) in which the members of one group (the fish) sit in the center of a circle and discuss an issue among themselves, while the outer circle (the bowl) observes and listens without interruption. A discussion can then ensue, allowing the outer circle to reflect on the perspective offered by the inner circle. In supervision, attention to the relationship, such as a built-in practice of looking at how the supervision and the relationship itself are working, could help mitigate or resolve problems (Mangione & Mears, 2008).

A more formalized, explicit way to teach about metaperspective might involve a mechanism such as the public conversations model (http://www.publicconversations.org), a meditation model such as described by Kabat-Zinn (1994), or Pantesco's (2008) model of difficult interaction skills for working with highly charged, evaluative material. In these, a technology of sorts or a process is offered that encourages people to learn to sit with strong feelings and open up to the views of others as well as negotiate conflict and disagreement.

During these middle years, much learning about relationship takes place on practicum, where students are often challenged with multiple professional relationships across disciplines and with support staff as well as with client–therapist and supervisor–supervisee relationships. Students need to be educated about the relational aspects of supervision and the practicum community through coursework and orientation to practicum. Supervisors need to be empowered to discuss relational aspects of supervision and clinical work. Such empowerment can be achieved through information and personal contact from the graduate school and through continuing education offered by the graduate program to the supervisors. Within a safe supervisory relationship, agreement on the expectations, goals, and tasks of supervision can be discussed. Developmentally, late practicum and internship years should constitute the greatest challenges to and opportunities for deepening the relationship competency.

By the last year of graduate training, it is hoped that students have acquired much knowledge about relationship; have developed a high level of self-awareness; are comfortable engaging with a variety of clients, faculty, supervisors, and colleagues; and have made progress in their ability to take a metaperspective within relationships. At this point, as they are working on

their dissertations and applying to internships, new relational challenges will arise, and the teaching and learning should become more individualized. Some challenges might have to do with issues around perceived competence, endings, and transition; taking a more adult role in the culture, competition and anxiety over internship; and the difficulty of finishing something meaningful. It is here when an individual advisor, mentor, supervisor, or dissertation chair might work most closely with a student on continuing to deepen their relational capacity and not closing off the meanings of current challenges or the relationships that can support the student in transition. Relevant self-disclosure by faculty, modeling openness and empathy, offering feedback, and helping the student to take a metaperspective might all provide consolidation and grounding. However, students could also benefit from revisiting relationship competency in a formalized way through a class or workshop that systematically looks at relational and personal and professional identity challenges at the end of graduate school and prepares the student for lifelong learning within and about relationship. A focus on relationship in a programmatic, planned manner at this stage transmits the message that relationship is both foundational and ongoing.

THE ASSESSMENT OF RELATIONSHIP

The assessment of a student's progress in relationship mirrors that of other competencies. Methods for multi-informant assessment include direct observation, standardized vignettes, supervisor ratings, and 360-degree evaluations along with self-assessment (Henderson Daniel, Roysircar, Abeles, & Boyd, 2002). A program must inform the student that this competency is being evaluated and how it is being evaluated, have a measurement device to evaluate it, and follow its stated procedures to ensure due process. There must be reasonable mechanisms delineated to improve or remediate a student's performance, and the bar for failure must be clear. Oliver, Bernstein, Anderson, Blashfield, and Roberts (2004) speak to such an interpersonal evaluation framework in more detail. Yet intangibles make evaluation of relationship amorphous and complicated. Next we offer general guidelines on evaluation, suggestions about remediation, and thoughts about the meaning of a competency focus in evaluation.

An evaluation-rich environment (Peterson, 2004) can remove some of the burden, stigma, and fear associated with evaluation, and we suggest a culture with a plethora of opportunities for small, immediate, formative kinds of evaluation and feedback. This should begin in admissions, in which applicants need to be aware that relational abilities are part of the admissions equation, and both formal and informal appraisals of relationship are noted. Letters of recommendation and personal statements require *interpretive* reading to glean information about personal adjustment and interpersonal

strengths and weaknesses. These documents can be augmented by an admissions exercise in which applicants work together on a project or by a more ambiguous task in which an applicant's capacity to sit with anxiety or make meaning of the task in relation with others is tested. More informal moments are also telling, given that applicants may be able to offer honed relationship skills for an interview. The DALs call for an admissions level of baseline competency in areas such as respectful communication, self-awareness, basic relationship skills, openness to others, and lack of obvious psychopathology. Each program must devise its own rubric for weighting viewpoints on applicants' relational skills, based on what the program deems important. Over time, a program can measure how well its selection process has done.

In the program, students should come to expect transparency about their work and their relational KSAs. They should know that how they treat people on practicum, in classes, and in the departmental office is part of the *professional relationship*, and that psychology has learned that the relationship is a significant variable in work with clients. Students need to know that they have limited confidentiality at best. Descriptors about relationship should appear on all course evaluations. For example, programs can consider an evaluation of professional demeanor and behavior, such that students get evaluated on issues such as openness to feedback, punctuality, appropriate self-reflection, thoughtfulness, attendance, and class demeanor. Some negative behaviors that bear close scrutiny are disrespect to staff, inflexibility, not cooperating with others, problems with punctuality, lack of insight into oneself, lack of awareness of effect on others, inability to receive or provide constructive feedback, lack of conflict resolution skills, inability to tolerate ambiguity, and discomfort with strong affect. Supervisors should be expected to engage in formative, ongoing evaluation of relational competency, particularly concerning the therapist–client relationship, to such a degree that the summative, end-point evaluations are not surprises. Practicum and internship evaluation forms need to be revised toward delineating competencies, particularly relationship. General questions can be supplemented with more specific ones. For example, "capacity to relate to clients" can be further described by ratings about ability to support, confront, elicit feelings, set limits, provide acceptance, and so forth. "Openness to supervision" and "conducts self in professional manner" would benefit from similar elucidation.

Advisors should routinely address relationship development with students. Faculty should be encouraged to speak with a disruptive, defensive, or monopolizing student and work with him or her to understand and change the behavior. Self-evaluation should become the norm—with students expecting that they will evaluate their relationship strengths and challenges. Multiple viewpoints are welcome. In fact, students are described as being on the front line with regard to peers and relationship, particularly in courses in which relationship is primary or in which group projects are expected. We

need to tap into this experience in a way that is not punitive, paranoia producing, or disruptive of community building.

During the first few months of school, a formal or informal diagnostic evaluation of the student's relational abilities and attitudes could be done. This could involve a scale or structured feedback from faculty and peers, but it should always include self-assessment and a face-to-face discussion with a faculty member. One such self-assessment tool for health psychology was proposed by Belar et al. (2001).

With regard to remediation, and the possibility of termination, a tension always exists around timing and the level of acceptable functioning. Are there certain actions that warrant immediate termination? How long does one work with a student? What is satisfactory progress? With relationship, given its inherent ambiguity and the uncertainty of the role normal development might take, we suggest moving into remediation quickly given the length of time that may be required for improvement and the necessity of competence for clinical functioning. Mitigating life events or circumstances, developmental stage, issues of diversity, and personality style and general level of functioning must all be considered in deciding whether a problem exists and how to respond. Remediation needs a thoughtful written plan developed in conjunction with the student and other faculty, with a clear sense of the problem and what would constitute improvement. The requirement of psychotherapy as part of a plan can be helpful if focused on clearly defined problems, if the department can help a student access affordable psychotherapy, and if there is clarity regarding boundaries between therapy and the department. An intensive professional or personal mentoring experience with a faculty member or supervisor with whom the student feels comfortable can also be facilitative, especially if it does not exist more routinely. This may be an opportunity for increased use of live observation and videotape and further focus on microskills training. Oliver et al. (2004) suggested interventions such as psychotherapy, increased supervision, leave of absence, repetition of courses, and/or practicum. In the end, it is up to faculty to take on the often straining issues of inability to remediate and to work through their own blocks to adequately addressing such complicated problems that involve a competency that goes to the core of who and what a person is. Pantesco's (2008) discussion of the system culture and strategies for intervention is enlightening about how to proceed with this.

In a competency framework, we need to actually see that the person can or cannot perform competently. It is not enough to have taken a course or to not have shown a problem. In this way, the department has to become a self-monitoring, self-reflective community with myriad possibilities for having, looking at, and evaluating relationships.

This renewed focus on relationship has ramifications for Domain E, Faculty and Student Relations, of the Committee on Accreditation's *Guidelines and Principles* (2005). Increased attention may certainly result in greater

attrition due to relational difficulties, but it should also add to a richer relational environment for all concerned. It is crucial that informed consent, due process, conflict resolution, appropriate procedures, and remediation are done well, which can result in enhanced protection of the public, our profession, the programs, students, and faculty.

REFERENCES

American Psychological Association. (2002). Ethical principles of psychologists and code of conduct. *American Psychologist, 57*, 1060–1073.

Association of Directors of Psychology Training Clinics. (2005). *Report on practicum competencies.* Paper presented at the Midwinter Meeting of ADPTC, March 25, 2004, Miami, FL.

Belar, C. D., Brown, R. A., Hersch, L. E., Horyak, L. M., Rozensky, R. H., Sheridan, E. P., et al. (2001). Self-assessment in clinical health psychology: A model for ethical expansion of practice. *Professional Psychology: Research and Practice, 32*, 135–141.

Committee on Accreditation. (2005). *Guidelines and principles for accreditation of programs in professional psychology.* Washington, DC: American Psychological Association.

Council of Chairs of Training Councils. (2004). *Recommended policy language for the comprehensive evaluation of student-trainee competence in professional psychology programs.* Retrieved March 5, 2009, from http://www.ccptp.org/trainingdirectorpage7.html

Hawes, S. E. (1998). Positioning a dialogic reflexivity in the practice of feminist supervision. In B. Bayer and J. Shotter (Eds.), *Material transactions: Disciplinary practices and the making of subjects* (pp. 94–110). London: Sage.

Henderson Daniel, J., Roysircar, G., Abeles, N., & Boyd, C. (2004). Individual and cultural-diversity competency: Focus on the therapist. *Journal of Clinical Psychology, 60*, 755–770.

Kabat-Zinn, J. (1994). *Wherever you go, there you are: Mindfulness meditation in everyday life.* New York: Hyperion.

Mangione, L., & Campbell, C. (2005). *Report of the relationship competency task force of the Education and Pedagogy Committee of NCSPP.* Unpublished document.

Mangione, L., & Mears, G. (2008) *The supervisory relationship when women supervise women: Questions of power, reflexivity, collaboration, and authenticity.* Manuscript submitted for publication.

McHolland, J. D. (1992). National Council of Schools of Professional Psychology core curriculum conference resolutions. In R. L. Peterson, J. D. McHolland, R. J. Bent, E. Davis-Russell, G. E. Edwall, K. Polite, et al. (Eds.), *The core curriculum in professional psychology* (pp. 155–166). Washington, DC: American Psychological Association.

Oliver, M. N. I., Bernstein, J. H., Anderson, K. G., Blashfield, R. K., & Roberts, M. C. (2004). An exploratory examination of student attitudes toward "impaired" peers in clinical psychology training programs. *Professional Psychology: Research and Practice, 35,* 141–147.

Pantesco, V. F. (2008). *Conducting difficult professional encounters: A competence whose time has come.* Unpublished manuscript.

Peterson, R. L. (2004). Evaluation and the cultures of professional psychology education programs. *Professional Psychology: Research and Practice, 35,* 420–426.

Peterson, R. L. (2007). *Standards for education in professional psychology: National Council of Schools and Programs in Professional Psychology resolutions through 1996.* Unpublished manuscript.

Polite, K., & Bourg, E. (1992). Relationship competency. In R. L. Peterson, J. D. McHolland, R. J. Bent, E. Davis-Russell, G. E. Edwall, K. Polite, et al. (Eds.), *The core curriculum in professional psychology* (pp. 83–88). Washington, DC: American Psychological Association.

Roberts, M. C., Borden, K. A., Christiansen, M. A., & Lopez, S. J. (2005). Fostering a culture shift: Assessment of competence in the education and careers of professional psychologists. *Professional Psychology: Research and Practice, 36,* 355–361.

Safran, J. D., & Muran, J. C. (2000). *Negotiating the therapeutic relationship.* New York: Guilford Press.

Singer, D., Peterson, R., & Magidson, E. (1992). The self, the student, and the core curriculum: Learning from the inside out. In R. L. Peterson, J. D. McHolland, R. J. Bent, E. Davis-Russell, G. E. Edwall, K. Polite, et al. (Eds.), *The core curriculum in professional psychology* (pp. 133–139), Washington, DC: American Psychological Association.

Spruill, J., Rozensky, R. H., Stigall, T. T., Vasquez, M., Bingham, R. P., & De Vaney Olvey, C. (2004). Becoming a competent clinician: Basic competencies in intervention. *Journal of Clinical Psychology, 60,* 741–754.

Whiston, S. C. & Coker, J. K. (2000). Reconstructing clinical training: Implications from research. *Counselor Education and Supervision, 39,* 228–254.

Yalom, I. (2005). *The theory and practice of group psychotherapy.* New York: Basic Books.

Yeskel, F. & Leondar-Wright, B., (1997). Classism curriculum design. In M. Adams, L. A. Bell, & P. Griffin (Eds.), *Teaching for diversity and social justice* (pp. 231–260). New York: Routledge.

5

THE ASSESSMENT COMPETENCY

RADHIKA KRISHNAMURTHY AND JED A. YALOF

Psychological assessment is a fundamental component of professional clinical psychology work, second only to psychotherapy in its centrality in clinical practice (Meyer et al., 1998). The National Council of Schools and Programs of Professional Psychology (NCSPP) educational model defines *assessment* as "an ongoing, interactive, and inclusive process that serves to describe, conceptualize, characterize, and predict relevant aspects of a client" (R. L. Peterson, D. R. Peterson, Abrams, & Stricker, 1997, p. 380). Assessment is a highly complex and comprehensive activity, such that the development of this competency requires extensive and carefully crafted training and practice (Krishnamurthy et al., 2004).

In clinical assessment contexts, effective assessors use a scientific method with its attendant knowledge, skills, and attitudes (KSAs) for identifying, evaluating, and responding to clinical problems and concerns. Assessors operate from an informed ethical base (American Psychological Association [APA], 2002) and consider multiple variables when developing inferences from assessment data that affects the welfare of clients and the public's perception of assessment applications (e.g., Meyer et al., 2001). Methods of assessment are quite broad ranging, extending from interviewing and diagnostic testing to review of records, systematic observation/monitoring of behavior, and various approaches to outcome measurement. Assessment competency

includes the ability to utilize diverse methods of evaluation and select the ones most applicable to the specific issue in question (Gold & De Piano, 1992), thus identifying the appropriate evaluation strategies, tools, measures, targets, and time lines across practice settings (Krishnamurthy et al., 2004).

In this chapter, we begin with an overview of recent developments in operationalizing the assessment competency and discuss the essential components of graduate-level assessment training. We proceed to delineate specific educational and practical training approaches and conclude with describing ways to evaluate competency attainment.

ASSESSMENT COMPETENCY STANDARDS AND EXPECTATIONS

The last 2 decades have witnessed progressive efforts by several educational and training councils to articulate professional psychology competencies with increased depth and precision and to establish clear standards for graduate psychology training. With specific reference to the psychological assessment competency, these developments have occurred concurrent with, and in response to, survey findings that have demonstrated inadequacies, gaps, and erosions in graduate assessment training. For example, Belter and Piotrowski's (2001) survey of clinical psychology graduate programs indicated reductions in assessment coursework in recent years. Other surveys have reported deficiencies, such as limited coursework topics and meager linkage between coursework and practical training (Childs & Eyde, 2002), insufficient training in testing and report writing prior to internship (Stedman, Hatch, & Schoenfeld, 2001), and overall, insufficient assessment skills for internship (Clemence & Handler, 2001). These findings appear alongside other survey findings indicating expectations of assessment competency during internship (e.g., Piotrowski & Belter, 1999) and substantial involvement by psychologists in assessment service among their practice activities (e.g., Watkins, Campbell, Nieberding, & Hallmark, 1995). It should be noted that although some survey findings have indicated some curtailment of assessment practice due to managed care constraints (e.g., Piotrowski, Belter, & Keller, 1998), the accumulated evidence suggests that overall impact is less pronounced than was anticipated (Weiner & Greene, 2007). Overall, internship training directors clearly want interns to be competent in psychological testing and assessment at the start of internship, even in tests and batteries that are being used less frequently by practitioners. Moreover, assessment practice has proliferated among some segments of the practicing community, and assessment experts have developed unique niches in the practice environment, warranting the need to ensure that graduates are competent in filling them.

NCSPP has played an active and pioneering role since the early 1980s in identifying core competencies in professional psychology and describing

standards of education and training to foster their development. In the context of NCSPP's delineation of the core curriculum, for example, Gold and De Piano (1992) discussed that assessment training, aimed at preparing students for "sophisticated, effective, ethical, professional functioning in a wide range of possible settings and contexts" (p. 92) should include competency in formulating the referral question, selecting suitable assessment methods, gathering and processing information, generating and integrating interpretive hypotheses, and disseminating the findings effectively. During the 1990s and since, several other professional training groups have advocated competency-focused education and training, and the APA's Committee on Accreditation (COA) has adopted a competency-based approach to graduate program and internship accreditation. The current COA guidelines and principles state, for example, that a graduate program's curriculum plan should provide a means for students to develop and demonstrate competency in "diagnosing or defining problems through psychological assessment and measurement" (APA COA, 2008, pp. 11–12), for which they should receive exposure to current knowledge in "theories and methods of assessment and diagnosis . . . and evaluating the efficacy of interventions" (p. 12).

Several recent conferences held or cosponsored by NCSPP have underscored competency development through the attainment of the requisite KSAs. For example, the 2002 Competencies Conference: Future Directions in Education and Credentialing in Professional Psychology hosted by the Association of Psychology Postdoctoral and Internship Centers involved a broad, collaborative effort by representatives from multiple organizations to build models of professional psychology competency training and evaluation. One schema that emerged from these efforts involved a "cube model" in which competency development was conceptualized in terms of independent but interrelated foundational domains, functional domains, and stages of development (Rodolfa et al., 2005). With regard to psychological assessment, Krishnamurthy et al. (2004) delineated eight core components of competency based on the work of the conference's psychological assessment work group that extended from knowledge of the scientific, theoretical, empirical, psychometric, and contextual bases of psychological assessment and the development of technical assessment skills to the ability to critically evaluate the multiple roles, contexts, and relationships of clients and professionals and their reciprocal impact on assessment activity.

The assessment competency received further elaboration in two recent NCSPP conferences. The 2005 Pedagogy Conference: Realizing Our Competencies Through Teaching and Learning focused on methods of instruction and evaluation of competency achievement, whereas the 2007 Clinical Training Conference: Developing Our Competencies in Clinical Training focused on identifying developmental achievement levels (DALs) that subsume appropriate KSAs expected at three milestones in training. The Pedagogy Conference assessment work group described, for instance, that con-

ducting culturally informed assessments and writing clear, descriptive, and concise assessment reports were essential components of assessment competence. The Clinical Training Conference's assessment work group described four key domains of the assessment competency: interviewing and relationships, case formulation, psychological testing, and ethics and professionalism. Table 5.1 presents the DALs for the assessment competency. The DALs describe the required KSAs across three stages of training: beginning practicum, beginning internship, and completion of degree.

A current effort toward further defining and measuring professional psychology competencies is represented in a document produced by the Assessment of Competency Benchmarks Work Group convened by the APA Board of Educational Affairs in collaboration with the Council of Chairs of Training Councils (Assessment of Competency Benchmarks Work Group, 2007). In this document, assessment competency is discussed as a functional competency that encompasses knowledge of measurement and psychometrics, use of different methods such as interviews and tests, communication of results, and integrative skills. Each of these facets is discussed in terms of its essential components, behavioral anchors, and methods of assessing its attainment across four developmental levels—readiness for practicum, readiness for internship, readiness for entry into practice, and readiness for advanced practice and specialization.

Other developments in recent years include position statements by assessment-related organizations about minimum standards for assessment training. For example, in 2006 the board of trustees of the Society for Personality Assessment (SPA) published a set of standards for education and training in psychological assessment based on the stance that psychological assessment is a specialty requiring intensive and continual education and training. The SPA statement discusses the need for establishing standards in light of the potential harm caused by incompetent assessment practice, delineates the minimum coursework and supervised training necessary for competency, and encourages ongoing honing of skills (SPA Board of Trustees, 2006). The National Academy of Neuropsychology (NAN) issued a position statement about the definition of a clinical neuropsychologist with reference to the necessary academic degree, practical training, experience, and licensure requirements for this professional specialty (NAN Board of Directors, 2001). These various articulations of standards and expectations for assessment competency have been bolstered by evidence of the validity and utility of psychological testing and assessment (e.g., Meyer et al., 2001).

ASSESSMENT TRAINING PRINCIPLES, GUIDELINES, AND APPROACHES

Training in psychological assessment requires more than learning interviewing techniques or psychological test administration and scoring. It

requires acquiring complex skills such as testing hypotheses, conceptualizing information, drawing inferences, and addressing referral questions (Krishnamurthy et al., 2004). Typical guidelines for assessment training cite instruction in psychological theory, developmental psychology, psychopathology, psychodiagnosis, test theory and statistics, and supervised practice and experience in testing as necessary components of training (Krishnamurthy et al., 2004). Survey data indicate that the majority of graduate programs require a course in intellectual assessment and coursework in personality assessment (Piotrowski & Zalewski, 1993), which seem to represent the minimum requirements, typically supplemented with practicum experiences in assessment. Peterson et al. (1997) emphasized that the assessment curriculum should not be restricted to specific individual content courses but should be integrated into a sequence of experiences encompassing training in general principles (e.g., measurement theory) and specific techniques (e.g., formulation of questions) together with supervised skill training. They added that assessment training requires awareness of ethical, sociocultural/diversity, legal, and administrative matters at all stages of training. Krishnamurthy et al.'s (2004) recommendations for assessment training included (a) providing coursework relevant to diverse assessment models that extend from foundational courses to those involving specific assessment methods; (b) offering coherent practicum training experiences in psychological assessment that are consistent with the program model, involve exposure to diverse populations and settings, and include intensive supervision offered through different modalities; (c) ensuring integration of coursework and practicum training experiences; and (d) fostering the development of essential psychological assessment skills within a framework of coherent, cumulative learning involving progressively increasing complexity.

Discussions in recent NCSPP conferences, such as the Pedagogy Conference, have shed light on typical approaches to assessment training used in graduate programs. For example, assessment knowledge, ranging from foundational concepts to advanced topics, is generally taught didactically and supported through the use of texts and other instructional materials. Interviewing and testing skills are often taught through demonstration and observation and developed through practice using volunteer participants prior to conducting actual clinical assessments with clients. Development of appropriate attitudes is often not addressed or trained directly but may be acquired in the course of practicum and internship training. Typical methods of evaluating the acquisition of assessment competency include course examinations and comprehensive examinations and evaluations by practicum and internship supervisors. (Hutchings, Crossman, Krishnamurthy, & Rabe, in preparation). The Benchmarks document (Assessment of Competency Benchmarks Work Group, 2007) offers expanded guidelines for evaluating students' assessment competencies, such as through the use of clinical case vignettes, patient satisfaction surveys, in vivo observations, case presentations styled

TABLE 5.1
Knowledge, Skills, and Attitudes and Domains for the Assessment Competency

Begin practicum	Begin internship	Complete doctoral degree
Interviewing and relationships domain		
K 1. Familiarity with models and techniques of interviewing, treatment planning, and goal setting 2. Familiarity with how the reason for referral drives the assessment 3. Working knowledge of how to appreciate own limitations (know what you do not know)	1. Working knowledge of models and techniques of clinical interviewing (e.g., structured, semi-structured, mental status exams) 2. Knowledge of the content of psychosocial history and mental status exam	1. Broad range of knowledge of models and techniques of interviews and relationships 2. Understanding of how a broad range of referral questions shapes interview 3. Broad knowledge of one's personal characteristics, as they impact the assessment process
S 1. Application of active listening to interviews and assessment 2. Use of empathic responses 3. Ability to begin to conduct a basic biopsychosocial evaluation or interview, with support/supervision	1. Ability to conduct a detailed assessment interview and gather data for a psychosocial history and mental status exam 2. Ability to assist client and referral source in developing a referral question and clarifying limitations of assessment 3. Ability to obtain historical information from collateral sources and to integrate it with self-report data 4. Ability to consult with supervisor as appropriate	1. Sophisticated integration of information and critical analysis of models 2. Flexible, empathic, and accurate utilization of a broad range of interview models and techniques based on referral question, client characteristics, and own self-knowledge
A 1. Respectful attitude toward others as part of enhancing assessment product	1. Willingness to tolerate ambiguity, conflict, and stress	1. Openness to the assessment information that can be derived from other disciplines
Case formulation domain		
K 1. Basic knowledge of the process of hypothesis generation and testing 2. Knowledge of information needed to formulate conceptualization	1. Working knowledge of diagnostic systems and awareness of the strengths and weaknesses of those systems 2. Working knowledge of	1. Knowledge of broad range of individual and system characteristics, (e.g., diversity, psychopathology, development, social context) and

3. Working knowledge of the person in context 4. Basic familiarity with human diversity, relative to the assessment process 5. Basic knowledge of psychopathology	models of psychological strength and psychological problems	how they impact case formulation and diagnosis
S 1. Ability to formulate and test hypotheses 2. Ability to collect and integrate information gathered in an organized manner 3. Ability to communicate findings clearly 4. Ability to utilize integrative and organizational skills to understand the referral question 5. Ability to consider diagnostic options when reflecting on assessment data	1. Ability to generate differential diagnostic possibilities 2. Ability to communicate findings in written form 3. Ability to identify strengths and weaknesses of individuals and systems being assessed 4. Ability to conduct a feedback session with the client and other relevant parties	1. Ability to integrate information gained from interview, collateral sources, and test data for case formulation and diagnosis 2. Ability to appropriately communicate, in writing and orally, to relevant audience 3. Ability to discuss strengths and limitations of assessment measures in report as needed 4. Ability to make appropriate referrals, based on assessment outcome
A 1. Commitment to curiosity and reflective thought to enhance understanding of assessment product	1. Willingness to think critically and with an open mind about alternative hypotheses	1. Commitment to systematically incorporate data from a broad range of sources into case formulation

Psychological testing domain

K 1. Basic knowledge of psychometric test and measurement theory (e.g., test construction, validity, reliability) 2. Basic knowledge of model of assessment/ strategy for assessment	1. Knowledge of constructs and theories underlying psychological tests and psychological testing methods 2. Knowledge of strengths, weaknesses, and limits of applicability of standard intellectual and personality measures 3. Knowledge of the methods of norming tests and implications for test usage with diverse populations	1. Advanced knowledge of strengths, weaknesses, and appropriateness of a broad range of psychological tests across a wide variety of individuals (diversity, psychopathology, development, and social context)

continues

TABLE 5.1
Continued

	Begin practicum	Begin internship	Complete doctoral degree
S	1. Basic foundation skills when performing psychological testing (e.g., administration, scoring, guided interpretation) 2. Ability to understand and convey results from individual tests	1. Ability to administer and score intellectual and personality measures, and to begin the process of integrated interpretation under supervision 2. Ability to identify appropriate measures and sources of information for referral questions in order to answer the questions 3. Ability to identify and adapt assessment methods for unique individuals and systems with supervision 4. With supervision, ability to use critical thinking in evaluating all sources of data in order to prepare an integrative report and offer feedback	1. Ability to choose, administer, score, and interpret tests, appropriate to the referral question with increasing levels of autonomy
A	1. Respectful objectivity and inquiry when conducting an assessment	1. Respect for value of psychological testing and assessment	1. Commitment to looking at the short-term and long-term usefulness of one's assessment work 2. Willingness to develop competency in administration and interpretation of new or revised tests that the psychologist intends to incorporate into own practice

	Ethics and professionalism domain		
K	1. Basic knowledge of ethical assessment 2. Familiarity with ethical issues and potential conflicts 3. Familiarity with external resources, including supervisor, and how to access them	1. Knowledge of legal and ethical principles and guidelines involved in assessment, and knowledge of potential courses of action	1. Refined and sophisticated knowledge of ethical and legal issues related to assessment

S	1. Ability to support decisions about actions 2. Ability to differentiate self needs from client needs when considering ethical dilemmas 3. Ability to use supervision constructively to further training and assessment goals	1. Ability to identify potential legal and ethical issues and address these with supervision	1. Ability to apply relevant legal and ethical principles to the assessment situation, and seeks supervision or consultation as appropriate 2. Ability to make referrals based on legal and ethical principles 3. Ability to seek consultation as needed 4. Ability to delineate limitations of assessment data sources in report
A	1. Respect for operable ethical standards throughout the assessment process	1. Willingness to critically examine test results in light of diverse populations and normative data 2. Willingness to examine the applicability of ethical and legal issues in the context of assessment with diverse populations	1. Integration of respectful attitudes and objectivity, such as curiosity and reflective thought into an ethical professional identity with a commitment to lifelong learning

Note. K = knowledge; S = skills; A = attitudes. From *Competency Developmental Achievement Levels (DALs) of the National Council of Schools and Programs in Professional Psychology (NCSPP)*, (pp. 4–8), by the National Council of Schools and Programs in Professional Psychology, 2007. Available at http://www.ncspp.info/DALof%20NCSPP%209-21-07.pdf. Copyright 2007 by the National Council of Schools and Programs in Professional Psychology. Reprinted with permission.

after the oral exam of the American Board of Professional Psychology, and self-assessments.

TEACHING AND TRAINING METHODS

NCSPP member programs appear mindful of the importance of sound assessment training. Indeed, recent survey data from 49 responding NCSPP programs indicate that approximately 92% have at least one required psychological assessment course within the curriculum and evaluating the competency within the course or curriculum, and nearly 76% formally evaluate assessment competency in both practica and internships (NCSPP and APA Research Office, 2006). In this section, we illustrate how the effective teaching and training of psychological assessment KSAs can lead to student outcomes that reflect a readiness to assume responsibilities as a psychological assessor in professional practice settings.

The Teacher's Role

Many NCSPP programs subscribe to a sequential, integrated, scholarly, and primarily practice-oriented philosophy in which program administrators and faculty strive to coordinate the teaching of scientific knowledge and clinical skill within the NCSPP core areas. Assessment training would therefore cover a wide range of contents, skills, and applications in keeping with established standards (e.g., American Educational Research Association, APA, & National Council on Measurement in Education, 1999) including assessment of different age groups (e.g., Sattler, 2001; Smith & Handler, 2006), linking assessment and intervention (e.g., Mortimer & Smith, 1983), and evidence-based practice in psychology (APA Presidential Task Force on Evidence-Based Practice, 2006). This information is disseminated under the direction of the assessment teacher. The teacher also sets the tone for the type of learning climate that either facilitates or impedes the acquisition of the aforementioned knowledge and skill domains.

The assessment teacher ideally aspires to bring a substantial degree of synthesis to the course area, paralleling the NCSPP model's goal of brining a high level of integration across the curriculum. Although course syllabi may be prescriptive with respect to the content areas within a particular subject domain, the manner in which this information is presented, deliberated, and critiqued establishes the essence of a positive learning environment. By modeling the NCSPP mission through the professionalism that defines the manner in which instructional content is delivered—that is, by functioning professionally, ethically, scholarly, and clinically in the classroom—the teacher provides students with opportunities to observe, emulate, and internalize important values and attitudes that are core components of the NCSPP education and training philosophy.

As students transverse these specialized areas, they build toward higher levels of integration in their assessment work as reflected ultimately in positive formative and summative outcomes. Formative outcomes include performance on tests and practice activities relative to particular classes. Summative measures are aligned closely with performance on comprehensive examinations as well as practicum and internship. Attainment of these ends places considerable pressure on the teacher's classroom management skills because of (a) the complexity of course content and the challenge of constructing reasonable, pragmatic, fair, and defensible evaluation measures; (b) the teacher's desire to share knowledge, feel affirmed, and make a significant contribution to student development—each of which can be accompanied by anxiety because of the meanings that teachers attach to student evaluations of the teacher's performance; and (c) student needs for affirmation, information, attention, and successful performance as well as their anxiety about being evaluated. Thus, when organizing a course and considering vari-

ous instructional strategies, the teacher crafts teaching interventions; that is, the teacher provides the timing, dosage, and tact that paves the way for a positive classroom experience.

Pedagogy and Practical Training

Teaching assessment within the NCSPP model implies that the core areas of relationship, intervention, research and evaluation, consultation and education, management and supervision, and diversity will be addressed as part of the assessment course sequence. Course and practicum requirements vary depending on the content domain (e.g., intellectual assessment vs. personality assessment courses), but typically involve reading and critiquing literature; learning and applying standardized test administration, scoring and interpretation rules; interviewing; writing reports; and providing feedback to clients. These are foundational skills for assessment psychologists. In this section, we discuss some ways to accomplish this end.

Test Administration, Scoring, and Interpretation

Students can practice test administration in the controlled classroom setting to gain confidence in handling different test materials and administering tests. The use of student role plays is one way to practice test administration. Students can practice giving different tests to each other and, with appropriate consent and the teacher's oversight, to testing volunteers. The teacher can play the role of the client as a demonstration and for instructional and practice purposes to show how to address typical situations that clinicians encounter in practice. Such role play permits quick and easy feedback to students on a variety of procedural issues and might involve the teacher as test examinee (a) purposefully providing ambiguous responses (e.g., on the vocabulary subtest that requires the student to apply standard prompts), (b) acting in a manner that requires the student to verbally intervene (e.g., becomes frustrated with the block design subtest), (c) continually rotating Bender-Gestalt cards to see how the student responds, or (d) giving responses to Rorschach inkblots. The teacher thereby observes the manner in which students adhere to procedure, inquire, and respond clinically to contrived, but challenging, interpersonal situations that the teacher develops as part of the learning exercise. Students can also be given roles to play with each other, with the teacher overseeing the practice and providing instructive feedback to the class as a whole. They can also observe the teacher in class during a mock administration, observe supervisors administering tests, and view instructional tapes.

Test scoring and interpretation can be taught and practiced by using protocols developed specifically for the course. For example, the teacher might do a walk-through of scoring an IQ test, review a Rorschach protocol for coding accuracy, share test protocols that have scoring errors and invite students to identify the mistakes, or challenge students to integrate the data points of different self-report measures (e.g., Minnesota Multiphasic Person-

ality Inventory–2 [MMPI-2], Personality Assessment Inventory, Millon Clinical Multiaxial Inventory). With respect to test interpretation, students move from basic to advanced interpretation as their understanding of the various data points that define the assessment process evolves. These data points include test variables, story narratives, clinical scales, and subtest scores, in conjunction with history, observations, and reactions to the client. The teacher's use of carefully selected protocols for interpretation purposes helps students learn the fundamentals of interpretation for each test and how to generate recommendations from test results. Moreover, the teacher's use of handouts, sample reports, sharing of insights, respectfulness of the class learning curve, and ability to answer what are often very sophisticated student questions makes it easier for students to relax and absorb information relevant to test interpretation.

There are two specific competency areas—ethical reasoning and multicultural awareness—that particularly anchor assessment applications in pedagogy. Competent assessment requires an understanding of ethical principles and standards (APA, 2002), and an appreciation for how these principles and standards interface with multiculturalism (APA, 2003). NCSPP programs strive to integrate these domains into the fabric of assessment training. The areas of professional ethics and multiculturalism are each represented extensively in the assessment literature, and it is the responsibility of programs to draw on this literature to support the development of ethical and multicultural sensitivity in students.

A sampling of some recent literature in both areas illustrates the way in which they can be understood as foundational to supporting the attainment of competency in psychological assessment. In the area of ethics education and practice, for example, de las Fuentes et al. (2005) summarized work group findings from the 2002 Competencies Conference and described the skills and knowledge that psychologists and psychologists in training need to acquire to be ethically competent. Yalof and Brabender (2001) described how ethical issues can be integrated into the teaching of personality assessment by using classroom experiences to illustrate ethical concepts. Claasen and Lovitt (2001) presented a decision-tree model for resolving ethical dilemmas that emerge when conducting psychological assessment in medical settings. In the area of multiculturalism, Dana's (1993) scholarly volume on multicultural assessment provides an essential foundation for KSAs in this domain, and Lopez (2002) described a didactic approach for teaching students about culturally informed assessment that includes a basic knowledge of tests and methods, minimization of inferences based on group labels, and formulation that considers cultural context.

Interviewing and Relationship Dynamics, Report Writing, and Feedback

We have grouped interviewing and relationship dynamics, report writing, and test feedback together because each area reflects a different type of

clinical skill that intersects particularly with the domains of intervention, relationship, supervision, and consultation. These are skills that mature over time. There are excellent sources on which the teacher can draw to support student skill development in the areas of interviewing (e.g., Craig, 2004), understanding the subtleties of client–assessor transaction through self-reflective skills (e.g., Schafer, 1954), report writing (e.g., Tallent, 1993), and feedback (e.g., Finn, 1996; Fischer, 1994). Classroom activities for teaching interviewing can include a review of basic interview components, the teacher's modeling how to conduct an interview, reviewing interview protocols, and conducting mock interviews (e.g., "Critique the way in which the mental status exam was conducted." "Did you think that there was positive rapport?" "How do you feel about the way the interviewer handled the situation where the patient declined to talk about whether or not he was hearing voices?"). Teaching report writing might involve the teacher's taking a series of test scores and background information presented initially as bullet points, talking aloud about how to best organize the information into a written narrative, and reviewing and critiquing reports developed for instructional purposes.

Supervisors who are familiar with the NCSPP model are positioned to understand program-based competencies and the sequence of program prerequisites that prepare students for direct service training. Supervisors who appreciate the various developmental needs of students at different points in training (e.g., Finkelstein & Tuckman, 1997) and who can particularize supervision interventions relative to student needs, foster a sense of self-confidence without overstimulating student anxiety. For beginning assessment students, supervisors may need to exercise more direct control over the supervision agenda. At the start of a student's assessment training, for example, supervisors may need to devote supervision time to activities that support the student's development of basic assessment skills. These activities may include observing interviews and test administrations, double-checking test scoring, reviewing the diagnostic manual, identifying the most relevant information from client charts and medical records, working on report edits, choosing tests, and coleading a feedback session. Assessment students with more advanced skill might not require the degree of supervisory oversight that a beginner requires. Advanced students might still require supervisory direction around basic assessment tasks, but, because of their progressive development in basic areas, they exercise more autonomy in directing the supervision agenda around specific needs that arise with clients.

OUTCOMES

The current "best practices" approach to education and training involves embedding methods of assessing learning outcomes into the structure of the training program. This enables educators and students to ensure that

specific milestones in competency building are reached along the way and that they serve as the foundations for subsequent stages of competency development.

Program Evaluation of Knowledge, Skills, and Attitudes

The evaluation of KSAs in the area of assessment is a complex process that draws on the program's sequential training model and the expertise of evaluators. NCSPP's 2007 articulation of assessment-related KSAs in clinical training provides a practice-oriented appreciation for the maturation of assessment competencies over time. We recommend three ways, discussed next, in which programs can assess student competency in assessment in relation to the NCSPP competency model.

Topic-Centered Evaluation

This type of evaluation is basic to core assessment classes (e.g., can the student provide a thoughtful critique of a test, interview, or test selection for a client; identify problems in a client-assessor interaction; spot scoring errors on a Wechsler Adult Intelligence Scale IV; correctly score a Beck Depression Inventory; analyze MMPI-2 validity and clinical scale patterns; code and interpret a Rorschach; identify core themes in a Thematic Apperception Test; identify behavior problems from a Child Behavior Checklist profile; or some combination thereof, depending on the nature of the course?). Faculty members are challenged to develop, demonstrate, and justify topic-centered evaluative measures of assessment knowledge and skill that have connection to actual clinical practice. There is the additional challenge of integrating content mastery, reasoning, interpersonal skill, and professional attitude into the classroom evaluation process. Faculty also receive evaluation of their performance via the program's feedback mechanisms and are therefore positioned to modify instructional methods in response to this feedback.

Competency-Based Evaluation

As students move toward the end point of formal education and training, carefully constructed, detailed, and competency-based clinical examinations test their ability to accurately score and interpret single measures and integrate information across tests and methods. Advanced examination of assessment skill, such as what might be required in a comprehensive examination format, can target the integration of multiple data points with other information related to cultural context, an ethical dilemma, and information about the client–therapist interaction. Here, students might be asked to organize a report, offer a written response to how they might advise the handling of the ethical dilemma if consulted, describe how they would supervise the therapist around a countertransference issue, reason a differential diagnosis, critique test selection, and articulate an approach for giving feed-

back to the client. Both written and oral components can be integrated into the examination. This type of outcome-oriented evaluative measure addresses formative competencies of research and evaluation, relationship and intervention, consultation and education, and management and supervision, while also engaging the student's self-reflective capacities in response to various clinical situations and questions that are likely to be commonplace occurrences in the real-world activities of a psychological assessor.

Supervisor Evaluation

Program reliance on supervisor evaluations is critical to determining areas of strength and need relative to desired program outcomes in the area of psychological assessment. Falender and Shafranske (2007) discussed the importance of supervisor competence and offered recommendations for competency-based supervision practice as a way of supporting the student's positive learning experience in a supervisory context. The use of evaluation forms that address various facets of the competency provides supervisors with an opportunity to review student progress in areas that the program deems especially relevant and provides clinical training directors with insights about the student's progress that might not be obvious from classroom performance.

SUMMARY

Psychological assessment has and will continue to occupy a prominent position in professional psychology, although the degree of attention given to it in clinical training and practice has waxed and waned slightly over the decades. Because assessment is inherently complex and requires considerable precision, conceptual ability, relational skill, and integrative capacity, as well as the maintenance of appropriate attitudes of inquiry, respect for diversity, and ethicality, the development of this competency has to be systematically and carefully shaped and nurtured in graduate psychology programs. NCSPP competencies can be integrated into the assessment curriculum to provide students with the KSAs for sophisticated assessment training at the doctoral level.

REFERENCES

American Educational Research Association, American Psychological Association, & National Council on Measurement in Education. (1999). *Standards for educational and psychological testing.* Washington, DC: American Educational Research Association.

American Psychological Association. (2002). Ethical principles of psychologists and code of conduct. *American Psychologist, 57,* 1060–1073.

American Psychological Association. (2003). Guidelines on multicultural education, training, research, practice, and organizational change for psychologists. *American Psychologist, 58,* 377–402.

American Psychological Association Committee on Accreditation. (2008). *Guidelines and principles for accreditation of programs in professional psychology.* Washington, DC: Author.

APA Presidential Task Force on Evidence-Based Practice. (2006). Evidence-based practice in psychology. *American Psychologist, 61,* 271–285.

Assessment of Competency Benchmarks Work Group. (2007). *A developmental model for defining and measuring competence in professional psychology.* Retrieved February 26, 2009, from http://www.apa.org/ed/graduate/comp_benchmark.pdf

Belter, R. W., & Piotrowski, C. (2001). Current status of doctoral-level training in psychological testing. *Journal of Clinical Psychology, 57,* 717–726.

Childs, R. A., & Eyde, L. D. (2002). Assessment training in clinical psychology doctoral programs: What should we teach? What do we teach? *Journal of Personality Assessment, 78,* 130–144.

Claasen, C. A., & Lovitt, R. (2001). Solving ethical dilemmas in medical settings during psychological assessment: A decisional model. *Journal of Personality Assessment, 77,* 214–230.

Clemence, A. J., & Handler, L. (2001). Psychological assessment on internship: A survey of training directors and their expectations for students. *Journal of Personality Assessment, 76,* 18–47.

Craig, R. (Ed.). (2004). *Clinical and diagnostic interviewing* (2nd ed.). New York: Aronson.

Dana, R. H. (1993). *Multicultural assessment perspectives for professional psychology.* Boston: Allyn & Bacon.

De las Fuentes, C., Willmuth, M. E., & Yarrow, C. (2005). Competency training in ethics education and practice. *Professional Psychology: Research & Practice, 36,* 362–366.

Falender, C. A., & Shafrankse, E. P. (2007). Competence in competency-based supervision practice: Construct and application. *Professional Psychology: Research & Practice, 38,* 299–306.

Finkelstein, H., & Tuckman, A. (1997). Supervision of psychological assessment: A developmental model. *Professional Psychology: Research & Practice, 36,* 92–95.

Finn, S. E. (1996). *Manual for using the MMPI-2 as a therapeutic intervention.* Minneapolis: University of Minnesota Press.

Fischer, C. T. (1994). *Individualizing psychological assessment.* Hillsdale, NJ: Erlbaum.

Gold, S. N., & de Piano, F. (1992). Assessment competency. In R. L. Peterson, J. D. McHolland, R. J. Bent, E. Davis-Russell, G. E. Edwall, K. Polite, et al., (Eds.), *The core curriculum in professional psychology* (pp. 89–95). Washington, DC: American Psychological Association and National Council of Schools and Programs of Professional Psychology.

Hutchings, P. S., Crossman, R. E., Krishnamurthy, R., & Rabe, D. M. (2005). *Pedagogy and outcome assessment for professional psychology competencies.* Unpublished manuscript.

Krishnamurthy, R., VandeCreek, L., Kaslow, N. J., Tazeau, Y. N., Miville, M. L., Kerns, R., et al. (2004). Achieving competency in psychological assessment: Directions for education and training. *Journal of Clinical Psychology, 60,* 725–739.

Lopez, S. R. (2002). Teaching culturally informed psychological assessment: Conceptual issues and demonstrations. *Journal of Personality Assessment, 79,* 226–234.

Meyer, G. J., Finn, S. E., Eyde, L. D., Kay, G. G., Kubiszyn, T. W., Moreland, K. L., et al. (1998). *Benefits and costs of psychological assessment in healthcare delivery: Report of the Board of Professional Affairs Psychological Assessment Work Group, Part I.* Washington, DC: American Psychological Association.

Meyer, G. J., Finn, S. E., Eyde, L. D., Kay, G. G., Moreland, K. L., Dies, R. R., et al. (2001). Psychological testing and psychological assessment: A review of evidence and issues. *American Psychologist, 56,* 128–165.

Mortimer, R. L., & Smith, W. H. (1983). The use of the psychological test report in setting the focus of psychotherapy. *Journal of Personality Assessment, 47,* 34–38.

National Academy of Neuropsychology Board of Directors. (2001). *Definition of a clinical neuropsychologist: Official position of the National Academy of Neuropsychology.* Retrieved February 21, 2009, from http://nanonline.org/NAN/ ResearchPublications/PositionPapers/DefinitionOfANeuropsychologist.aspx

National Council of Schools and Programs of Professional Psychology and American Psychological Association Research Office (2006). *2005 NCSPP self study: Final results.* Washington, DC: American Psychological Association.

Peterson, R. L., Peterson, D. R., Abrams, J. C., & Stricker, G. (1997). The National Council of Schools and Programs of Professional Psychology educational model. *Professional Psychology: Research and Practice, 28,* 373–386.

Piotrowski, C., & Belter, R. W. (1999). Internship training in psychological assessment: Has managed care had an impact? *Assessment, 6,* 381–385.

Piotrowski, C., Belter, R. W., & Keller, J. W. (1998). The impact of "managed care" on the practice of psychological testing: Preliminary findings. *Journal of Personality Assessment, 70,* 441–447.

Piotrowski, C., & Zalewski, C. (1993). Training in psychodiagnostic testing in APA-approved PsyD and PhD clinical psychology programs. *Journal of Personality Assessment, 61,* 394–405.

Rodolfa, E., Bent, R., Eisman, E., Nelson, P., Rehm, L., & Richie, P. (2005). A cube model for competency development: Implications for psychology educators and regulators. *Professional Psychology: Research and Practice, 36,* 347–354.

Sattler, J. M. (2001). *Assessment of children: Cognitive functions* (4th ed.). San Diego, CA: Author.

Schafer, R. (1954). *Psychoanalytic interpretation in Rorschach testing.* New York: Grune & Stratton.

Smith, S. R., & Handler, L. (Eds.) (2006). *The clinical assessment of children and adolescents: A practitioner's handbook.* Mahwah, NJ: Erlbaum.

Society for Personality Assessment Board of Trustees. (2006). Standards for education and training in psychological assessment: Position of the Society for Personality Assessment. *Journal of Personality Assessment, 87,* 355–357.

Stedman, J. M., Hatch, J. P., & Schoenfeld, L. S. (2001). The current status of psychological assessment training in graduate and professional schools. *Journal of Personality Assessment, 77,* 398–407.

Tallent, N. (1993). *Psychological report writing* (4th ed.). Englewood Cliffs, NJ: Prentice-Hall.

Watkins, C. E., Campbell, V. L., Nieberding, R., & Hallmark, R. (1995). Contemporary practice of psychological assessment by clinical psychologists. *Professional Psychology: Research and Practice, 26,* 54–60.

Weiner, I. B., & Greene, R. L. (Eds.). (2007). *Handbook of psychological assessment.* New York: Wiley.

Yalof, J., & Brabender, V. (2001). Ethical dilemmas in personality assessment courses: Using the classroom for in vivo training. *Journal of Personality Assessment, 77,* 203–213.

6

THE INTERVENTION COMPETENCY

JEFFREY L. BINDER AND FREDRICK S. WECHSLER

Competency in intervention typically refers to an area of activity and has been broadly defined as "activities that promote, restore, sustain, and/or enhance positive functioning and a sense of well-being in clients through preventive, developmental, and/or remedial services" (Peterson, Peterson, Abrams, & Stricker, 1997, p. 380). *Competency* also implicitly refers to a level of performance that is context sensitive, requiring judgment, acumen, and flexibility (Barber, Sharpless, Klostermann, & McCarthy, 2007; Binder, 2004). In an earlier book addressing the professional program training model and curriculum, Bent and Cox (1991) focused on widening the boundaries defining the intervention competency beyond the traditional area of psychotherapy. Whereas intervention does, indeed, cover wider boundaries now, there still is much to learn about and improve in the training of the core intervention competence, psychotherapy. Consequently, we focus on psychotherapeutic interventions by defining this competency in terms of a core cluster of knowledge, skills, and attitudes (KSAs) and by tracking its developmental benchmarks. We also suggest elements of a prototypic curriculum, discuss pedagogical issues associated with psychotherapy training, and describe issues associated with evaluating intervention competence.

During the past several years, stakeholders in clinical psychology training have attempted to define the components of core clinical competencies,

including an intervention competency, and establish benchmarks for assessing progressive acquisition of these competencies during the course of doctoral training. Reflecting the typical curricula of professional training programs, benchmarks have been proposed for determining when a student is (a) ready to begin a clinical practicum, (b) ready to begin an internship, and (c) ready to apply for licensure to enter independent clinical practice. These benchmarks can be used by training programs as guidelines for establishing and measuring student learning outcomes for each phase in training as well as the final program learning outcomes that should be achieved for a student to graduate.

The foundation document from which schools or programs affiliated with the National Council of Schools and Programs in Professional Psychology (NCSPP) can obtain guidance in establishing competency-based student learning outcomes is the "Developmental Achievement Levels" (DALs) document (NCSPP, 2007) approved at the August 2007 NCSPP meeting. The intervention competency is one of seven core competencies, each consisting of a cluster of specific body of knowledge, set of skills, and set of attitudes. The intervention competency is conceptualized in four domains: (a) planning, (b) implementation, (c) evaluation, and (d) ethics. Each domain is operationalized by specific tasks and outcomes across the three dimensions of KSAs. The American Psychological Association (APA) Presidential Task Force on Evidence-Based Practice (2006) also proposed a list of competencies that define *clinical expertise*, which along with knowledge of relevant research findings compose the foundation of evidence-based practice. This task force's conception of clinical competencies overlaps substantially with the NCSPP DALs. Another effort to address clinical competencies was the Assessment of Competency Benchmarks Work Group established by the APA Board of Educational Affairs in collaboration with the Council of Chairs of Training Councils (CCTC). This group used the competencies enumerated by the authors of the "cube" model of competency development (Rodolfa et al., 2005), focused on developing behavioral anchors, and suggested assessment methods. This work group produced A Developmental Model for Defining and Measuring Competence in Professional Psychology (Assessment of Competency Benchmarks Work Group, 2007) as a guideline for establishing and assessing student learning outcomes. The competencies enumerated in this document also overlap substantially with those in the NCSPP document, including comparable dimensions of KSAs as well as comparable stages of training that require learning benchmarks. The intervention competency also had similar domains that included planning, implementation, evaluation, and ethics. The APA document does not provide as detailed a description of the competencies as the NCSPP document, but it does provide more concrete behavioral anchors and suggests more specific assessment methods.

To provide an overview of the current consensus about the nature of the intervention competency, we draw primarily from the NCSPP DALs and

incorporate content from the other two documents where adding to the DALs description would enrich the concept or provide ideas for assessment. Following the format of the DALs, we present the intervention competency organized into the four domains: (a) planning, (b) implementation, (c) evaluation, and (d) ethics. For each domain, we enumerate a set of KSAs that a student should have attained at three major stages of training: (a) beginning practicum, (b) beginning internship, and (c) completing a doctoral degree. The composition of the intervention competency is presented in Table 6.1 to aid readers in assimilating the information.

THE CURRENT CONCEPTION OF THE INTERVENTION COMPETENCY

During the course of students' formal clinical training, the training program must support the achievement of some fundamental learning outcomes.

The Student's Professional Development

A high proportion of students are drawn to clinical psychology because they see themselves as natural helpers and enjoy this role. Once in a clinical training program, many of these students discover to their dismay that the role of professional helper is far more difficult and emotionally taxing than they envisioned. A clinical psychology student must absorb an enormous amount of information and master many skills over several years of training. In addition, the student must successfully negotiate a breathtakingly wide variety of interpersonal relationships and internalize new ethical and multicultural sensibilities. Perhaps the most intimidating challenge involves learning to be intimately and nonjudgmentally attuned to the emotional experiences and lives of clients who are suffering as well as to his or her own emotional reactions to these people. At the same time, the student must collaborate with a client on planning treatment and executing changes to the plan when indicated. This requires continuous adjustments to changing circumstances inside and outside of the therapy setting or what Schön (1983, p. 165) called "reflective conversations" with the problem context. The student also must manage difficulties that arise in the therapeutic relationship, involving strains or ruptures in the therapeutic alliance (Safran & Muran, 2000). In addition, the student should develop the ability to engage in what Messer (2008, p. 365) called "assimilative integration," the incorporation of therapeutic techniques from different models into a primary treatment model.

The faculties of training programs in professional psychology recognize that the evolution from novice student to competent professional requires the acquisition of knowledge and skills as well as psychological maturity. This recognition is reflected in the guidelines for "comprehensive student

TABLE 6.1
Knowledge, Skills, and Attitudes and Domains for the Intervention Competency

Begin practicum	Begin internship	Complete doctoral degree
Intervention planning domain		
K 1. Basic knowledge of theories of therapy and their interventions 2. Knowledge of biopsychosocial data necessary for diagnosis and case formulation 3. Knowledge of biopsychosocial data necessary to plan interventions	1. Knowledge of ways biopsychosocial factors create and maintain risk and protective factors involved in mental health 2. Knowledge of theories of therapy and their application 3. Understanding of history, benefits, and limitations of Evidence-Based Practice (EBP)	1. Knowledge of biopsychosocial factors across variety of populations, presenting problems, contexts and settings, and their impact on presenting problems 2. Understanding of the influence of a chosen theory and interventions on the process of therapy 3. Reliable understanding of factors that limit or influence one's own ability to carry out a treatment plan
S 1. Ability to identify relevant biopsychosocial data for diagnosis, case formulation, and intervention 2. Ability to apply basic diagnostic information 3. Display of empathy, active listening, rapport building, history taking and other information gathering, and other interviewing abilities 4. Beginning ability to apply theory and interventions to a case vignette or role play 5. Ability to select appropriate interventions for a case vignette based on assessment considerations	1. Ability to prioritize biopsychosocial factors maintaining the presenting problem 2. Ability to apply a theory to guide development of a treatment plan 3. Ability to apply increasingly sophisticated interviewing skills across a broader range of populations and settings 4. Ability to modify case formulation in collaboration with a supervisor 5. Ability to collaborate with clients on a treatment plan and orient client to treatment process 6. Ability to explain rationale for selection of a treatment strategy and ability to change strategy as necessary	1. Ability to reliably prioritize biopsychosocial factors across a variety of populations, presenting problems, contexts, and settings 2. Ability to modify a treatment plan when necessary 3. Ability to negotiate challenges to a treatment alliance and integrate nonspecific factors into treatment approach 4. Ability to seek and utilize consultation strategically when formulating cases 5. Ability to independently collaborate with client on a treatment plan and collaborate on changes to treatment plan or specific strategies 6. Ability to integrate interventions from more than one

	7. Ability to utilize appropriate interventions with clients based on diagnostic and case formulation considerations 8. Ability to conceptualize a case from one theoretical model	theoretical model considering diagnoses and case formulation
A 1. Curiosity, openness, empathic stance, desire to serve, respect, and nonjudgmental attitude 2. Appreciation for complexity and ambiguity of clinical problems 3. Acceptance of a range of possible interventions and ability to change course	1. Openness to multidisciplinary consultation, multiple sources of information and scientific inquiry 2. Appreciation of affective nature of treatment and potential ambiguity, ambivalence, and negative feeling states 3. Belief in possibility of change and attitude of hope and optimism 4. Increased acceptance of use of self as instrument of change 5. Deepened appreciation of client's life experience	1. Valuation of and desire for multidisciplinary consultation and seeking additional sources of information 2. Intellectual curiosity 3. Greater commitment to incorporating affect into therapy and commitment to therapist self-development to increase this awareness 4. Realistic sense of what is possible in therapy and one's own ability/limitations to create change 5. Balance of humility and confidence 6. Increased tolerance of successful and unsuccessful outcomes

---

Intervention implementation domain

K 1. Knowledge of how outcomes are affected by the treatment alliance, as well as relational and communication skills 2. Awareness of multiple psychological theories and modes of intervention 3. Knowledge of the sources and utility of scientific literature 4. Knowledge of therapeutic processes 5. Knowledge of issues involved in termination	1. Expanding knowledge of appropriate treatment interventions for various clients and presenting problems, based in the scientific literature and clinical experience 2. Advanced knowledge of therapeutic processes 3. Growing awareness of one's personal abilities and limits in regard to various interventions 4. Advanced knowledge of issues and tasks in termination	1. Knowledge of the appropriate treatment intervention for particular clients and presenting problems (including some knowledge of appropriate psychopharmaco-therapy) 2. Knowledge of the rationale for clinical decisions, based in the scientific literature and clinical experience 3. Advanced awareness of one's personal abilities and limits in

continues

TABLE 6.1
Continued

Begin practicum	Begin internship	Complete doctoral degree
		regard to various treatment interventions and their outcomes
		4. Knowledge of complex termination issues and interventions to address them
S 1. Ability to use appropriate and effective relational skills to establish and maintain therapeutic relationships	1. Increased mastery of communication and relational skills	1. Proficiency of communication and relational skills
2. Ability to use appropriate and effective communication skills	2. Ability to carry out more complex interventions in context of a working professional relationship	2. Ability to carry out complex interventions in context of a working professional relationship
3. Ability to establish a treatment alliance	3. Ability to establish and maintain a treatment alliance	3. Ability to establish and maintain a treatment alliance while addressing complex clinical issues
4. Ability to tolerate and deal with ambiguity	4. Ability to consider various interventions for client and presenting problems	4. Ability to select appropriate interventions for client and presenting problems
5. Ability to role-play basic clinical interventions	5. Ability to prioritize problems to be addressed	5. Ability to prioritize problems to be addressed and plan interventions accordingly
6. Ability to identify clinical issues through vignettes and role plays	6. Ability to plan, evaluate, or modify interventions using supervision, consultation, and/or the literature	6. Ability to flexibly apply various interventions
7. Ability to use supervision, consultation, and/or literature to guide or modify interventions	7. Ability to be reflective and mindful of one's abilities and limits, and how they affect interventions and outcomes	7. Ability to plan, evaluate, and modify interventions with increasing independence
	8. Ability to reflect more globally on one's own self in relation to clinical work	8. Ability to recognize and appreciate the similarities and differences of self and client(s) and have the ability to address these in clinical work (i.e., adjusting clinical formulations and interventions)
	9. Ability to terminate appropriately, with sensitivity to the issues at hand	9. Ability to use the self as a clinical instrument and understand how

			one's self may affect interventions and outcomes 10. Ability to more independently guide interventions and to reflect more globally on one's self in relation to clinical work 11. Ability to terminate appropriately, with sensitivity to the issues at hand 12. Ability to educate others to promote and improve aspects of mental health (i.e., clients, institutions, systems, society)
A	1. Desire to help others resolve problems 2. Appreciation of client strengths, resiliency, and effectiveness 3. Openness to new experiences and new learning 4. Willingness to explore one's own role and influence in the clinical encounter 5. Openness to receiving supervision and direction from others 6. Appreciation of the empirical basis for clinical interventions	1. Desire to help others resolve problems within the bounds of a professional relationship 2. Appreciation of client strengths, resiliency, and effectiveness 3. Appreciation of the value of continued new experiences and learning 4. Willingness to explore attitudes and feelings about therapeutic process issues 5. Desire to explore one's own role and influence in the clinical encounter 6. Appreciation of the value of receiving supervision, consultation, and guidance 7. Openness to reflecting on clinical errors and a desire to adjust interventions as necessary 8. Openness to negative or critical feedback 9. Appreciation of the empirical basis for clinical interventions, and a desire to integrate this with professional experience	1. Desire to help individuals and the systems in which they reside 2. Appreciation of the roles, responsibilities, and boundaries of being a helping professional 3. Appreciation and acceptance of one's own knowledge and experience in understanding human differences 4. Appreciation of client strengths, resiliency, and effectiveness 5. Appreciation of the value of a lifelong pursuit of new experiences and learning 6. Appreciation of the ongoing value of exploring attitudes and feelings about therapeutic process issues 7. Commitment to ongoing exploration of one's own role and influence in the clinical encounter 8. Valuation of ongoing consultation and guidance, and

continues

TABLE 6.1
Continued

Begin practicum	Begin internship	Complete doctoral degree
		appreciation of the value of being a supervisor or consultant to others
		9. Openness to reflecting on critical feedback or clinical errors, and a desire to adjust interventions as necessary
		10. Appreciation of the empirical basis for clinical interventions, a desire to integrate this knowledge and contribute to it

Intervention evaluation domain		
K 1. Rudimentary knowledge of theoretical, methodological, and research literature relevant to approaches to intervention evaluation 2. Understanding of research relevant to appropriate diagnostic procedures 3. Knowledge of research on emotional states, associated treatment paradigms, and outcomes	1. Knowledge of research methodology 2. Knowledge of broad repertoire of conceptual/theoretical frames that inform and structure intervention evaluation	1. Awareness of the connection between one's own issues and effectiveness of interventions 2. Meta-knowledge—knowing what one knows and does not know 3. Knowledge of application of research to specific treatment populations and associated treatment issues 4. Knowledge of a range of methods for self-evaluation
S 1. Familiarity with instruments that inform interventions 2. Basic ability to discuss clinical intervention skills	1. Ability to ask for, incorporate, and implement critical feedback 2. Ability to monitor ongoing treatment program 3. Ability to seek evidence for and against treatment effectiveness 4. Ability to use outcome assessment measures as error-correcting feedback to improve therapy skills	1. Consolidation of prior experience into practice and identity as a professional 2. Ability to discern appropriate evaluation methods 3. Ability to self-monitor and self-correct with regard to intervention efficacy

A 1. Intellectual curiosity and openness to multiple perspectives, contexts, and approaches to evaluation	1. Openness and non-defensiveness of examining one's own attitudes, behaviors, and impact on others 2. Appreciation of the impact of one's internal states on assessment of clinical outcomes 3. Tolerance of ambiguity and affects 4. Willingness to incorporate and discern multiple perspectives and approaches to evaluation	1. Greater comfort in role of professional psychologist related to trusting one's judgment on intervention, process, and outcome 2. Commitment to ongoing evaluation of knowledge, skills, and attitudes toward development of a professional identity 3. Commitment to integrating and discerning emerging approaches to evaluation

Ethics domain

| K 1. Knowledge of the ethical/legal guidelines that inform practice
2. Awareness of licensure requirements without knowledge of specifics
3. Awareness of basic documentation procedures, agency policies, and other practice management skills
4. Understanding of importance of self-awareness in terms of one's own biases and their possible effects on client(s)
5. Initial exposure to specialization options in the field | 1. Expanded knowledge of ethical/legal guidelines based on real experience with clients
2. Knowledge of practice management skills across various settings
3. Knowledge of strategies for self-reflection and self-care
4. Increased knowledge of specific licensure requirements
5. Awareness of clinical interests and strengths
6. Awareness of the legal and ethical considerations in handling special situations (e.g., homicidality, suicidality, abuse, neglect, ethical challenges) and the need for supervision in handling them | 1. Knowledge of ethical and legal guidelines from various sources (e.g., APA, state board, various clinical settings)
2. Knowledge of practice management skills from an administrative perspective
3. Self-knowledge at an advanced level that allows one to utilize this information to impact one's behaviors
4. Knowledge of specific licensure requirements
5. Knowledge of specialization options
6. Knowledge of legal and ethical considerations in handling special situations in the applicable jurisdictions (e.g., homicidality, suicidality, abuse reporting, neglect, ethical challenges) |
| S 1. Ability to apply the ethical/legal guidelines to vignettes
2. Identification of practice and case management skills | 1. Ability to apply the ethical/legal guidelines to real clients with supervisory assistance
2. Demonstration of professional | 1. Ability to integrate ethical and legal guidelines from various sources (e.g., APA, state board, various clinical settings) |

continues

TABLE 6.1
Continued

Begin practicum	Begin internship	Complete doctoral degree
3. Ability to recognize special situations (e.g., homicidality, suicidality, abuse, neglect, ethical challenges) and report them with supervision	management skills in applied setting with regular supervision 3. Ability to observe and discuss one's responses to therapeutic interventions or clients with supervision 4. Ability to recognize special situations (e.g., homicidality, suicidality, abuse, neglect, ethical challenges), report them when appropriate, and with supervision, address them clinically	2. Ability to maintain self-care and self-awareness sufficient for ethical practice 3. Ability to apply the ethical/legal guidelines to real clients more independently (occasionally seeking consultation or supervision) 4. Demonstration of practice management skills in applied settings with occasional supervision 5. Implementation of practice management skills sufficient for ethical practice 6. Ability to recognize special situations (e.g., homicidality, suicidality, abuse, neglect, ethical challenges); handle the situations with appropriate forethought, a reasonable strategy, and rationale (including getting consultation when necessary); and integrate these procedures with clinical considerations 7. Appropriate advocacy for clients and consumer groups (i.e., in institutions, systems, and society)
A 1. Appreciation of professional responsibility and ethics 2. Willingness to comply with ethical/legal guidelines 3. Awareness of necessity of practice management skills	1. Valuation of ethical/legal guidelines 2. Appreciation of practice management skills across various settings 3. Willingness to self-reflect through supervision	1. Internalization of moral duties and ethical decision making 2. Commitment to ongoing self-reflection and self-care 3. Commitment to lifelong learning 4. Internalized sense of professional identity.

| 4. Openness to self-exploration and self-critique, especially as relates to one's own beliefs and biases
5. Valuation of higher education | 4. Appreciation of the concept of lifelong learning
5. Internalized sense of professional responsibility and ethics | including legal and ethical responsibilities |

evaluation" developed by the APA CCTC (2004). These guidelines include the ability to manage various personal and professional relationships in an effective and appropriate manner; the capacities for self-awareness, self-reflection, self-evaluation, and self-care; an openness to supervisory feedback; and the ability to resolve personal issues that could interfere with professional development. The student must learn to self-monitor the ongoing interaction between client and self, as well as how his or her own reactions are affecting one's evolving understanding of the client and the implementation of interventions. The ability to self-monitor is particularly important because the therapist as a performer of complex skills has a substantial impact on treatment outcome (Wampold & Brown, 2005). Self-monitoring includes a realistic view of one's therapeutic abilities and limitations, which may be a far greater challenge than clinicians typical presume (Dunning, 2005). Self-evaluation also includes appreciation of and ongoing attempts to identify heuristics as well as cognitive biases that can affect clinical judgment, such as biases that can impede recognition of treatment strategies that are not working (APA Presidential Task Force on Evidence-Based Practice, 2006). Consequently, many training programs have explicitly adopted the CCTC guidelines as part of their formal student evaluation procedures.

A variety of strategies are used in intervention training to introduce students to the psychological challenges of conducting psychotherapy. For example, watching video recordings of actual therapy sessions offers practice in identifying salient issues and themes found in therapeutic interactions in addition to practice in reflecting on one's own personal reactions to what is occurring. Role-playing exercises offer practice in actually trying to conduct a therapeutic inquiry while remaining attuned to the personal reactions evoked by the situation. In addition, a widely held belief is that personal therapy is a crucial part of training because it enhances self-reflection and self-acceptance and it provides firsthand experience of how therapy works (Ladany, 2007). Although the sparse empirical evidence that exists provides no substantial support for the idea that personal therapy contributes to the training of competent and effective therapists (Macran & Shapiro, 1998), faith in this belief undoubtedly will remain strong.

Developing an Intervention Competency Curriculum

A prototypic intervention competency curriculum poses a number of challenges to educators, including the complexity of skills to be learned combined with the lack of empirically supported teaching methods and measures to guide the development of such a curriculum. Another challenge is training students to conduct individual, couples, family and group therapies while concurrently engaging in interventions and consultations to various community groups and organizations. Training in intervention competency also requires the acquisition of basic technical skills along with the capacity to flexibly and creatively respond to unexpected clinical problems and emergencies. The ability to choose an appropriate treatment strategy and interventions for a particular client and therapeutic context is based on accumulating supervised clinical experiences and reflects the gradual development of *analogic thinking* (Holyoak, 1992), that is, the automatic transfer of relevant knowledge from prior problem situations that resemble the current situation to the immediate problem context. Another form of analogic thinking may be the advanced awareness of one's personal abilities and limits in regard to various treatment interventions and therapeutic situations. The general format for training in intervention competency involves offering coursework on theories of intervention, specific intervention models, or both, followed by, or concurrent with, practice in the form of supervised clinical practica at real clinical settings. There are various strategies for organizing the sequence and content of intervention courses. A composite intervention curriculum would look something like this:

1st Year

A one- or two-course sequence on the fundamentals of clinical interviewing and therapeutic inquiry is a required introduction to intervention. These courses would include some or all of the following topics: structured interviewing to establish a formal diagnosis, unstructured interviewing to establish an idiographic case formulation, basic helping skills (e.g., active listening, asking open-ended questions, restatements and reflections), components of an interpersonal stance associated with the development of a therapeutic alliance (e.g., respect, warmth, curiosity, nonjudgmental), and markers and skills associated with recognizing and managing therapeutic alliance ruptures. These basic courses have extensive experiential components (typically through role playing or structured assignments in in-house training clinics) in which new students practice applying the knowledge and skills being taught.

1st Through 3rd Years

Beginning in their 1st or 2nd years, students begin to learn about theory-guided, or research-informed treatment models, or both, including the change

processes and technical strategies and tactics associated with different models. Training programs will typically require from three to five required intervention courses. The balance of didactic and experiential teaching strategies varies across courses and programs. The strategies for organizing course content also vary. The traditional strategy is to organize the content of courses around theoretical schools (e.g., psychoanalytic, cognitive–behavioral, humanistic). An alternative approach is to organize intervention course content around research-informed basic therapeutic principles (e.g., common relational factors, specific technical strategies proven differentially effective with specific personality characteristics, change processes common across different types of treatment). Another source of variability is the relative proportion of time spent on theories of personality and psychopathology, theories of therapy, and relevant treatment research. Interventions with different age groups and different modalities (e.g., groups, families, couples, organizations) are taught either as required or as elective courses.

In the first decade of the 21st century, there is a lively debate concerning how much to emphasize *empirically supported* treatment models for specific disorders versus *evidence-based* intervention approaches that are applicable to a relatively broader range of people. We recommend that along with whatever specific texts are chosen for an intervention curriculum, the students should be exposed to the latest empirical findings regarding case formulation, the role of relationships factors, changes processes, and treatment efficacy and effectiveness. It is also important for students to learn to evaluate systematically the effectiveness of their efforts to implement both empirically supported treatment models and evidence-based intervention approaches. Evaluating outcomes in the field may reduce the gap between laboratory research and actual practice, which will foster more relevant treatment research and place clinical practice on a more solid scientific foundation.

3rd and 4th Years

Most programs offer their advanced students a selection of elective courses to begin establishing a specialization or to broaden general clinical knowledge and skills. Elective intervention courses include such topics as assessment and treatment of substance abuse, brief psychotherapies, advanced psychoanalytic or cognitive–behavior theory therapies, trauma, and child maltreatment.

Clinical Practica

The best setting for controlling the student's initial intervention practice is an in-house teaching clinic, where program faculty provide most of the supervision and have more control over the types of clinical problems to which new student–therapists are exposed. An in-house training clinic also allows for consistency between coursework and clinical training. If there is

an in-house training clinic, students typically begin getting exposure to clients through a practicum during their 1st year. However, many clinical programs do not have teaching clinics, in which case students typically obtain supervised therapy experience in 2nd and/or 3rd year practicum arrangements as well as an optional 4th year practicum. When a program has only community practicum placements, the faculty needs to provide practicum seminars that complement on-site supervision in community clinic placements. These practicum seminars provide an opportunity for thorough discussions of clinical issues that arise during the students' clinical work at their practicum sites as well as a bridge from treatment philosophies associated with community settings to the treatment philosophies of program faculty members.

CURRENT TRAINING STRATEGIES AND RECOMMENDATIONS FOR THE FUTURE

Interest in developing pedagogic theories to guide training for intervention competency has waxed and waned. At the beginning of the 21st century, systematic investigations of intervention training were sparse (Kazdin, 2000), but nearly a decade later there appears to be renewed interest in evaluating and improving training methods. Over the past 3 decades, the major training innovations have been the introduction of audio and video recordings (recordings of exemplary therapists can serve as role models, and recordings of student therapists can be used to provide more specific feedback in supervision), and the use of treatment manuals (such manuals provide more precise specification of therapeutic principles and procedures). These enhancements to training, however, have not been organized by an explicit pedagogic theory that would guide instruction in acquisition of an intervention competency.

The clinical student's typical intervention training experience involves an abrupt transition from sitting in a classroom and learning about intervention theories and procedures to practicing with real clients in real clinical settings (a common exercise involves students role-playing client and therapist, but this rough simulation of real therapy is unlikely to have ecological validity [Beutler & Harwood, 2004]). This disconnect between the acquisition of knowledge and its application in clinical contexts breeds what cognitive scientists call *inert knowledge*, that is, concepts, principles, rules, and procedures lacking guidelines regarding when and how to implement them in real clinical contexts (Bransford, Franks, Vye, & Sherwood, 1989). In regard to intervention training, inert knowledge will impede students in progressively developing intervention skills. Perhaps a starting place for developing a coherent pedagogic framework relevant to training in an intervention competency is the limited existing body of research on intervention training. The findings from this research suggest that the most effective com-

ponents are a combination of structured didactic and experiential activities designed to teach specific procedures and skills in a progression from simple to more complex performances (Beutler, 1997; Binder, 1993).

Research by cognitive scientists on the development and nature of expertise in different performance domains, as well as evaluation of instructional methods for facilitating expert performance, provides specific guidance for improving the way in which knowledge is acquired as a foundation for developing intervention skills (Binder, 1999). We have discussed how certain attitudes are crucial elements of an intervention competency and important for maintaining the competency over time. It also has been found that the ways in which students understand new information as well as their receptivity to new ideas are deeply influenced by their existing knowledge and preconceptions about the subject. If instructors do not identify and encourage discussion about and evaluation of this preexisting body of knowledge and attitudes, the students may not accurately and firmly grasp the new concepts and information (Bransford, Brown, & Cocking, 2000). For example, a student's negative preconceptions about the value of short-term forms of psychotherapy may impede acquiring sufficient knowledge to develop the therapeutic skill required of this form of intervention. On the other hand, previously developed KSAs can be a bridge to learning new skills. Students struggling to understand how to conduct a therapeutic inquiry are often helped by comparing this task with preexisting interpersonal skills and an attitude of curiosity associated with listening to a friend describe a personal problem, then helping that person figure out ways to deal with it.

It is recommended that instructors of intervention courses avoid barraging students with content in the name of comprehensiveness or presenting material according to a superficial organizational principle (e.g., presenting treatment models in chronological order of development). Students are more likely to retain content in a form that will serve as a usable foundation for the development of performance skills if the content is organized around basic concepts or "big ideas" (Bransford et al., 2000). For example, in a course on psychoanalytic therapy, students would not be exposed to a detailed review of all of the specific varieties of psychoanalytic theory and therapy going back to Freud's drive/structural theory of personality and classic psychoanalysis. Instead, students would acquire an in-depth understanding of several basic concepts, such as the unconscious, the internal representational world, maladaptive interpersonal patterns, a developmental perspective, the roles of transference and countertransference, the role of the therapeutic alliance, and the roles of insight and corrective emotional experiences in therapeutic change. A research-informed, transtheoretical course on change processes might focus on the components of *therapeutic responsiveness*, the ability to recognize and attend to patient experiences and needs. Component skills associated with this ability include interpersonal pattern recognition and nonjudgmental attunement to one's own reactions (*mindfulness*; Fauth, Gates,

Vinca, Boles, & Hayes, 2007). Instructors should consider exposing the student only to information that is essential as a foundation for understanding a specific intervention (e.g., treatment approach, intervention strategy) and to basic concepts that would be the most effective way of organizing this information. A focus on teaching a smaller selection of essential content and basic concepts along with many concrete illustrative examples, rather than a wider coverage of material, helps students to develop a knowledge base that is more likely to translate into effective performance skills. Students can elect to expand their knowledge of a subject when circumstances and their interests inspire them.

Those who are training students in intervention competency are increasingly recognizing that a crucial component of this training is the student's acquisition of *metacognitive skills*, that is, the ability to monitor one's personal reactions to clients and situations in addition to the ability to monitor one's ongoing performance to make error-correcting adjustments based, in part, on changing contexts (Binder, 2004). A promising pedagogic strategy for modeling and encouraging the development of metacognitive skills is the use of *formative assessment*, in which students are evaluated frequently on their acquisition of circumscribed knowledge and skills, to provide frequent feedback about how well they are learning (Bransford et al., 2000).

The acquisition of an intervention competency, like any complex performance, requires that trainers provide precise feedback during training. Cognitive scientists who have studied the development of expertise across various performance domains have discovered that an extended period of *deliberate practice* is essential to the development of expertise (Ericsson, 2006). Deliberate practice has three components: (a) performance of well-defined tasks at an appropriate level of difficulty, (b) informative feedback, and (c) opportunities for repetition and correction of performance errors. These conditions are impossible to arrange if the practice setting involves conducting therapy with actual patients but receiving supervision at other times. An arrangement more consistent with the pedagogic strategy of deliberate practice would be simulated clinical settings in which students could practice circumscribed intervention skills that were ordered from basic to more complex and in which students could receive immediate feedback with opportunities to immediately re-practice the skills. Students would be exposed to these simulations as part of their didactic courses on intervention—before they ever were exposed to real patients. The simulations would be based on computer interactive technology that currently exists combined with material from real therapies (Beutler & Harwood, 2004; Binder, 1999; Caspar, Berger, & Hautle, 2004).

ASSESSMENT OF INTERVENTION COMPETENCY

To assess the intervention competency during training and to guide the construction of assessment instruments, there must be a clear, specific defi-

nition of the competency that can be operationalized and benchmarks at crucial points in the curriculum that reflect progressive development of the competency. These requirements are being achieved (e.g., Assessment of Competency Benchmarks Work Group, 2007; NCSPP, 2007). The benchmarks provide guidelines for assessing competency from the perspective of the quality of a student's performance (e.g., adherence to prescribed interventions, tact demonstrated in interventions) and from the perspective of the effectiveness of the student's performance (e.g., treatment outcome). Although various competence measures have been published, there are no widely accepted and established measures with which training programs assess their students (Barber et al., 2007). One example of a method for assessing intervention competency from the perspective of treatment outcome is the use of the Outcome Questionnaire, OQ-45, a self report instrument, to gather outcome data from the treatments of one therapist to assess overall effectiveness (Okiishi et al., 2006). We recommend, and we hope, that teachers of intervention competency partner with psychotherapy researchers who are attempting to develop and/or refine intervention competency measures, as well as with cognitive scientists who study and evaluate expert performance, to develop measures that can be successfully used to evaluate students' development of this competency.

REFERENCES

APA Presidential Task Force on Evidence-Based Practice. (2006). Evidence-based practice in psychology. *American Psychologist, 61*, 271–285.

Assessment of Competency Benchmarks Work Group. (2007). *A developmental model for defining and measuring competence in professional psychology.* Retrieved February 26, 2009, from http://www.apa.org/ed/graduate/comp_benchmark. pdf

Barber, J. P., Sharpless, B. A., Klostermann, S., & McCarthy, K. S. (2007). Assessing intervention competency and its relation to therapy outcome: A selected review derived from the outcome literature. *Professional Psychology: Research and Practice, 38*, 493–500.

Bent, R. J., & Cox, R. (1991). Intervention competency. In R. L. Peterson, J. D. McHolland, R. J. Bent, E. Davis-Russell, G. E. Edwall, K. Polite, et al. (Eds.), *The core curriculum in professional psychology* (pp. 97–102). Washington, DC: American Psychological Association.

Beutler, L. E., (1997). The psychotherapist as a neglected variable in psychotherapy: An illustration by reference to the role of therapist experience and training. *Clinical Psychology: Science and Practice, 4*, 44–52.

Beutler, L. E., & Harwood, T. M. (2000). *Prescriptive psychotherapy: A practical guide to systematic treatment selection.* Oxford, England: Oxford University Press.

Beutler, L. E., & Harwood, T. M. (2004). Virtual reality in psychotherapy training. *Journal of Clinical Psychology, 60,* 317–330.

Binder, J. L. (1993). Is it time to improve psychotherapy training? *Clinical Psychology Review, 13,* 301–318.

Binder, J. L. (1999). Issues in teaching and learning time-limited psychodynamic psychotherapy. *Clinical Psychology Review, 19,* 705–719.

Binder, J. L. (2004). *Key competencies in brief dynamic psychotherapy: Clinical practice beyond the manual.* New York: Guilford Press.

Bransford, J. D., Brown, A. L., & Cocking, R. R. (2000). *How people learn: Brain, mind, experience, and school.* Washington, DC: National Academy Press.

Bransford, J. D., Franks, J. J., Vye, N. J., & Sherwood, R. D. (1989). New approaches to instruction: Because wisdom can't be told. In S. Vosniadou & A. Ortony (Eds.), *Similarity and analogical reasoning* (pp. 470–497). New York: Cambridge Univesity Press.

Caspar, F., Berger, T., & Hautle, I. (2004). The right view of your patient: A computer-assisted, individualized module for psychotherapy training. *Psychotherapy: Theory, Research, Practice, Training, 41,* 125–135.

Council of Chairs of Training Councils. (2004, March). *Comprehensive student evaluation policy.* Retrieved February 26, 2009, from http://www.appic.org/downloads/CCTC_Comprehensive_Ev82AA3.pdf

Dunning, D. (2005). *Self-Insight. Roadblocks and detours on the path to knowing thyself.* New York: Psychology Press.

Ericsson, K. A. (2006). The influence of experience and deliberate practice on the development of superior expert performance. In K. A. Ericsson, N. Charness, P. J. Feltovich, & R. R. Hoffman (Eds.), *The Cambridge handbook of expertise and expert performance* (pp. 683–704). New York: Cambridge University Press.

Fauth, J., Gates, S., Vinca, M.A., Boles, S., & Hayes, J.A. (2007). Big ideas for psychotherapy training. *Psychotherapy: Theory, Research, Practice, Training, 44,* 384–391.

Holyoak, K. J. (1992). Symbolic connectionism: toward third-generation theories of expertise. In K. A. Ericsson & J. Smith (Eds.), *Toward a general theory of expertise: Prospects and limits* (pp. 301–335). New York: Cambridge University Press.

Kazdin, A. E. (2000). Evaluating the impact of clinical psychology training programs: Process and outcome issues. *Clinical Psychology: Science and Practice, 7,* 357–360.

Ladany, N. (2007). Does psychotherapy training matter? Maybe not. *Psychotherapy: Theory, Research, Practice, Training, 44,* 392–396.

Macran, S., & Shapiro, D. (1998). The role of personal therapy for therapists: A review. *British Journal of Medical Psychology, 7,* 13–25.

Messer, S. B. (2008). Unification in psychotherapy: A commentary. *Journal of Psychotherapy Integration, 18,* 363–366.

National Council of Schools and Programs in Professional Psychology (NCSPP). (2007). *Competency developmental achievement levels (DALs) of The National*

Council of Schools and Programs in Professional Psychology. Retrieved September 21, 2007, from http://www.ncspp.info/pub.htm

Okiishi, J. C., Lambert, M. J., Eggett, D., Niesen, L., Dayton, D. D., & Vermeersch, D. A. (2006). An analysis of therapist treatment effects: Toward providing feedback to individual therapists on their clients' psychotherapy outcome. *Journal of Clinical Psychology, 62,* 1157–1172.

Peterson, R. L., Peterson, D. R., Abrams, J. C., & Stricker, G. (1997). The National Council of Schools and Programs of Professional Psychology educational model. *Professional Psychology: Research and Practice, 28,* 337–386.

Rodolfa, E. R., Bent, R. J., Eisman, E., Nelson, P. D., Rehm, L., & Ritchie, P. (2005). A cube model for competency development: Implications for psychology educators and regulators. *Professional Psychology: Research and Practice, 36,* 347–354.

Safran, J. D. & Muran, J. C. (2000). *Negotiating the therapeutic alliance: A relational treatment guide.* New York: Guilford Press.

Schön, D. A. (1983). *The reflective practitioner.* New York: Basic Books.

Wampold, B. E. & Brown, G. S. (2005). Therapist variability in practice. *Journal of Consulting and Clinical Psychology, 73,* 914–923.

7

THE RESEARCH AND EVALUATION COMPETENCY: THE LOCAL CLINICAL SCIENTIST—REVIEW, CURRENT STATUS, FUTURE DIRECTIONS

STEVEN J. TRIERWEILER, GEORGE STRICKER,
AND ROGER L. PETERSON

The *local clinical scientist* originally was framed as a model for training professional psychologists in the research and evaluation competency (Trierweiler & Stricker, 1992). In contrast to the vagueness of the traditional scientist–practitioner training model for clinical psychology (Raimy, 1950), the local clinical scientist model identified how a clinician psychologist is supposed to be scientific in actual practice by drawing attention to the scientific issues intrinsic to a locally specific domain of inquiry. In addition to training in standard academic science and methodology, research training was seen to involve complex identity, attitude, knowledge, and critical thinking issues. A realistic portrayal of the phenomena that clinical practitioners actually confront in their daily activities suggests that practice is more than simply applied science. Local clinical inquiry is scientific inquiry: The task of the local clinical scientist is constantly to seek linkages between psychological science and the empirical realities of practice and to identify phenomena

within the practice setting that are central to the intervention and are potentially in need of scientific clarification (Trierweiler & Stricker, 1998; Trierweiler, 2006; see also D. R. Peterson & Peterson, 1997). In this sense, the local clinical scientist model provides a bridge between science and practice that had not previously been explicated (Stricker & Trierweiler, 1995; cf. Shakow, 1976; Kanfer, 1990; D. R. Peterson, 1991). But even more, in keeping with the helping goal that is intrinsic to the professional practice, the local clinical scientist model demands that the empirical truths of particular cases in particular clinical settings provide the ultimate criteria for the success of professional inquiry (Trierweiler, 2006; Trierweiler & Stricker, 1998). The action component of the local clinical scientist model is not statistical. Rather, it involves the ongoing, localized identification of important empirical phenomena and their interpretation in terms of relevant scientific hypotheses. Accordingly, training in the model is strongly naturalistic, empiricist, hypothesis-focused, logical, and pragmatic.

This chapter discusses the research and evaluation competency. In 2007, the National Council of Schools and Programs of Professional Psychology (NCSPP) created developmental achievement levels (DALs) for each core competency. Table 7.1 describes the domains of the research and evaluation competency and the knowledge, skills, and attitudes needed for each domain at the prepracticum, preinternship, and degree completion levels.

This chapter focuses on the local clinical scientist and related training models for the research and evaluation competency and discusses some of the issues raised by this conceptualization. In particular, we focus on the ways the model has been misunderstood by contrasting it with its alternatives, highlighting some of the promising ways it has been implemented, and discussing the extensive work still needed to realize its potential.

SCIENTIFIC TRAINING FOR THE PROFESSIONAL PSYCHOLOGIST

Over the years, the most serious controversies and misunderstandings surrounding the NCSPP model have concerned the role of science in the education of professional psychologists (e.g., Bieshke, Fouad, Collins, & Halonen, 2004; Dawes, 1994; Hays, 1986; Hoshmand & Polkinghorne, 1992; McFall, 1991, 1996; Messer, 2004; D. R. Peterson, 1985, 1991, 1996a, 1996b; Stricker, 1992; Trierweiler, 1987, 2006; Trierweiler & Stricker, 1998). Allegations to the contrary notwithstanding (e.g., McFall, 1991, 1996), no one has ever questioned the notion that all professional psychologists, whether PhD or PsyD, are to be scientifically educated and trained in all aspects of their education, not just when they are conducting research or evaluation. However, adopting a metaperspective on scientific training, NCSPP has made it clear that a scientific training model must be compatible with the realities

TABLE 7.1
Knowledge, Skills, and Attitudes and Domains for the Research and Evaluation Competency

Begin practicum	Begin internship	Complete doctoral degree
Critical evaluation of research domain		
K 1. Familiarity with different research methodologies (e.g., qualitative, quantitative) 2. Foundation knowledge of psychometric theory underlying frequently used measures (e.g., reliability, validity) 3. Understanding of important link between critical thinking and clinical decisions	1. Understanding of the strengths and limitations of different research methodologies (i.e., quantitative and qualitative; efficacy and effectiveness) and sources of information 2. Understanding of advanced statistical procedures as they are found in the psychological literature 3. Understanding of the process of psychometric research	1. Understanding of different epistemologies, including an understanding of western science in its cultural context 2. Maintenance and expansion of breadth and depth of knowledge statistics and research design
S 1. Ability to read research articles and critically evaluate truth claims at an introductory level 2. Grasp of basic library search techniques and ability to locate appropriate sources of information	1. Ability to critically evaluate literature (discriminate solid and relevant articles from others) and apply to clinical work 2. Grasp of advanced library search techniques 3. Ability to independently conduct a comprehensive literature review on a topic of interest	1. Ability to critically evaluate research literature in terms of applicability to specific clinical questions 2. Ability to smoothly explain relevant professional research literature to a client 3. Ability to critically evaluate different epistemologies
A 1. Ability to distinguish scientific evidence from personal opinion	1. Recognition of the value of staying current in the literature 2. Maintenance of an attitude of healthy skepticism 3. Openness to multiple ways of knowing	1. Incorporation of scientific attitudes and values in work as a psychologist
Conducting and using research in applied settings domain		
K 1. Knowledge of basic statistical concepts 2. Beginning understanding of how personal biases can limit inquiry and research	1. Recognition of own limitations in research 2. Understanding of the importance and value of consultation	1. Understanding of how to build new practice methods and adjust interventions based on evidence

continues

TABLE 7.1
Continued

Begin practicum	Begin internship	Complete doctoral degree
S 1. Beginning ability to identify personal biases that impact the design and implementation of research 2. Ability to explain how a psychologist would collect data to address a local clinical issue	1. Able to design appropriate data collection methods in local clinical settings 2. Engagement in data analysis and synthesis 3. Ability to collect and analyze both qualitative and quantitative data 4. Ability to detect and correct errors in conducting research 5. Ability to develop and manage a major scholarly project 6. Identification of personal biases that impact the design and implementation of research and the application of research findings in clinical settings	1. Ability to design and conduct outcome research (individual client and/or larger participant group) in an applied setting 2. Ability to function as a peer consultant in research design and evaluation 3. Completion of a major scholarly research project 4. Dissemination of scholarly findings to the professional community 5. Ability to identify and attempt to control for personal biases that impact the design and implementation of research and the application of research findings in clinical settings 6. Application of research in local clinical settings
A 1. Appreciation of the role of psychologists in conducting research in applied settings	1. Reflection on personal biases brought to the research process by oneself and by important stakeholders 2. Ability to offer feedback to peers on research design through supervision or consultation	1. Assumption of a leadership role as an evaluator and/or researcher in applied settings 2. Investment in the application of research findings in local clinical settings

Ethics and professional competence domain

Begin practicum	Begin internship	Complete doctoral degree
K 1. Demonstration of a basic working knowledge of ethical principles of research 2. Basic knowledge of the impact of individual and cultural diversity on research	1. Knowledge of ethical principles in research 2. Understanding of the role of diversity issues in the evaluation design and analysis of research	1. Inclusion of diversity issues in the development, implementation, and interpretation of research
S 1. Ability to evaluate research with respect to conformity to ethical standards	1. Ability to design research in conformity with ethical standards	1. Ability to conduct research according to accepted ethical

2. Description of epistemological model of the integration of science and practice in own program	2. Ability to make mid-course corrections in clinical and research practice based on data 3. Application of ethical principles in research	principles and standards 2. Ability to function as a local clinical scientist in an applied setting
A 1. Openness to Institutional Review Board feedback and research ethics	1. Investment in presenting scientific work for the scrutiny of others 2. Investment in offering constructive feedback to peers 3. Commitment to mid-course corrections in clinical and research practice based on data 4. Endorsement of the importance of the local clinical scientist model to own training as a psychologist	1. Commitment to the importance of research and evaluation in ongoing inquiry and lifelong learning

Note. K = knowledge; S = skills; A = attitudes. From *Competency Developmental Achievement Levels (DALs) of the National Council of Schools and Programs in Professional Psychology (NCSPP),* (pp. 31–34), by the National Council of Schools and Programs in Professional Psychology, 2007. Available at http://www.ncspp.info/DALof%20NCSPP%209-21-07.pdf. Copyright 2007 by the National Council of Schools and Programs in Professional Psychology. Reprinted with permission.

of empirical inquiry in the practice setting (R. L. Peterson, Peterson, Abrams, & Stricker, 1997).

Rigorous professional activity has traditionally been conceived as the application of scientific knowledge developed through laboratory experiments or controlled field research to the understanding and solution of human problems. Although the methodological tools and critical questions associated with controlled research can contribute to clinicians' thinking about their work (Stricker & Trierweiler, 1995; Trierweiler & Stricker, 1992, 1998), something more is needed for clinical inquiry itself. In addition, the local clinical scientist model encourages practitioners to engage the challenge of the individual human condition directly. Starting with an accurate description of the needs of each client, the local clinical scientist model requires that practitioners bring the best available theoretical conceptions, the most useful available research, their careful scientifically constructed understanding of the local circumstances of the case, and their individual and collective professional experience to bear in studying and improving the functional condition of the client. Professional activity as framed by the local clinical scientist model is not just the application of knowledge derived from a separate scientific research process; it is a form of scientific research in its own right, dealing with a range of phenomena largely outside the ken of academic science.

There have been a number of related views on the scientific process of professional work. Most of these discussions focus on the importance of a

critical and careful clinician thought process as a scientific foundation for expert clinical assessment and intervention. Schön (1983, 1987) emphasized expertise as "reflection-in-action." In his work on disciplined inquiry, D. R. Peterson (1991, 1995, 1996b; see also Kanfer, 1990) emphasized a detailed process in clinical work that paralleled what was done in the production of university science. Much later, based on the 2002 Competencies Conference: Future Directions in Education and Credentialing in Professional Psychology, Bieshke et al.'s (2004) work summarized the committee's activities in characterizing the outlook of the person of the psychologist as "scientifically minded." Critical thought is very much a part of the local clinical scientist model as well. But the local clinical scientist model also points to the scientific difficulties in translating statistical science into practice, to the extent it is actually applicable (Cronbach, 1975), and to the realities of accessing empirical phenomena in specific clinical situations. Critical thought for the local clinical scientist is not simply the extension of theoretical and analytic tools from scientific and professional tradition; it is also a performance of careful empirical inquiry in a particular space–time local circumstance. Accurate, realistic description of that circumstance, which is essentially an issue of accurate assessment and measurement, is the foundation for any application of theory or scientific hypothesis (Trierweiler, 2006).

This shift in viewpoint toward the local clinical scientist model carries profound implications for the education of professional psychologists. Instead of mandating statistical, dissertation research—which is often incorrectly equated with nomothetic knowledge and the sole means for contributing to general scientific knowledge in psychology (Lamiell 2003)—as the central requirement of scientific education and training for all practitioners, the local clinical scientist model emphasizes the examination of the empirical realities of the situations and issues actually encountered by practicing professional psychologists.

DISSERTATIONS, SCHOLARLY PRODUCTS, AND RESEARCH CURRICULUM

As presented in detail in chapter 1 of this volume, on the NCSPP model, programs have taken an array of positions regarding the importance of scholarly products for scientific education, ranging from requiring relatively small, clinically oriented doctoral projects to dissertations of the level and quality that might be found in traditional PhD programs. Those programs that require dissertations usually emphasize an applied focus that embodies a broader array of investigative approaches and a wider range of dissertation topics, all of which demonstrate an omnipresent emphasis on disciplined inquiry as basic to clinical education.

The great majority of PsyD programs require a minimum of two courses in research. Variations include a semester of qualitative and another of quantitative; some programs emphasize the consumption of research; some emphasize certain kinds of applied research, such as evaluation or action research; and others focus on local clinical science. Most programs award additional credits to students for preparation of their dissertations in collaboration with a mentor.

THE LOCAL CLINICAL SCIENTIST POSITION

Because the focus was on the research and evaluation competency, the design of the local clinical scientist model stressed scientific and methodological training with an eye toward the investigation of local phenomena. In contrast to the traditional model of the academic scientist working in a university laboratory, local clinical scientists are trained to be

> critical investigators of local (as opposed to universal) realities (a) who are knowledgeable of research, scholarship, personal experience, and scientific methodology; and (b) who are able to develop plausible, communicable formulations for understanding essentially local phenomena using theory, general world knowledge including scientific research, and, most important, their own abilities as skeptical scientific observers.
>
> Although largely compatible with traditional scientific methodological training, this view calls for differing educational practices because it emphasizes (a) being a generalist of knowledge and method, as opposed to a specialist; (b) focusing on local realities, in which data are gathered as they apply to a particular case and may be limited in the extent to which they generalize to other cases; and (c) developing an active inquiring mind as opposed to concentrating on technical expertise with scientific methods. In effect, methodological training can neither be put aside, nor can it simply continue to echo traditional university training. Rather, it must be explicitly integrated with the interests of the active professional. (Trierweiler & Stricker, 1992, p. 104)

The local clinical scientist model conceptualizes a collection of phenomena that previously had not been identified as relevant to scientific inquiry in practice and are rarely even discussed in our science, inasmuch as academic science has almost exclusively emphasized statistical description of quantitative variables as opposed to specific individual descriptions. These broad classes of empirical observation in the local clinical situation include the description of (a) specific instances of empirical phenomena in an individual's life that can be described by categories from psychological theory or scientific hypotheses; (b) specific instances of how sociocultural, economic, gender, or ethnicity considerations may affect data gathering and interpretation in a particular local clinical situation; (c) specific aspects of an individual's

personal experience, communication, biography, and development that may be germane to the case and to data gathering within the case; and (d) specific aspects of space-time moments in the clinical interaction and relationship that may affect intervention, outcome, and ongoing inquiry (Trierweiler, 2006; Trierweiler & Stricker, 1998).

The scientific data of practice primarily involve behavioral observations and face-to-face communications with clients and significant others. Formal psychological assessment procedures also may be used. If richly described, the classes of local empirical observation would provide a sizable and thorough database from which to engage scientific hypotheses and for conceptualizing clinical problems and interventions regardless of the theoretical or empirical background of a particular clinical problem or therapeutic approach. Alternatively, when these classes of observation are ignored or incompletely described or linked to the empirical realities of time-extended client behavior and self-report, it might be said that the clinical endeavor is straying from a rigorous scientific approach (Trierweiler, 2006).

By implication, we do not consider application of theory or the findings of psychological research studies to constitute rigorous scientific practice unless they are carefully coordinated with the local empirical realities of a clinical case (namely, specific self-reports and behavioral observations). For example, yes-and-no answers to a few generic diagnostic questions—as is often encouraged in the *Diagnostic and Statistical Manual of Mental Disorders* (4th ed.; *DSM–IV*; American Psychiatric Association, 1994) diagnosis—do not provide sufficient scientific foundation for specific clinical diagnoses without extensive and careful coordination of those answers with the particulars of the case (e.g., to ensure that the clinician and patient are talking about the same phenomena in the individual's life). This is especially true when the underlying classification system itself is scientifically weak (e.g., Follette & Houts, 1996). Pretending that a system like the *DSM–IV* takes precedence over other approaches because it looks, or is asserted to be, scientific when reliabilities are low (albeit asserted to be adequate) and validity is virtually unknown does not make for dependable science. Any generalized taxonomy is only as good as its ability to completely describe and classify naturally occurring empirical phenomena. With human psychology, there is little evidence that the *DSM* or any other system comprehensively classifies the unique mental health related issues and situations that humans confront in their lives (e.g., Messer, 2004; Wakefield, 1992; Westen, 1998). Aggregating an already weak classification system using statistical techniques does not improve on the fundamental issues of connecting conceptual understanding and intervention to real phenomena in the lives and experience of individuals. As was understood in the early days of the scientist–practitioner model, only a wise and well-informed scientific practitioner, using methodological tools appropriate to the situation, can accomplish such individualized preci-

sion (American Psychological Association [APA], Committee on Training in Clinical Psychology, 1947).

In short, contrary to much recent rhetoric about scientific evidence in practice, statistical studies do not provide strong empirical and logical foundation for simplified applications of scientific study procedures to the local circumstances of clinical practice (Chronbach, 1975; Lamiell, 1981; Shakow, 1976; Trierweiler, 2006, Trierweiler & Stricker, 1998). Similarly, clinicians' usage of clinical theories, fashionable clinical hypotheses, or cultural stereotypes (e.g., dreams reflect unconscious transference issues, memory blocks mean some prior trauma, relationships between the sexes are usually about power issues, Hispanic patients are family-oriented) requires careful coordination with specific clinical data to be rigorously applied. Overly free usage of theories and research results (which come to the clinical situation as working hypotheses), as is often seen in the popular media, can, without careful assessment, actually be antiscientific and potentially misguided.

The local clinical scientist model suggests that assessment of empirical realities of a case is more involved than is suggested by simple Q & A diagnostic procedures (e.g., the patient says he is sad and has sleep problems; therefore, medication is needed). It must be remembered that such methods originate in the instrumental requirements of large-scale population studies, and, therefore, they are often deficient in procedures for uncovering the information needed to coordinate the meaning of research (e.g., diagnostic) concepts with local data (Trierweiler, 2006). Extensive individualized data are required as grounds for making scientifically sound diagnostic interpretations. At the same time, rigorous assessment based on the local clinical scientist model is more involved than is typically found in clinical practice models. As a scientific perspective relevant to any theory or mode of practice, it is more empirically focused and event-driven than is often found in therapy training models, in which theoretical perspectives govern the clinical process and conclusions may be drawn prematurely (e.g., the patient mentioned a time that she cannot remember, therefore, she was abused). To be well grounded in life particulars, all self-report and behavior-based interpretations need to be understood in terms of the individual's life as he or she actually experienced it across time and situation—not in terms of a clinician's or clinical system's belief or conjecture about how that life was experienced. The most powerful tools the local clinical scientist has in the assessment process are a good relationship with the patient, which enhances the probability that the needed information can become available, and the ability to ask exactly what a particular event or idea means to the person in the service of a clinical intervention. The local clinical scientist is, first, a gatherer of clinical data from a complex individual life stream and only later an interpreter of those data.

Trierweiler (2006) called this careful coordination between empirical observations in the local clinical situation and research or theory-based hy-

potheses *methodological realism*. From this perspective, it is hard to imagine a typical mental health medical visit in the contemporary United States that is more than cursorily scientific. Instead of acknowledging and scientifically overcoming the complexities of human self-report, many professionals seemed to have succumbed to the social and economic press to be scientific by adopting procedures that lend the appearance of science without careful attention to the issues and weaknesses involved. Too often, it is form without substance. Psychologists working in medical settings or with patients with prior medical experience often have to manage the consequences of this lack of psychological rigor in the typical medical examination. The local clinical scientist model has far-reaching implications for defining the empirical evidence of psychological practice, coordinating those data with scientific study results and with clinical theories, and determining the level of training that would be required to accomplish these complex interpretations (it is relevant to all clinical endeavors but best realized only at the highest level of scientific and clinical training in the field). The model is highly compatible with the traditional scientist–practitioner and practitioner–scholar models but more explicit about the methodological issues involved in extending psychological science into the realities of lived experience.

Insofar as the local clinical scientist model fully incorporates both the strengths and weaknesses of scientific methods, including critiques such as those by Manicas and Secord (1983) or Hoshmond and Polkinghorne (1992), it is not surprising that the literature since the original statement of the local clinical scientist model has been somewhat confused about the scientific commitments of the model and the extent to which it conceives of practitioners as only consumers of the scientific knowledge products of academic scientists. Also, there have been suggestions that the model merely represents attempts to implement scientific evaluations in clinical contexts or that, at least in informal comments, it condones the status quo in the ways clinicians and scientists operate. Whereas we endorse scientific endeavors of all stripes, we want to say unequivocally here that such limited characterizations of the local clinical scientist model are inaccurate and avoidant of central issues and critiques of conventional practice identified by the model. The local clinical scientist model has always had much greater ambitions than just advocating the "consumption" of existing science, focusing instead on (a) the longstanding problem of teaching the root logic of scientific methods to practitioners, (b) a critical analysis of scientific approaches as widely implemented in contemporary psychology and psychiatry, and (c) the adequacy of scientific presentations to the needs of practitioners. Some seem to imply that only those working in academic settings, producing "knowledge" by publishing in peer-reviewed journals, can claim scientific status. Again, we take issue with such characterizations: Major scientific and technical advancements are being made in the private sector in a variety of fields, and psychology is no exception, having long demonstrated a rich tradition of scholarly

discourse that influences both scientific and clinical endeavors. The local clinical scientist raises serious questions about the ongoing practices of both existing scientists and practitioners. As such, it is antithetical to any version of guild-level parochialism, be if from practice or academic science. Only open, critical dialogue that is true to the scholarly traditions of psychology can lead to needed advances in managing the science–practice interface (Peterson & Trierweiler, 1999; Trierweiler, 2006).

As was pointed out in the original statement of the model, the local clinical scientist is very much a scientist in our vision but with a focus different from his or her academic colleagues:

> Historically, training has emphasized skills necessary for scientific knowledge production, whereas scientific skills related to local clinical analysis have received relatively less explicit attention. In contrast to traditional training models, we propose that professional psychology programs develop and expand the early insight that the professional psychologist is a local clinical scientist (e.g., Shakow, 1976). We take as self-evident the need to continue also to train clinicians who will be devoted to the production of scientific psychological knowledge. The major difference between the traditional training model and the model we propose is that, in our model, the capacities necessary for local clinical science and scientific knowledge production do not need to be developed fully in the same individuals.
>
> We also differ from the Boulder formulation [i.e., the original statement of the scientist–practitioner model as documented in Raimy (1950)] because we do not agree with the grim implication that scientific "adaptability" to local circumstances requires "suspension of highly critical, analytic concern [in response to the] 'unscientific' demands of clinical reality" (Raimy, 1950, p. 86). Indeed, the essence of the training problem is to help students to conceptualize clinical judgment and decision making in a way that critical analysis of the local evidence, required to establish a fit between clinical theory, data, and action, is in the foreground of the clinician's concerns. We can accomplish this if we conceptualize research training explicitly as training in critical thinking, and as a means to instill scientific attitudes. (Trierweiler & Stricker, 1992, p. 105)

Most important, the local clinical scientist model is grounded in logic of scientific methodologies as they have developed in psychology, including accomplishments and controversies, appropriate extensions and limitations. But, in contrast to traditional training, these tools are taught as a contribution to developing the attitude and thinking skills needed for localized inquiry and individualized analysis as opposed to conducting research that describes properties of statistical variables for packaging in a scientific journal. Trierweiler and Stricker (1998) wrote the *Scientific Practice of Professional Psychology* in support of this endeavor, to elaborate the broad and rigorous

conceptual foundation for extrapolating methodological thought into practice that has long existed in psychology. In conjunction with other comprehensive methodology textbooks, the book establishes a vision of scientific professional inquiry that is well grounded in the core methodological scholarship of scientific psychology, brings together in one place the full range of quantitative and qualitative approaches to scientific inquiry in psychology, and directly addresses both critical strengths and weaknesses of different methods. It is the only work to date in the literature to address the complexities of such an integration of core scientific methodological thought and the empirical realities of practice. And, it represents one of the few discussions in the literature of the logical problems associated with drawing individual clinical inferences from statistical results (see also, Cronbach, 1975; Lamiell, 1981, 2003; Trierweiler, 2006).

However, this process moves beyond simply following the suggestions from scientific outcome studies. Even these seemingly directly practice-relevant studies require careful translation into the local clinical situation (Trierweiler, 2006). Such translation will be more or less complicated and involved depending on similarities between the operation of a particular clinical intervention and the characteristics of study samples. Beyond these outcome and therapy process formulations, any scientific finding is potentially relevant as clinicians attempt to understand and interpret the time-extended realities of clients. One might say that the task is to understand the clinical situation in terms of an empirically grounded conceptualization that is consistent with the general picture of the reality that science suggests surrounds us.

THE LOCAL CLINICAL SCIENTIST IN PRACTICE SETTINGS

The local clinical scientist model encourages clinicians to actively model the reality of the clinical situation using empirical observation, careful analysis of self-reports, and knowledge from science and practice traditions. There are myriad examples of the local clinical scientist functioning in clinical settings. We can divide them into three general categories: (a) the individual practitioner, (b) the helpful review, and (c) the research program.

The individual practitioner is the ultimate focus of this model. With the increasing number of graduates of professional schools and the frequent adoption of the local clinical scientist by these programs (cf., the NCSPP model, chap. 1, this volume), we can expect to see more and more individual practitioners who have been influenced by this approach. Because the work goes on in the privacy of individual offices in local settings, it is difficult to document the prevalence of practice, but we are hopeful that there are an increasing number of practitioners who do function as local clinical scientists. Certainly, the authors of this chapter have been told on many occa-

sions by individuals that they appreciated the articulation of the model and are influenced by it; unfortunately, when they describe what they do, as we have tried to spell out, it may not be what we had in mind.

Research reviews geared to the practitioner are also quite helpful in aiding the individual practitioner in keeping relevant research findings in mind when they devise treatment plans and strategies. APA publishes a monthly newsletter, the *Clinician's Research Digest*, which presents summaries of research that is relevant to the practitioner. Individual practitioners are made aware of these studies and can request reprints if there is direct application to their practice. The journal of APA's Division of Psychotherapy (29), *Psychotherapy: Theory, Research, Practice, Training*, has begun to publish Practice Reviews (e.g., Mobini & Grant, 2007), articles that summarize research literature relevant to a particular area of practice. In addition to these innovative approaches, there are many traditional research reviews for the practitioner to draw on (e.g., Westen, 1998).

The most ambitious implementations of the local clinical scientist model are research programs designed to aid the practitioner in daily functioning, combining the value of the statistical findings with the local needs of more individual inquiry. One such approach consists of the construction of Practice Research Networks (PRNs; e.g., Borkovec, Echemendia, Ragusea, & Ruiz, 2001), a program that combines the research acumen of scientists with the daily experience of practitioners who function in local settings. Data drawn from these practices are combined to develop indications of general practices and their outcomes. An additional approach that can be recommended is the lengthy program designed by Lambert (Harmon, Lambert, Slade, Hawkins, & Whipple, 2005; Lambert, Harmon, Slade, Whipple, & Hawkins, 2005). In this program, data are accumulated from a large number of practitioners, and, from this, expected progress can be charted and provided to each individual practitioner. If a particular case is not showing expected progress, the treatment plan can be modified. Clients have shown increased positive change as a result of these alterations in the plan. It is one thing to exhort the practitioner to learn from experience. It is entirely another to document that experience so that faulty heuristics (Tversky & Kahneman, 1974) do not lead to errors in memory. Both PRNs and the Lambert program are approaches to systematic documentation and will serve the local clinical scientist well.

THE LOCAL CLINICAL SCIENTIST IN TRAINING SETTINGS

As has been said, the local clinical scientist model is an important aspect of the practitioner–scholar model, (or, when the words are reversed) the scholar–practitioner model and the practitioner model (R. L. Peterson et al., 1997; chap. 1, this volume). Because most clinical training programs do not

limit their model statement to naming the local clinical scientist, there is no reliable source of data on the prelevance of the model's implementation. Based on data obtained from the APA Center for Psychology Workforce (J. Kohout, personal communication, January 9, 2008), at least 62 doctoral programs identify their model as one of these variants. Still, because of the way the question was worded, these data may not be reliable. There are at least 18 programs that identify their programs as having been influenced by the local clinical scientist vision (J. Skidmore, personal communication, January 8, 2008), including other programs that have e-mailed author R. Peterson independently). When Peterson was on the Committee on Accreditation (1999–2004), it was his impression that a large number of internships identified part of their training model as local clinical scientist, though no formal numbers were kept. The Citations Index reports that between 1996 and 2007, the Stricker and Trierweiler *American Psychologist* (1995) article was cited an average of 5.23 times per year. Although this is a fairly sizable number of citations for an article on training, it appears that the local clinical scientist model has been much more influential in the training community than in more general psychological writing.

FUTURE DIRECTIONS

As Trierweiler (2006) has suggested, a clear next step is to develop a clinical and scientific literature describing how scientific studies can be meaningfully extended into local clinical situations. Such a literature should involve three areas of development. First, the limitations of statistical research conclusions for the local clinical scientist need to be addressed directly in studies that might pertain to clinical practice (Trierweiler, 2006). Theory appropriate to translation of research studies into the clinical setting must be developed. Second, we need to strengthen our understanding of self-report and behavior observation in the clinical setting as the most direct empirical methods for accessing the realities of clients' time-extended lives. In part, this work will involve examination of how concepts clients use are attached to the directly experienced and remembered aspects of their lives (Trierweiler, 2006; Trierweiler & Donovan, 1994). Third, the clinical endeavor is almost entirely about observation, recognition, and interpretation of mental health-related life issues in the context of a developing professional relationship with the client. These performance aspects of information gathering and clinical judgment need to be acknowledged as central to the larger project of scientifically describing clinical thought both as they pertain to traditional issues such as diagnosis (e.g., Trierweiler, 2006) and as they affect conceptualization of clinical process and intervention. The local clinical scientist model is more than just a training concept: It points to a realm of naturalistic scientific inquiry that is dauntingly familiar to novice and expe-

rienced clinicians alike. The wish to bring science into practice will only come to fruition when this realm is realistically and fully included in the larger training, scholarly, and scientific discourse of psychology along with the well-established and currently dominant output of statistical science. Much work remains to be done.

REFERENCES

American Psychiatric Association. (2000). *Diagnostic and statistical manual of mental disorders* (4th ed., text revision). Washington, DC: Author.

American Psychological Association, Committee on Training in Clinical Psychology. (1947). Recommended graduate training program in clinical psychology. *American Psychologist, 2*, 539–558.

Bieschke, K. J., Fouad, N., Collins, F., & Halonen, J. (2004). The scientifically-minded psychologist. *Journal of Clinical Psychology, 60*, 713–724.

Borkovec, T. D., Echemendia, R. J., Ragusea, S. A., & Ruiz, M. (2001). The Pennsylvania practice research network and future possibilities for clinically meaningful and scientifically rigorous psychotherapy effectiveness research. *Clinical Psychology: Science and Practice, 8*, 155–167.

Cronbach, L. J. (1975). Beyond the two disciplines of scientific psychology. *American Psychologist, 30*, 116–127.

Dawes, R. M. (1994). *House of cards: The collapse of modern psychotherapy*. New York: Free Press.

Follette, W. C., & Houts, A. C. (1996). Models of scientific progress and the role of theory in taxonomy development: A case study of the DSM. *Journal of Consulting and Clinical Psychology, 64*, 1120–1132.

Harmon, C., Lambert, M. J., Slade, K., Hawkins, E. J., & Whipple, J. S. (2005). Improving outcomes for poorly responding clients: The use of clinical support tools and feedback to clients. *Journal of Clinical Psychology/In Session, 61*, 175–185.

Hays, S. C. (1986). A training model in search of a rationale. *American Psychologist, 41*, 593–594.

Hoshmand, L. T., & Polkinghorne, D. E. (1992). Redefining the science–practice relationship in professional training. *American Psychologist, 47*, 55–66.

Kanfer, F. H. (1990). The scientist–practitioner connection: A bridge in need of constant attention. *Professional Psychology: Research and Practice, 21*, 264–270.

Lambert, M. J., Harmon, C., Slade, K., Whipple, J. S., & Hawkins, E. J. (2005). Providing feedback to psychotherapists on their patients' progress: Clinical results and practice suggestions. *Journal of Clinical Psychology/In Session, 61*, 165–174.

Lamiell, J. T. (1981). Toward an idiothetic psychology of personality. *American Psychologist, 36*, 276–289.

Lamiell, J. T. (2003). *Beyond individual and group differences: Human individuality, scientific psychology, and William Stern's critical personalism.* Thousand Oaks, CA: Sage.

Manicas, P. T., & Secord, P. F. (1983). Implications for psychology of the new philosophy of science. *American Psychologist, 38,* 399–413.

McFall, R. M. (1991). Manifesto for a science of clinical psychology. *The Clinical Psychologist, 44,* 75–88.

McFall, R. M. (1996). Making psychology incorruptible. *Applied and Preventive Psychology, 5,* 9–16.

Messer, S. B. (2004). Evidence-based practice: Beyond empirically supported treatments. *Professional Psychology: Research and Practice, 35,* 580–588.

Mobini, S., & Grant, A. (2007). Clinical implications of attentional bias in anxiety disorders: An integrative literature review. *Psychotherapy: Theory, Research, Practice, Training, 44,* 450–462.

Peterson, D. R. (1985). Twenty years of practitioner training in psychology. *American Psychologist, 40,* 441–451.

Peterson, D. R. (1991). Connection and disconnection of research and practice in the education of professional psychologists. *American Psychologist, 46,* 422–429.

Peterson, D. R. (1995). The reflective educator. *American Psychologist, 50,* 975–983.

Peterson, D. R. (1996a). Making conversation possible. *Applied and Preventive Psychology, 5,* 17–18.

Peterson, D. R. (1996b). Making psychology indispensable. *Applied and Preventive Psychology, 5,* 1–8.

Peterson, D. R., & Peterson, R. L. (1997). Ways of knowing in a profession: Toward an epistemology for the education of professional psychologists. In D. R. Peterson, *Educating professional psychologists: History and guiding conception* (pp. 191–228). Washington, DC: American Psychological Association.

Peterson, R. L., Peterson, D. R., Abrams, J. C., & Stricker, G. (1997). The National Council of Schools and Programs of Professional Psychology educational model. *Professional Psychology: Research and Practice, 28,* 373–386.

Peterson, R. L., & Trierweiler, S. J. (1999). Scholarship in psychology: The advantages of an expanded vision. *American Psychologist, 54,* 350–355.

Raimy, V. C. (Ed.). (1950). *Training in clinical psychology.* New York: Prentice Hall.

Schön, D. A. (1983). *The reflective practitioner: How professionals think in action.* New York: Basic Books.

Schön, D. A. (1987). *Educating the reflective practitioner: Toward a new design for teaching and learning in the professions.* San Francisco: Jossey-Bass.

Shakow, D. (1976) What is clinical psychology? *American Psychologist, 31,* 553–560.

Stricker, G. (1992). The relationship of research to clinical practice. *American Psychologist, 47,* 543–549.

Stricker, G., & Trierweiler, S. J. (1995). The local clinical scientist: A bridge between science and practice. *American Psychologist, 50,* 995–1002.

Trierweiler, S. J. (1987). Practitioner training: A model with rationale intact. *American Psychologist, 42,* 37–45.

Trierweiler, S. J. (2006). Training the next generation of psychologist clinicians: Good judgment and methodological realism at the interface between science and practice. In C. D. Goodheart, A. E. Kazdin, & R. J. Sternberg (Eds.), *Evidence-based psychotherapy: Where practice and research meet* (pp. 211–238). Washington, DC: American Psychological Association.

Trierweiler, S. J., & Donovan, C. M. (1994). Exploring the ecological foundations of memory in psychotherapy: Interpersonal affordance, perception, and recollection in real time. *Clinical Psychology Review, 14,* 301–326.

Trierweiler, S. J., & Stricker, G. (1992). Research and evaluation competency: Training the local clinical scientist. In R. L. Peterson, J. McHolland, R. J. Bent, E. Davis-Russell, G. E. Edwall, E. Magidson, et al. (Eds.), *The core curriculum in professional psychology* (pp. 103–113). Washington, DC: American Psychological Association and National Council of Schools of Professional Psychology.

Trierweiler, S. J., & Stricker, G. (1998). *The scientific practice of professional psychology.* New York: Plenum.

Tversky, A., & Kahneman, D. (1974). Judgment under uncertainty: Heuristics and biases. *Science, 185,* 1124–1131.

Wakefield, J. C. (1992). The concept of mental disorder: On the boundary between biological facts and social values. *American Psychologist, 47,* 373–388.

Westen, D. (1998). The scientific legacy of Sigmund Freud: Toward a psychodynamically informed psychological science. *Psychological Bulletin, 124,* 333–371.

8

THE CONSULTATION AND EDUCATION COMPETENCY

MARK STANTON

This chapter provides an overview of the consultation and education competency, beginning with the definition and historical context, proceeding to the subsequent development and current status of the competency, noting barriers and methods for its inclusion in graduate education and training, and concluding with the depiction of emerging issues.

DEFINITION AND TYPES

The original definition of the consultation and education competency (McHolland, 1992) details the specific nature of the competency, the knowledge base required, and the educational experiences expected to develop the competency:

> Consultation refers to the planned collaborative interaction between the professional psychologist and one or more clients or colleagues, in relation to an identified problem area or program. Psychological consultation is an explicit intervention process that is based on principles and procedures found within psychology and related disciplines, in which

143

the professional psychologist has no *direct* control of the actual change process. Psychological consultation focuses on the needs of individuals, groups, programs, or organizations. Education is the directed facilitation by the professional psychologist of the growth of knowledge, skills, and attitudes in the learner. (p. 165)

Consultation and education were paired because they were understood to be different means of psychological intervention for a similar purpose. For instance, a psychologist engaged to assist an organization in dealing with workplace diversity may both consult (i.e., conduct a needs assessment and provide science-based recommendations regarding practices and procedures) and educate (i.e., provide diversity seminars or workshops).

The types of consultation and education have increased since the inception of the competency. Early attention focused on mental health consultation, but that has now expanded to include a wider variety of mental health applications (e.g., psychological consultation in primary care, law enforcement, business), behavioral, school-based (parent, teacher) consultation, and organizational consultation (Brown, Pryzwansky, & Schulte, 2001). Education includes psychoeducation seminars on various psychological issues (e.g., coping with anxiety or depression) or life cycle transitions (e.g., premarital preparation, divorce recovery) and training (e.g., diversity workshops, team development, personality in the workplace) in multiple settings (e.g., counseling centers, community clinics, nonprofit organizations, business), as well as Web-based education efforts (e.g., mental health information Web sites). Higher education roles were originally a minimal consideration but are now an emerging interest.

DEVELOPMENT OF THE CONSULTATION AND EDUCATION COMPETENCY

The consultation and education competency continued to evolve as professional organizations determined more thoroughly the need for clear competency standards and pathways to achieve the competency. Over time, it became clear that the competency required a developmental progression through the training stages.

National Council of Schools and Programs of Professional Psychology

The chapter on consultation and education competency in the text *Core Curriculum in Professional Psychology* (Illback, Maher, & Kopplin, 1992) summarizes the conceptualization of the competency at that time and delineates the knowledge, skills, and attitudes (KSAs) essential for competence. The authors noted that consultation and education constitute a substantial

portion of actual practice in professional psychology, yet "professional training programs traditionally have not placed great emphasis on explicit training in this area" (p. 115). In subsequent development of the competency, the National Council of Schools and Programs of Professional Psychology (NCSPP) stressed the need for increased emphasis on emerging competencies, suggesting that the education and training currently available in consultation and education are minimal when compared with their potential career importance (R. Peterson, Peterson, Abrams, & Stricker, 1997). They indicated that the ability of psychology to expand its scope of practice to promote new roles in response to needs is critical for the profession.

The 1999 NCSPP Charleston conference on New Competencies intended to clarify the nature of developing competencies (e.g., consultation, supervision) and to explore other potentially important competencies in professional psychology (e.g., administration, advocacy). Discussion in the work group on the consultation competency confirmed a continuing deficiency of coverage in member schools. Traditional forms of consultation (e.g., clinical consultation) were included in the curriculum, but newer forms (e.g., consultation in organizations) were not uniformly addressed. The emergence of consultation practice by graduates and increased student interest in consulting psychology was noted, but most programs represented in the work group had not implemented thorough education and training mechanisms for the competency. The work group recommended further development of the curriculum in consultation.

Society of Consulting Psychology

Discussions about consulting psychology as a "special proficiency" under clinical, counseling, or school psychology, or as a separate specialty began in Division 13 of the American Psychological Association (APA), the Society of Consulting Psychology (see Lowman, 1998a). The Society of Consulting Psychology hypothesized that organizational consulting psychology is more than a proficiency, yet standards did not exist for consultation competencies at the individual, group, and organization levels, and few doctoral programs existed that prepared students in consulting psychology. They conceded that there may be multiple pathways to competency in consulting psychology, even allowing that graduates of clinical or counseling psychology programs might add specialty training at the doctoral or postdoctoral levels, yet advocated for consulting psychology to transcend its status as a subspecialty of other fields. Lowman (1998a) noted that the "large influx of mental health practitioners into managerial consultative roles" (p. 263) demands appropriate training of such individuals.

Division 13 proceeded to specify education and training principles at the doctoral and postdoctoral level (APA, 2007; Cooper, 2002; Lowman et

al., 2002). The foreword recognizes that academic training in "clinical or counseling psychology can provide considerable training that is relevant for the practice" of consulting psychology (Lowman et al., 2002, p. 213). They specified three broad domains of expertise (individual, group, and organizational) and competencies in each domain that interact with each other, such as assessment, relationship, process skills, and multicultural competency. The overlap with other models of the core competencies is readily apparent, but the principles specify more exact competencies in a manner that may exceed the typical education in consultation provided by most clinical and counseling psychology programs.

Shullman (2002) reacted to the Division 13 principles by arguing for the historical primacy of consultation in counseling psychology and suggesting that education and training in counseling psychology adequately prepares one for entry into consulting psychology.

Competencies Conference

On another front, the 2002 Competencies Conference was convened to identify general competencies within psychology (Collins, Kaslow, & Illfelder-Kaye, 2004). One of the work groups focused on consultation and interprofessional collaboration (Arredondo, Shealy, Neale, & Winfrey, 2004). This group defined the terms as follows:

> Psychological Consultation focuses on the needs of individuals, groups, programs, and organizations. It refers to planned interactions between the professional psychologist (consultant) and one or more representatives of clients, colleagues, or systems (consultees) relative to a problem, person, area, or program. Psychological consultation is based on principles and procedures found within psychology and related disciplines in which a professional psychologist applies his/her areas of expertise in response to the presenting needs and stated objectives of consultees. (p. 789)

There are clear correlates between this definition and the NCSPP definition of consultation. The consultation workgroup delineated four competency components: foundational knowledge, the culturally self-aware consultant, skill sets, and implementation skills. Finally, the work group provided education and training implications based on the recognition of common foundational competencies across the primary general practice specialties (clinical, counseling, and school) that suggest that consultation is a generic competency construct with various applications in the different specialty areas. They recommended training that includes personal and professional development; practical, supervised experience; coursework in systems theory; and coursework in ethics and assessment relevant to consultation informed by diversity guidelines and standards.

Developmental Progression

Many of the contemporary models of professional competency advocate developmental progression in the competency through a series of stages: beginner, advanced beginner, competent, proficient, and expert. These models suggest that education and training in the competencies must facilitate progression across the stages and that assessment of competency must be developmental (Arredondo et al., 2004; Collins et al., 2004). Programs may not simply insert one course into the curriculum and assume competency; rather, programs move students through the stages of development over time in the program, including coursework, practicum, and predoctoral internship. NCSPP created developmental achievement levels (DALs) for the core competencies in 2007, specifying the required KSAs in the competency needed to begin practicum, to begin internship, and to complete the doctoral degree (NCSPP, 2007). Table 8.1 describes the DALs for the consultation and education competency.

The recognized components of the consultation competency (Arredondo et al., 2004; Sears, Rudisill, & Mason-Sears, 2006) have now evolved into clusters: (a) knowledge of evidence-based theories, models, and interventions (Lowman, 2005); (b) relationship skills (Glasser, 2002); (c) diversity and cross-cultural competency in consultation (Manley & Holiwski, 2003; Rogers, 2000; Steward, 1996); (d) problem-solving and implementation skills (Glasser, 2002; O'Roark, 2002); and (e) ethical and professional practice skills (Lowman, 1998b).

CURRENT STATUS OF THE CONSULTATION AND EDUCATION COMPETENCY

The 2005 NCSPP Self Study (Paskiewicz et al., 2006) suggests that consultation and education continues to lag behind other competencies in the curriculum of member schools. All schools include mandatory courses in assessment, intervention, diversity, and research and evaluation; almost all require a course in the relationship competency. In contrast, only 78% require a course in consultation and education. Although another 18% offer an elective course in this competency, it ranks as the lowest in emphasis in the curriculum among the competencies.

Nevertheless, the 2005 Self Study (Paskiewicz et al., 2006) indicated that over 60% of faculty respondents reported engaging in external consultation, the third most frequent faculty scholarship activity. This suggests that NCSPP schools have faculty experienced in consultation.

An informal review of implementation of the competency in NCSPP member schools was completed for this document. Online curriculum and course descriptions were reviewed, and it was found that many programs of-

TABLE 8.1
Knowledge, Skills, and Attitudes and Domains for the Consultation and Education Competency

Begin practicum	Begin internship	Complete doctoral degree
Knowledge of evidence-based theories, models, and interventions domain		
K 1. Knowledge of consultation and education as core competencies of professional psychology	1. Familiarity with examples of consultation and education at the individual, group, organizational, and community levels 2. Knowledge of a range of educational methods and approaches to the delivery of instruction (e.g., lecture, small group, tutorial, independent study, blended, online) 3. Understanding of relevant principles applicable to consultation and education (e.g., learning theory)	1. Knowledge of how to select and apply appropriate consultation and education models and evidence-based interventions, taking into account contextual and diversity variables 2. Understanding of the indications and contraindications for specific educational approaches, techniques, and technologies (e.g., lecture, small group, tutorial, independent study, blended, online)
S 1. Ability to think conceptually and beginning ability to make sense of behavioral patterns	1. Beginning ability to use consultation and educational evaluation and assessment tools	1. Ability to recognize situations in which consultation and/or education is appropriate 2. Ability to select and conduct appropriate needs assessment and interventions taking into account individual and group differences, contextual and diversity variables 3. Ability to use appropriate consultation and educational evaluation and assessment tools
A 1. Interest in understanding principles of consultation and education	1. Curiosity about conceptual models of consultation and education	1. Motivation to sustain lifelong learning about methods/models of consultation and education

K	1. Basic understanding of the scientific method and its application to psychology	1. Basic understanding of relevant concepts and theories of consultation and education based upon the scientific literature, including foundational knowledge of systemic conceptualizations 2. General knowledge of outcome research and evaluation in consultation and education	1. Detailed knowledge of individual and programmatic outcome research and evaluation methods in consultation and education
S	1. Beginning ability to apply the scientific method to problems within psychology	1. Beginning ability to write reports, under supervision, that provide useful recommendations to consultees 2. Beginning skill in conducting and evaluating instructional activities provided by self and others using principles of instructional design 3. Ability to participate in interdisciplinary and/or criterion-based evaluation of education and consultation	1. Ability to write consultative reports that are well organized, succinct, and provide useful recommendations 2. Ability to evaluate educational models utilizing existing and emerging technology, such as online course development software and collaborative learning environments 3. Ability to develop and evaluate consultation and education evaluation and assessment tools and summarize/present results 4. Ability to provide rationale based in scientific principles and theoretical understanding and experience for consultation interventions
A	1. Appreciation of the importance of scientific evidence	1. Appreciation of the value of evaluation and assessment tools in education and consultation	1. Willingness to research and adopt innovative approaches to consultation and education

continues

TABLE 8.1
Continued

Begin practicum	Begin internship	Complete doctoral degree
Problem solving and intervention domain		
K 1. Recognition of the role of consultation and education in addressing social problems	1. Recognition of how consultation and education can address social problems	1. Knowledge of the roles and methods of consultation and education in seeking resolution of social problems
S 1. Development of basic relational skills prerequisite to consultation and educational interventions	1. Beginning ability to apply consultation and education processes, models, and approaches at multiple levels	1. Ability to apply consultation and education to social issues for improving individual, small group, organizational, and societal functioning
A 1. Concern for others and respect for consultation and education competency	1. Commitment to recognizing and addressing social problems of individuals and groups in society	1. Motivation to use consultation and education as tools of psychology in the public interest, in social responsibility, and in addressing social problems
Performing consultation and education roles and building relationships domain		
K 1. Beginning knowledge of individual and cultural differences in learning styles	1. Knowledge of the educator and consultant's roles and their unique features as distinguished from other professional roles	1. Basic understanding of the application of consultation and education theory to specific human context
S 1. Ability to solicit and receive peer consultation 2. Ability to develop positive relationship skills foundational to consultation and education 3. Beginning development of appropriate professional conduct and identity (e.g., organization, awareness of self, professional presence) 4. Ability to communicate basic respect	1. Ability to solicit and offer appropriate peer consultation 2. Ability to accommodate individual and cultural differences in learning and consultee styles 3. Ability to maintain personal control, tolerance, and integrity in routine practice situations	1. Ability to select and conduct appropriate consultation and education models and interventions taking into account individual and group differences and contextual variables 2. Ability to engage in a collaborative consultative relationship with others within psychology and other disciplines 3. Ability to summarize and present results in a clear, useful manner

regarding the
fundamental worth and
dignity of learners,
clients, and consultees
5. Mastery of
fundamental oral and
written communication
skills foundational to
consultation and
education practice

A	1. Attitude of curiosity toward others and one's personal impact in the context of consultation and education 2. Readiness to participate in basic consultation and education activities with supervision 3. Openness to supervision in consultation and education and willingness to problem solve with others 4. Flexibility and tolerance of ambiguity in the context of consultation and education 5. Belief in the ability of individuals, organizations, institutions, and other social systems to change through collaborative planning and systematic consultation and/or educational intervention	1. Willingness to engage in critical thinking and openness to consideration of multiple perspectives within the complexities of consultation and educational problems 2. Willingness to seek consultation or additional training as necessary	1. Adoption of the role of consultant and educator into one's professional identity as a psychologist 2. Confidence in one's ability to function in the role of consultant or educator

Ethical and professional practice domain		
K 1. Understanding of the importance of ethical and legal issues in consultation and education	1. Understanding of ethical and legal issues in consultation and education	1. Knowledge of the complexities of consultation and education, including ethical and legal issues
S 1. Ability to ask questions and seek information relevant to ethical and	1. Beginning skill in formulating ethical and legal issues in	1. Skill in the appropriate recognition and application of ethical

continues

TABLE 8.1
Continued

Begin practicum	Begin internship	Complete doctoral degree
S legal issues in consultation and education	consultation and education	and legal issues in education and consultation
A 1. Openness to consideration of legal and ethical issues in consultation and education	1. Care and concern regarding the appropriate application of legal and ethical issues in consultation and education	1. Recognition of the importance of lifelong education and training and quality improvement in the maintenance of competence in education and consultation practice

Note. K = knowledge; S = skills; A = attitudes. From *Competency Developmental Achievement Levels (DALs) of the National Council of Schools and Programs in Professional Psychology (NCSPP),* (pp. 42–47), by the National Council of Schools and Programs in Professional Psychology, 2007. Available at http:// www.ncspp.info/DALof%20NCSPP%209-21-07.pdf. Copyright 2007 by the National Council of Schools and Programs in Professional Psychology. Reprinted with permission.

fer one combined course in consultation and supervision, the two emerging competencies. Course descriptions suggest that education and management, components of those competencies, are underrepresented in the content of the courses.

APA accreditation requires that the consultation and education competency be addressed in order to demonstrate satisfaction of the specified content areas. This may be fulfilled by a specific course or by content incorporated systematically into other courses and practicum training.

BARRIERS TO CURRICULUM AND TRAINING INCLUSION

The results of the 2005 NCSPP Self Study (Paskiewicz et al., 2006) indicate the continued relative importance placed on the core competencies in research, assessment, intervention, and diversity in contrast to less emphasis placed on consultation and education. It is likely that the same arguments made in the 1992 faculty survey (Borden & Mitchell, 1992) are made today in faculty meetings, arguing against taking units away from established competencies to increase emerging competencies.

Although many NCSPP faculty have professional experience in the consultation and education competency (Paskiewicz et al., 2006), it is unlikely that many have completed formal academic coursework in the competency because it is a recent development in the psychology curriculum. Adjunct faculty may be contracted to teach in this area, but they will not have the influence to raise the visibility and importance of the competency in the program.

One crucial difficulty in preparing students for consultation is the lack of external project sites easily accessible to beginners. Although recommendations for development of the competency consistently include actual consultation experiences (Arredondo et al., 2004; Illback et al., 1992), it is difficult to provide access to the number of projects needed for all students. Sample syllabi reviewed require students to develop venues by offering free services, but access, time, and commitment from organizations are still needed for training projects.

Another barrier is the deficit of practicum sites in consultation with appropriate supervision. The nature of independent consultation makes it difficult for experienced consultants to easily incorporate an inexperienced student into delivery of services. It may be easier to develop psychoeducation possibilities within clinics, schools, and organizations.

Finally, students voice concerns about possible bias by predoctoral internship sites in the evaluation of practica that emphasize consultation and education versus clinical skills or assessment. In the era of an internship supply-and-demand imbalance, it is perceived that the number of hours of practicum and the type of hours achieved are important to selection by internship sites (Kaslow, Pate, & Thorn, 2005). A survey of academic and training directors found that "virtually all respondents included clinical intervention and clinical assessment as legitimate practicum activities, while roughly half of respondents included supervision activities and community consultation, advocacy, and training as acceptable practicum experiences" (Kaslow et al., 2005, p. 309). Teaching was separated from consultation in the survey, and only 11.8% of internship site directors considered it a legitimate practicum experience. The survey further delineated specific types of practicum experience and asked respondents to rate the importance of each type of experience in that category; this analysis found that only 10% of internship programs rated consultation highly but that consultation experience in particular settings (e.g., schools, medical settings, academic institutions, community agencies) was ranked somewhat higher when the internship type matched the type of experience (e.g., Veterans Affairs medical centers rank consultation in medical settings more highly). These data demonstrate that consultation experience may be helpful in selection if it matches the type of site, but students must cultivate exact match. Kaslow, Pate, and Thorn (2005) challenged training directors to recognize that "psychologists are increasingly called on to conduct systems-oriented interventions and consultations" (p. 315), so more training is needed in order to prepare students for this role.

CONVINCE FACULTY

To include the consultation and education competency more thoroughly and consistently in doctoral curriculum and training, it will be necessary to

convince faculty of the importance of these emerging competencies. New courses require subtraction of existing courses; it may be easier to incorporate aspects of consultation and education into existing courses in a manner consistent with the developmental achievement of the competency. The data on graduates' entry into consultation and education positions must be recognized by programs, so that faculty will actively adopt the following methods for increased inclusion of the competency in graduate education.

TEACH SYSTEMS THEORY

Transition to organizational consulting will be facilitated if programs emphasize interventions at the larger level (group, organization). Foundational knowledge of systems theory and systemic conceptualization (Arredondo et al., 2004; Carlson, Kubiszyn, & Guli, 2004; Lowman, 2005; Stanton, in press) provides the theoretical base for understanding the complexity and reciprocity of dynamics in larger social organizations. This content should be required in all doctoral programs (Arredondo et al., 2004).

Increase Resources

More resources are needed that are specifically applicable to preparation for the consultation and education competencies in doctoral programs. Some faculty have capitalized on their experience to produce models for teaching the consultation competency that include theory, case examples, technical information, and skills development (Sears et al., 2006). These resources are needed to facilitate incorporation of this content into the curriculum.

Develop Initial Competency in Existing Opportunities

Students may begin to develop consultation and education competency in clinical practica, clinical courses, and in the general coursework if the faculty deliberately builds it into these opportunities (e.g., develop psychoeducation workshop on aging in gerontology course, practice primary care consultation in clinical training course). Corporate training or presentation skills for psychoeducation may be included in these courses, just as report writing is included in assessment courses.

Teach Technology

The use of technology (DeLeon, Crimmins, & Wolf, 2003; Kerr & Murthy, 2004; Naglieri et al., 2004) needs to be incorporated into the curriculum to enhance the consultation and education competencies. Contemporary consultation and education both require the ability to present infor-

mation in a sophisticated and engaging manner and to use Internet and computer-based delivery systems. Task-technology fit theory needs to be applied to roles and behaviors in these competencies to determine the appropriate use of computer-mediated communication and other methods of interaction (Kerr & Murthy, 2004). Assignments that develop technology competency may readily be incorporated into courses across the curriculum.

Create Projects and Venues

One way around the paucity of consultation sites is the development of projects that focus on university or program entities (e.g., clinics, programs, departments) over which the program has direct influence or control. Some consultation syllabi reviewed for this chapter incorporate assignments that involve provision of consultation to administrators and programs in a manner that benefits both student and institution. Additional venues may be developed for pro bono consultation and education for 501 charitable or nonprofit organizations, since these organizations may not typically have access to such resources. Faculty who provide consultation services may be able to develop segments of their consultation work that can accommodate students, but clear guidelines will need to be established regarding ethics, professional relationship, supervision, and financial arrangements. There are similarities here to long-standing arrangements around clinical psychotherapy training, but few programs have developed formal documents or handbooks around consultation training standards.

Use Existing Courses in Other Programs

A review of doctoral program Web sites indicates that schools offer a variety of options to enhance the consultation and education competency, but most are separate from the APA-accredited program (e.g., certificates or degrees in organizational/industrial consultation, consulting psychology, or business psychology). These faculty and curricula need to be more closely aligned with the APA-accredited programs, perhaps by creating elective tracks in addition to single mandatory courses in these competencies to allow students the option of expanding their education in the competency at the doctoral level.

EMERGING ISSUES

The continued emergence of consultation as a practice area requires more consistent education and training for professional psychologists (Kaslow et al., 2004). It is no longer reasonable to relegate the core competency in consultation and education to an elective, as if it is something that only select psychologists will include in practice.

Technology Issues

Increased use of technology for the provision of consultation and education raises concerns about empirical support for these practices and the need for national licensure or national standards that facilitate provision of services across geographic boundaries. Technology "compels us to conceive of boundaries in other than geographical terms" (DeLeon et al., 2003, p. 168). These issues need to be researched and standards determined.

Preparation Needed for Higher Education Roles

The education competency currently focuses on psychoeducation, but there appears to be a need for PsyD programs to expand the competency to include preparation for academic roles.

Data from the APA Research Office indicate that PsyD graduates do find employment in academic settings but at a lower rate than PhD recipients (APA, 2003). In university settings, 14% of 2003 PhD recipients found employment versus only 3.2% of PsyD recipients. The margin narrows in 4-year colleges (PhD 2.8% vs. PsyD 1.3%), medical schools (PhD 4.7% vs. PsyD 2.5%), and other academic settings (PhD 1.9% vs. PsyD 1.3%). The sum for PsyD graduates in primary employment in academic settings is 8.3%. In addition, another 8.3% had secondary employment in academic settings, suggesting adjunct or clinical faculty status, for a total of 16.6% employed in academia. This contrasts with 34.1% total for PhD graduates. These data are important because they suggest a need to prepare PsyD students for this role.

A review of online program descriptions suggests that few PsyD programs offer courses specifically for the development of competencies to enter academic teaching positions. At a minimum, PsyD students need to be exposed to pedagogical principles for teaching psychology, curriculum themes, course development, student evaluation methods, ethical issues, the technology of teaching, and continuous evaluation of the quality and effectiveness of teaching (Lucas & Bernstein, 2005). Programs need to challenge students to become "scholars of teaching" who are theorists and practitioners of teaching and learning, incorporating technologies and conducting research on outcomes (Mitterer, 2006). Teaching experience and the ability to teach the specific courses needed by a department are important factors in the candidacy process (Landrum & Clump, 2004). PsyD programs that facilitate teaching experience may benefit their graduates who want to consider employment in academia.

CONCLUSION

More education and training in consultation and education is needed in doctoral programs today. Programs must find creative ways to include the

development of this competency in an already full curriculum and training program. Because graduates are increasingly moving into consultation and education roles, programs need to prepare them for those roles.

REFERENCES

American Psychological Association. (2003). *Demographic shifts in psychology*. Retrieved August 9, 2007, from http://www.research.apa.org/demoshifts.html

American Psychological Association. (2007). Guidelines for education and training at the doctoral and postdoctoral level in consulting psychology/organizational consulting psychology. *American Psychologist, 62*, 980–992.

Arredondo, P., Shealy, C., Neale, M., & Winfrey, L. L. (2004). Consultation and interprofessional collaboration: Modeling for the future. *Journal of Clinical Psychology, 60*, 787–800.

Borden, K., & Mitchell, C. (1992). Faculty opinions on the core curriculum: A survey. In R. L. Peterson, J. D. McHolland, R. J. Bent, E. Davis-Russell, G. E. Edwall, K. Polite, et al. (Eds.), *The core curriculum in professional psychology* (pp. 56–63). Washington, DC: American Psychological Association and National Council of Schools of Professional Psychology.

Brown, D., Pryzwansky, W., & Schulte, A. (2001). *Psychological consultation: Introduction to theory and practice* (5th ed.). Boston: Allyn & Bacon.

Carlson, C., Kubiszyn, T., & Guli, L. (2004). Consultation with caregivers and families. In R. Brown (Ed.), *Handbook of pediatric psychology in school settings* (pp. 617–635). Mahwah, NJ: Erlbaum

Collins, F., Kaslow, N., & Illfelder-Kaye, J. (2004). Introduction to the special issue. *Journal of Clinical Psychology, 60*, 695–697.

Cooper, S. (2002). Perspectives and reactions to the principles for education and training in organizational consulting psychology. *Consulting Psychology Journal: Practice and Research, 54*, 211–212.

DeLeon, P., Crimmins, D., & Wolf, A. (2003). Afterword—The 21st century has arrived. *Psychotherapy: Theory, Research, Practice, Training, 40*, 164–169.

Glasser, J. K. (2002). Factors related to consultant credibility. *Consulting Psychology Journal: Practice and Research, 54*, 28–42.

Illback, R., Maher, C., & Kopplin, D. (1992). Consultation and education competency. In R. L. Peterson, J. D. McHolland, R. J. Bent, E. Davis-Russell, G. E. Edwall, K. Polite, et al. (Eds.), *The core curriculum in professional psychology* (pp. 115–120). Washington, DC: American Psychological Association and National Council of Schools of Professional Psychology.

Kaslow, N. J., Borden, K., Collins, F., Forrest, L., Illfelder-Kaye, J., Nelson, P., et al. (2004). Competencies conference: Future directions in education and credentialing in professional psychology. *Journal of Clinical Psychology, 60*, 699–712.

Kaslow, N. J., Pate, W., & Thorn, B. (2005). Academic and internship directors' perspectives on practicum experiences: Implications for training. *Professional Psychology: Research and Practice, 36,* 307–317.

Kerr, D., & Murthy, U. (2004). Divergent and convergent idea generation in teams: A comparison of computer-mediated and face-to-face communication. *Group Decision and Negotiation, 13,* 381–399.

Landrum, R., & Clump, M. (2004). Departmental search committees and the evaluation of faculty applicants. *Teaching of Psychology, 31,* 12–17.

Lowman, R. (1998a). New Directions for graduate training in consulting psychology. *Consulting Psychology Journal: Practice and Research, 50,* 263–270.

Lowman, R. (Ed.). (1998b). *The ethical practice of psychology in organizations.* Washington, DC: American Psychological Association.

Lowman, R. (2005). Executive coaching: The road to Dodoville needs paving with more than good assumptions. *Consulting Psychology Journal: Practice and Research, 57,* 90–96.

Lowman, R., Alderfer, C., Atella, M., Garman, A., Hellkamp, D., Kilburg, R., et al. (2002). Principles for education and training at the doctoral and postdoctoral level in consulting psychology/organizational. *Consulting Psychology Journal: Practice and Research, 54,* 213–222.

Lucas, S., & Bernstein, D. (2005). *Teaching psychology: A step-by-step guide.* Mahwah, NJ: Erlbaum.

Manley, T., & Holiwski, F. (2003). Teaching on racism: Tools for consultant training. *Journal of Educational and Psychological Consultation, 14,* 387–399.

McHolland, J. (1992). National Council of Schools of Professional Psychology Core Curriculum Conference Resolutions. In R. L. Peterson, J. D. McHolland, R. J. Bent, E. Davis-Russell, G. E. Edwall, K. Polite, et al. (Eds.), *The core curriculum in professional psychology* (pp. 153–176). Washington, DC: American Psychological Association and National Council of Schools of Professional Psychology.

Mitterer, J. (2006). Ask not what post-secondary education can do for psychology; ask what psychology can do for post-secondary education. *Canadian Psychology, 47,* 57–62.

Naglieri, J., Drasgow, F., Schmit, M., Handler, L., Prifitera, A., Margolis, A., et al. (2004). Psychological testing on the Internet: New problems, old issues. *American Psychologist, 59,* 150–162.

National Council of Schools and Programs in Professional Psychology. (2007). *Competency developmental achievement levels (DALs) of the National Council of Schools and Programs in Professional Psychology (NCSPP)* [Electronic Version], 52. Retrieved December 22, 2007, from http://www.ncspp.info/DALof%20NCSPP%209-21-07.pdf

O'Roark, A. (2002). The quest for executive effectiveness: Consultants bridge the gap between psychological research and organizational application. *Consulting Psychology Journal: Practice and Research, 54,* 44–54.

Paskiewicz, W., Rabe, D., Adams, W., Gathercoal, K., Meyer, A., & McIlvried, J. (2006, January). *2005 NCSPP self study with complementary data*. Paper presented at the National Council of Schools and Programs of Professional Psychology, Lake Las Vegas, NV.

Peterson, R., Peterson, D., Abrams, J., & Stricker, G. (1997). The National Council of Schools and Programs of Professional Psychology educational model. *Professional Psychology: Research and Practice, 28,* 373–386.

Rogers, M. (2000). Examining the cultural context of consultation. *School Psychology Review, 29,* 414–418.

Sears, R., Rudisill, J., & Mason-Sears, C. (2006). *Consultation skills for mental health professionals*. Hoboken, NJ: Wiley.

Shullman, S. (2002). Reflections of a consulting counseling psychologist: Implications of the principles for education and training at the doctoral and postdoctoral level in consulting psychology for the practice of counseling psychology. *Consulting Psychology Journal: Practice and Research, 54,* 242–251.

Stanton, M. (in press). The systemic epistemology of family psychology. In J. Bray & M. Stanton (Eds.), *Handbook of family psychology*. Oxford, England: Wiley-Blackwell.

Steward, R. (1996). Training consulting psychologists to be sensitive to multicultural issues in organizational consultation. *Consulting Psychology Journal: Practice and Research, 48,* 180–189.

9

THE MANAGEMENT AND SUPERVISION COMPETENCY: CURRENT AND FUTURE DIRECTIONS

KATHLEEN A. MALLOY, JAMES E. DOBBINS, KELLY DUCHENY, AND LAPEARL LOGAN WINFREY

When people think about tasks that are routinely performed by professional psychologists, therapy and assessment are generally the first activities that come to mind. However, supervision and management tasks also comprise a significant number of those routine functions. An American Psychological Association (APA) doctorate employment survey indicated that 42% of professional school graduates spent at least 25% of their professional time engaged in management and supervision activities (Kohout & Wicherski, 1991). In spite of longstanding findings indicating that psychologists regularly engage in management and supervision, neither area has been well represented in graduate education or in the accreditation process. Management has seldom been endorsed as an essential aspect of professional psychology doctoral training, and supervision has only recently received attention as a core domain for clinical training. While the APA *Guidelines and Principles (G&P) for Accreditation* address standards for education in the area of supervision at all levels of training (doctoral, internship, and postdoctoral), it is not until the postdoctoral level of training that the G&P address compe-

tency in "organization, management and administration issues" (APA Committee on Accreditation, 2002, p. 22). Delegates to the 2002 Competencies Conference: Future Directions in Education and Credentialing in Professional Psychology, who represented leading organizations that oversee doctoral training in clinical psychology in the United States and internationally, agreed that supervision was a core competency for professional psychologists and called for a developmental approach to assess it across the professional life span (Falender et al., 2004). However, the Competencies Conference failed to address management as a competency at any developmental stage. In examining doctoral level clinical training, Lewis, Hatcher, and Pate (2005) surveyed 263 graduate practicum sites and found that only 27.8% of sites offered experiences in supervision and only 13.9% offered experiences in management. Kaslow, Pate, and Thorn (2005) reported that 46% of internships and 62% of academic programs considered supervision to be a legitimate practicum experience. However, only 9% of internships and 17% of academic programs considered administration to constitute legitimate practicum activities.

As early as 1987, the National Council of Schools and Programs of Professional Psychology (NCSPP), as a national leader in professional psychology training, had identified the need to include management and supervision as core competencies in professional psychology education (Bent & Cannon, 1987). In 1992, in its Standards for Education in Professional Psychology, NCSPP formally adopted the management and supervision competency as a component of graduate training in professional psychology (Peterson et al., 1992). In 2007, NCSPP adopted the developmental achievement levels (DALs), which list five domains of this competency: (a) assuring the well-being of the client or organization, (b) training and mentoring of supervisees or employees, (c) evaluation/gatekeeping, (d) ethics, and (e) health care leadership and advocacy (NCSPP, 2007). Table 9.1 describes the DALs for the management and supervision competency. The DALs describe the required knowledge, skills and attitudes (KSAs) across three stages of training: beginning practicum, beginning internship, and completion of degree.

As a competency, management and supervision should be regarded as domains of activity that permeate most, if not all, aspects of professional work. Management and supervision are conceptualized to represent a broad functional domain that includes definable aspects of professional self-care, care of clients, training of students, and administration of organizations. This approach shifts away from the historical view of management and supervision as narrowly defined, specialized areas of training. Instead, NCSPP's educational model defines management as a broad domain of KSAs that subsumes supervision activities as a related, but more focused aspect of management (Bent, Schindler, & Dobbins, 1992). This model acknowledges the similarities that exist between supervision and management; however, there are also clear differences between the two. NCSPP defines *management* as consisting of "those activities that direct, organize, or control the services

TABLE 9.1
Knowledge, Skills, and Attitudes and Domains for the Management and Supervision Competency

Begin practicum	Begin internship	Complete doctoral degree
Assuring client and organizational welfare domain		
K 1. Understanding of need for supervision 2. Understanding that diversity plays a role in organizations 3. Knowledge of one's limitations in functioning within an organization	1. Knowledge of one or more models of supervision 2. Basic knowledge of how personal and cultural values can influence supervision and management 3. Knowledge of organizational operations and the functions and limitations of roles therein	1. Knowledge of supervision practices and agency policies that enhance client and staff welfare 2. Knowledge of at least one model or theory and associated research and applications. 3. Sophisticated knowledge of how diversity issues and personal and cultural values influence supervision and management
S 1. Demonstration of awareness of self and others in relationship to leaders 2. Articulation of the importance of diversity in organizations 3. Demonstration of self-control and flexibility in new situations	1. Demonstration of ability to think critically and analytically about self and others as a manager, supervisor, and supervisee 2. Attention to issues of diversity within the organization 3. Demonstration of ability to determine when to seek extra supervision	1. Ability to implement at least one model of supervision 2. Integration of knowledge of diversity issues into supervisory and management process 3. Management and maintenance of own self-care and promotion of the wellness of others 4. Effective work with organizational structure, hierarchical relationship, and multidisciplinary colleagues
A 1. Appreciation for diversity 2. Enthusiasm for learning to function in clinical role 3. Valuation of leaders and supervisors as guides for effective service delivery 4. Active approach to learning about self in systems	1. Awareness of self and role in larger system 2. Interest in learning about organizational systems and how they influence individuals within them	1. Concern for and commitment to well-being of supervisees' clients 2. Tolerance of role expectancies and ambiguities 3. Valuation of the incorporation of diversity issues in supervisory and organizational decision making

continues

TABLE 9.1
Continued

Begin practicum	Begin internship	Complete doctoral degree
Training/mentoring domain		
K 1. Knowledge of the purpose of training and the roles of apprentice and supervisee	1. Knowledge of multiple roles in the supervisory process 2. Knowledge of research evidence relevant to supervision and management of organizations 3. Knowledge of individual and cultural differences in supervision 4. Knowledge of and developing expertise in clinical areas in which one is supervising	1. Basic knowledge of monetary implications of a health care service delivery system 2. Knowledge of at least one business model that lends itself to health care delivery systems 3. Understanding of the importance of training and mentoring in the professional development of individuals and in the quality enhancement of organizations
S 1. Ability to articulate basic roles of supervisor and supervisee 2. Effective function within organizational context 3. Active search for opportunities to learn from clinical placement and from supervisor 4. Acceptance of and incorporation of feedback from instructors and peers	1. Demonstration of ability to think critically and analytically 2. Ability to establish a supervisory alliance 3. Ability to use and integrate feedback within the supervisory relationship 4. Ability to apply research knowledge to health care systems and supervision 5. Ability to articulate primary mission and limits of setting	1. Ability to take an active part in developing or changing public policy 2. Ability to apply research findings to suggest changes in organizational policies and planning 3. Ability to perform and balance multiple roles in supervision, (e.g. teaching, evaluation, mentoring, modeling) 4. Ability to provide effective formative and summative feedback 5. Ability to integrate and evaluate feedback within the supervisory relationship 6. Ability to assess learning needs of trainees
A 1. Demonstration of interest in learning 2. Demonstration of interest in self-reflection 3. Openness to considering advocacy	1. Desire to supervise others 2. Valuation of professional collaboration within supervisory relationships	1. Willingness to take an active part in developing or changing public policy 2. Valuation of training and mentoring as professional activities

as a professional responsibility

3. Valuation of flexibility
4. Commitment to lifelong learning and quality improvement
5. Interest in advocacy efforts

Evaluation/gatekeeping domain

K 1. Understanding of purposes of evaluation
2. Understanding of responsibilities of agencies to larger bodies for accreditation and approval

1. Knowledge of basic formative and summative methods of evaluating clinical work of supervisees
2. Knowledge of how diversity and individual differences can influence approaches to evaluation
3. Knowledge of evaluation and feedback methods used in organizations

1. Knowledge of best practices in evaluation
2. Knowledge of one's own value system and the implications for management
3. Knowledge of evaluation of health care delivery systems

S 1. Appropriate response to supervisor and agency expectations
2. Demonstration of constructive use of formative feedback
3. Provision of basic constructive feedback to peers
4. Provision of needed information in a timely manner

1. Assessment of clinical strengths and areas needing improvement for self and others
2. Evaluation of how issues of diversity impact the supervision process
3. Ability to seek, use, provide, and integrate feedback
4. Prompt response to supervisory requests

1. Development of new evaluative skills as needed to serve the health care organization
2. Oversight of program evaluations with the aid of a more experienced manager
3. Modeling of an accurate and reflective self-assessment process
4. Stimulation of self-reflection and self-evaluation in others

A 1. Demonstration of non-defensive openness to both formal and informal formative feedback
2. Valuation of self-reflection and an active approach to self-discovery
3. Demonstration of cooperative attitude regarding supervisor's priorities and agency's policies and expectations

1. Interest in increasing self-knowledge and experience
2. Valuation of and respect for the dignity and autonomy of others
3. Valuation of own skills
4. Openness to providing and receiving feedback from peers and supervisors

1. Valuation of role in organizational system and demonstration of beginning comfort with role of manager/supervisor
2. Investment in offering others feedback
3. Investment in receiving feedback from others

continues

TABLE 9.1
Continued

Begin practicum	Begin internship	Complete doctoral degree
Ethics domain		

K
1. Basic knowledge of ethics codes
2. Understanding of need for and purpose of accurate record keeping
3. Knowledge of own limitations in experience and skills

1. Knowledge of professional ethics, statutes, and rules and regulations regarding supervision
2. Knowledge of limits of one's supervisory and clinical skills
3. Knowledge of differences between therapy, consultation, supervision, and management roles

1. Knowledge of legal and ethical requirements, case law, and risk management relevant to supervision
2. Knowledge of limitations of one's own supervisory competence

S
1. Ability to recognize legal and ethical issues in clinical and organizational contexts
2. Ability to function within appropriate professional boundaries in an organizational context
3. Beginning skill in accurate and useful record keeping

1. Demonstration of appropriate professional assertiveness related to ethical issues
2. Search for appropriate information and consultation about ethical issues in supervision
3. Evaluation of and appropriate response to ethical and legal issues associated with supervision or organizational demands
4. Ability to comply with legal requirements
5. Ability to promptly complete necessary records with minimal supervision of methods

1. Integration of legal and ethical awareness in planning and implementation of programs
2. Ability to help supervisees and others recognize ethical dimensions of clinical decision making
3. Ability to develop record keeping methods that aid the organization's functioning
4. Ability to resolve supervisory role conflicts

A
1. Demonstration of appreciation for and commitment to ethical practice
2. Recognition of the influence of value systems to ethical decision making
3. Appreciation for the need to function within the policies and procedures of an organization

1. Commitment to ethical practice as supervisee and supervisor
2. Appreciation for professional and business codes of conduct that influence service delivery

1. Commitment to ethical practice in all aspects of supervisory behavior
2. Encouragement of supervisees and organizations in the development of ethical practices

K 1. Basic knowledge about health care systems	1. Understanding of impact of reimbursement on treatment provided and service delivery system 2. Knowledge of one or more models of leadership /management 3. Basic knowledge of monetary implications in service delivery	1. Knowledge of systemic implications of financial issues for health care service delivery 2. Knowledge of leadership and management roles 3. Basic knowledge of health care service delivery system options 4. Knowledge of at least one business model that lends itself to health care delivery systems
S		1. Ability to take an active part in developing or changing public policy 2. Ability to apply research findings to suggest changes in organizational policies and planning 3. Beginning ability to provide leadership in program planning and development
A 1. Openness to considering advocacy as a professional responsibility	1. Interest in advocacy efforts	1. Willingness to take an active part in developing or changing public policy

Note. K = knowledge; S = skills; A = attitudes. From *Competency Developmental Achievement Levels (DALs) of the National Council of Schools and Programs in Professional Psychology (NCSPP),* (pp. 35–40), by the National Council of Schools and Programs in Professional Psychology, 2007. Available at http://www.ncspp.info/DALof%20NCSPP%209-21-07.pdf. Copyright 2007 by the National Council of Schools and Programs in Professional Psychology. Reprinted with permission.

of psychologists and others offered or rendered to the public," and defines self-management as concerning "the application of similar principles to effective functioning in a professional role" (McHolland, 1992b, p. 165). *Supervision* is defined as "a form of management blended with teaching in the context of relationship directed to the enhancement of competence in the supervisee" (McHolland, 1992b, p. 165).

Unique to the NCSPP definition of management is *self-management* or management of the professional self (Bent & Cannon, 1987; Bent et al., 1992). Self-management includes management of time and information, prioritizing obligations, personal organization to meet professional requirements, and stress management. Self-management also includes functioning within the "consensual standards" (Bent et al., 1992, p. 122) of the profession (i.e., ethics, regulations) and concerns controlling the activities of psychologists

so that they can apply their KSAs to develop and maintain functional relationships. Many NCSPP programs teach self-management as part of socialization seminars, ethics courses, and professional behavior activities on practicum.

To form the foundational relationships necessary to manage and supervise others, psychologists must be able to competently work with people from diverse backgrounds within diverse cultural contexts. Moreover, psychologists must be trained to function effectively within the diverse roles of therapist, supervisor, administrator, educator, and consultant within diverse contexts. As stated in NCSPP's standards, "Issues of diversity and the development of alternative management and supervisory models should be emphasized. Diversity and multicultural issues should inform all aspects of the management and supervision competency areas" (McHolland, 1992b, p. 166).

The remainder of this chapter addresses the need to train future psychologists in management and supervision, the KSAs that should be addressed in such training, the ways in which professional psychology programs are providing such training, and future directions for training.

MANAGEMENT

Although a significant number of psychologists have management and administration as part of their careers, very little formal training in management is occurring in professional psychology graduate programs. Even when students are exposed to managerial domains of practice, that exposure often does not occur in an organized and thoughtful manner. For example, graduate students participate with faculty members in committees that are empowered to manage various elements of the training program. Those students, however, are seldom made aware that they are participating in managerial tasks, and little time is spent helping them to understand the theory underlying the completion of those tasks. Students on practicum or internship are in settings in which management is occurring all around them. They often participate in tasks that would be considered administrative, such as offering input on a new intake form or helping to develop policies or procedures. These tasks are not labeled as *managerial* and not discussed as a domain of practice. Instead, these tasks are invisible and are assumed to be expendable. Students are rarely taught the importance of mastering the skills needed to manage others, required to complete coursework to develop managerial skills, or taught the theory and research that underlies the competent performance of such tasks.

By incorporating management into professional psychology training programs, graduates of those programs will be better prepared to perform the wide array of tasks expected of them as psychologists. The settings in which psychologists are called on to perform managerial or administrative tasks in-

clude, but are not limited to, private practice, mental health clinics, hospitals, inpatient mental health facilities, managed care organizations, behavioral health settings, universities, clinical training programs, professional associations, and psychology internship programs (O'Donohue & Fisher, 1999). In addition, many psychologists are continually developing new roles and types of practice that require management and administration skills. Examples of entrepreneurial endeavors include such things as life coaching, practices based solely on self-pay income sources, interdisciplinary team membership, shared group practice, and consultation-based practices.

The more frequently psychologists are involved in management and administration, the more opportunities they will have to impact policy development, health care delivery, and information management practices (Dyer, 1999; Freeman, 1999). In both public and private agencies, psychologists are among the most educated personnel. Adding training in management and administration to the advanced clinical training that they receive will not only position them well to fill higher paying jobs but will also offer psychologists greater opportunities to be involved in program and organizational policy development. Understanding human motivation and learning can allow a manager to assist those she or he manages to enhance their performance. As a result of the training that graduate students in professional psychology receive in understanding and working with diverse individuals, they will be prepared not only to manage such individuals but also to participate in developing best practices that address the needs of diverse groups of people.

Knowledge and Skills

Psychologists in clinical practice need to possess an array of managerial and administrative skills, and an understanding of the theory underlying those skills. Strong marketing skills are necessary to survive in an increasingly competitive market (APA, 1996). Skills in human resources and budget management and, as federal and state monies become tighter, the ability to generate funds through grants and contracts is important for psychologists in many settings. Even psychologists who are not interested in making management a significant piece of their careers must understand federal and state regulations (e.g., Health Insurance Portability and Accountability Act) and how to implement those regulations. A lack of understanding about the risks involved in offering a public service can result in extremely serious consequences, including sanctions from professional organizations, loss of licensure, and lawsuits (Bennett, Bryant, VandenBos, & Greenwood, 1990). Psychologists must also be prepared to manage their client case loads (Bent et al., 1992). This includes individualized service planning, knowledge and use of ancillary resources, contracting, fee setting, appropriate application of ethical and legal standards in informed consent, and privileged communication.

For those trainees interested in moving toward careers in mental health management, administration and program and policy development, it is helpful to understand the impact of a market economy on the availability of mental health services and the ways in which national and state politics affect financial decisions (Swift, 1996). Integrating classroom learning in economics, financial management, strategic planning, administration, and managing organizational change with students' clinical training would help interested individuals prepare for such careers (Swift, 1996). Training in management and administration would also prove helpful to psychologists interested in working in academic settings. Such skills help faculty members with income generation (generally through grants and contracts), programmatic learning assessment and program development.

Attitudes

For some psychologists, one impediment to embracing the role of manager is the belief that such a role is not in keeping with their identity as a therapist and as a psychologist. Swift (1996) noted that psychologists sometimes fear that "we will lose the deep and rich training we've worked so hard for to the demands of business, management and financial exceptions" (p. 149). Relationships are seen as central to the practice of psychology, whereas, for some, management is seen as defining relationships as secondary to goal achievement. As a manager, the well-being of organizations must be considered, at times leading to decisions that may not seem to be in the best interest of individual employees or agency clients (i.e., reprimanding or firing an employee, cutting services offered due to financial constraints).

If management is to be accepted as a legitimate practice domain, psychologists must understand that training in management can deepen and enhance their identity, can infuse administrative roles with psychological principles and values, and can add to the variety of roles open to psychologists. Once management is accepted as an acknowledged domain of practice for psychologists, it will become more obvious that many of the attitudes that make one a strong clinician also make one a strong manager.

To provide high quality management services, psychologists should hold themselves accountable to the people with whom they work and the organizations and communities within which they work. Integrity plays a critical role in the development of a trusting administrative relationship. Without attitudes of integrity, empathy, and justice, psychologists engaged in management activities risk doing harm, and stunting the growth of their organization, employees, and communities (APA, 2002). Managing psychologists should value and acknowledge the time and contributions of others. In addition, critical to any administrative relationship is a clear articulation of expectations and a commitment to the accurate, objective assessment of performance. A focus on the value of professional growth, avoidance of burnout,

acknowledgement of achievement, and encouragement of innovation and creativity will build a strong, effective manager. Psychologists who manage should value all organizational stakeholders and should be committed to self-reflection (Bent et al., 1992). An awareness of the impact of privilege and power should assist managers in examining the impact and meaning of their administrative decisions and in increasing the cultural competence of their work environments. Psychologists should be attuned to the impact of individual and cultural difference and the effects of oppression and discrimination (i.e., racism, sexism, age discrimination) in the workplace. This awareness will allow them to critically examine their own biases and the discrimination occurring within the environment in an effort to create a workplace that respects the experience of others and provides culturally adept services.

SUPERVISION

Over the past 50 years, a substantial body of literature has been published that acknowledges the importance of supervision in training future psychologists to become competent therapists. However, there has been significantly less attention paid to training psychologists in the KSAs necessary to provide that supervision (Bent et al., 1992; Borders, 2006, Falender et al., 2004; Watkins, 1997). NCSPP was the first training council to define the provision of supervision as a core competency in professional psychology training (Bent et al., 1992; Peterson et al., 1992). Early on, NCSPP identified the need to prepare students for the increased emphasis on administrative and supervisory roles in managed care environments (Cummings, 1999) and to enlarge the realms of supervision beyond the traditional areas of psychotherapy and assessment. NCSPP also recognized that professional psychologists were more frequently serving as members of interdisciplinary health care teams with professionals and trainees from diverse disciplines and diverse cultures (Canfield et al., 2000) and that a broader focus on supervisory and cultural competence was needed to best meet the demands of these expanded roles.

Currently, supervision is accepted as a core competency in professional psychology that is critical to each professional's lifelong learning (Kaslow et al., 2004). Supervision has been incorporated as part of the profession's ethics (APA, 2003) and as a curricular standard for accreditation (APA, Committee on Accreditation, 2002). There is also a growing emphasis on the need to train future supervisors to provide supervision in a culturally competent manner (APA, Council of Representatives, 2002 ; Falender et al., 2004; Hird, Tao, & Alberta, 2007).

Knowledge

Individuals preparing to supervise others should be familiar with definitions of supervision that address the relationship between supervisor and su-

pervisee, the focus and goals of supervision activities, and important relational variables. Functional domains for which the supervisor is responsible include the ability to form an effective training relationship, provide evaluations, monitor the quality of professional services, and provide a critical gatekeeping function for those who are not well-suited for working in the profession (Watkins, 1997).

Although not producing a concrete definition, the 2002 Competencies Conference identified six areas of knowledge required for mastery of supervision, including knowledge of supervision models, theories, and modalities, and research on supervision; information on how psychologists and supervisees develop from novice to master; the ethics and legal issues relevant to supervision; evaluation of supervision and process outcomes; and an understanding of the impact of diversity in all its forms on the supervisory process and context (Falender et al., 2004). In addition, supervisors must demonstrate content-specific knowledge in the clinical area being supervised (e.g., therapy with children and adolescents).

Skills

Becoming a competent supervisor requires mastering a complex set of skills. Watkins (1997) asserted that one of the most essential skills for clinical supervisors is the ability to model and use their own values as a tool to create change in the supervisee. To do this effectively, supervisors must have well-articulated professional values and deliver their lessons with precision and observable skill. Competent supervisors should sensitively monitor the multiple roles they have with supervisees and effectively perform and balance those roles. Supervisors should also be able to assess their own performance as a supervisor and encourage and use evaluative feedback from their trainees. Supervisors should set appropriate professional and interpersonal boundaries, seek consultation when supervisory issues are outside of their competence, and remain flexible in their approach to supervision. Competent supervisors should also be able to assess the learning needs and developmental level of their supervisees, provide effective formative and summative feedback to and about supervisees, and promote growth and self-assessment in supervisees (Falender et al., 2004). A skillful supervisor integrates strong relational skills with self-awareness and the need for competence in working with diverse individuals and cultures (APA, Council of Representatives, 2002; Garrett et al., 2001). Supervisors must be aware not only of the impact of identity variables presented by supervisees and their clients but also how the supervisor's own identity affects supervision (Ladany, Constantine, Miller, Erickson, & Muse-Burke, 2000).

Additional skills required of supervisors include being able to explain their working models and to integrate psychological theory and intervention (Watkins, 1997). They must also possess strong teaching and didactic skills,

be able to think scientifically, and be able to translate scientific findings into practice (Falender et al., 2004).

Along with defining the skills necessary to master the supervision competency comes the task of studying how to measure supervisory skills. Toward that end, McHolland (1992a) presented examples of how the supervision competency could be observed and measured. He stated that in the domain of self-supervision, trainees should be able to accurately evaluate personal strengths and weaknesses in their clinical work. When supervising others, trainees should be able to describe their supervision approach in clear, concrete terms.

Attitudes

The vast majority of the attitudes that were described as important for learning in management are also important components of competence in supervision. For example, supervisors must also hold themselves accountable to the people with whom they work, including the supervisee and client and the organization and community within which they work. Attitudes that embrace integrity, empathy, and justice are as important to supervisors as to administrators (APA, 2002). It is also vital that supervisors-in-training are taught to embrace the need for cultural competence (APA, Council of Representatives, 2002; Fong & Lease, 1997; Garrett et al., 2001). Supervisors must remain aware of privilege and power in their relationships with supervisees. They must also be committed to helping supervisees explore the impact those variables have on their relationships with their clients.

It is also critical to understand that the responsibility for the well-being of both supervisees and their clients lies with the supervisor. The supervisor must be able to balance clinical and training needs. Supervisors are expected to approach the supervisory relationship in a respectful and empowering manner and must value a balance between challenging a trainee to stretch and grow and supporting the trainee's efforts. Supervisors must commit to lifelong learning and professional growth, value ethical principles, and know and utilize available psychological science related to supervision as well as evidence a commitment to understanding and respecting their own limitations (Falender et al., 2004).

PROVIDING TRAINING IN MANAGEMENT AND SUPERVISION

The most obvious method of including training in management and supervision in graduate programs is to ensure their presence within the curriculum (Marwich DeMuth, Yates, & Coates, 1984; Sales, 1984). In observing the NCSPP educational model, 80% of member programs include coursework in management and supervision (Paszkiewicz, 2006). For students

who are interested in making management, administration, or program development a significant part of their professional lives, advanced seminars or a series of electives should be made available (Bent et al., 1992). Information from other fields should also be made available to students, whether integrated into the standard psychology curriculum or offered as separate courses in other departments (e.g., marketing, business management; Marwich DeMuth et al., 1984). Some NCSPP programs have developed joint degrees with business schools in their universities or provided students with the opportunity to complete business coursework to satisfy curricular requirements for the management competency. Including such experiences in academic offerings makes vital information available to students and conveys the message that the role of manager is a valuable and appropriate one for psychologists.

In classes that address supervision, students should first learn what to expect as a supervisee and how to be an active participant in the supervision they receive (Bent et al., 1992; Schindler & Talen, 1996). Addressing their experiences as supervisees allows them to capitalize on their own experiences to help them better understand the supervision theories and models they are learning. It also allows them to gain the greatest benefit from the supervision they are receiving, accelerating their learning and development. Students can then focus on applying the models of supervision that they have learned to the work of a supervisor. Role playing is one way to allow students to practice implementing the models they are learning, to receive feedback on their skills from the instructor, and to observe and critique other students as they practice their supervision skills.

Outside the classroom, a range of opportunities within academic programs arise for less traditional training in management and supervision. For example, most program or institutional committees include student members. Faculty and administrators should view this participation as an opportunity for students to learn administrative and managerial KSAs that will carry over into their future careers. Whether through student government meetings, curriculum committee membership, guest speaker coordination, or participation in an accreditation site visit, opportunities abound for intentional learning in these areas. Programs could integrate learning about management and supervision into teaching, research, and faculty assistant training. Work–study positions could include managerial or administrative responsibilities that would contribute to students' mastery of the management and supervision competency. For students especially interested in management and administration, more intensive experiences could be developed.

Management and supervision skills must also be taught on practicum and internship. Clinical training opportunities within service delivery settings could easily be broadened to include management and supervision. Placements could be developed that allow students the opportunity to observe or work with psychologists in jobs that include management and supervision.

Within these settings, managers and supervisors would serve as role models and teach students the skills necessary to be successful. For example, involving students in a meeting of clinical supervisors would allow them to observe professionals performing the managerial tasks that are a part of supervision. Students would be given the opportunity to observe psychologists who have integrated management and supervision with service delivery as central elements of their professional identities, thus reinforcing the value and worth of such activities. Management and supervision would then no longer be seen by psychologists-in-training as mysterious activities that occur behind closed doors. Such opportunities can be designed to occur at any level of training, including practicum, internship, and postdoctoral training.

Students could also provide supervision to less advanced students under the supervision of an experienced supervisor (Rau, 2002; Schindler & Talen, 1996; Watkins, 1999) during practicum, internship, or postdoctoral training. The experience could be coordinated with coursework in supervision or with seminars that are part of clinical training experiences.

In further developing the management and supervision competency area, several things must happen. The DALs must be refined and practical ways to assess competency in management and supervision across the developmental spectrum must be created. Assessment approaches that allow programs to accurately measure students' mastery in the areas of supervision and management across time and level of training must be developed and evaluated (Kaslow et al., 2004). Additional work in refining and assessing existing training models, developing new approaches to training, and incorporating other methodologies, such as 360 degree assessments, will continue to improve the field's ability to educate professional psychologists for leadership roles in the evolving workforce. In addition, resources and nuanced tools for education, training, and assessing competency must be made available. Finally, continued attention must be given to how issues of cultural and individual differences, power, and oppression, inform proficiency and expertise in this area.

REFERENCES

American Psychological Association. (1996). *Marketing your practice: Creating opportunities for success.* Washington, DC: Author.

American Psychological Association. (2002). Ethical principles of psychologists and code of conduct. *American Psychologist, 57,* 1060–1073. Washington, DC: Author.

American Psychological Association, Committee on Accreditation. (2002). *Guidelines and principles for accreditation of programs in professional psychology.* Washington, DC: Author.

American Psychological Association, Council of Representatives. (2002). *Guidelines on multicultural education, training, research, practice, and organization change for psychologists.* Washington, DC: Author

Bennett, B. E., Bryant, B. K., VandenBos, G. R., & Greenwood, A. (1990). *Professional liability and risk management.* Washington, DC: American Psychological Association.

Bent, R. J., & Cannon, W. G. (1987). Key functional skills of a professional psychologist. *Standards and evaluation in the education and training of professional psychologists: Knowledge, attitudes, and skills.* Norman, OK: Transcript Press.

Bent, R., Schindler, N., & Dobbins, J. (1992). Management and supervision competency. In R. L. Peterson, J. D. McHolland, R. J. Bent, E. Davis-Russell, G. E. Edwall, K. Polite, et al. (Eds.), *The core curriculum in professional psychology* (pp. 121–126). Washington, DC: American Psychological Association.

Borders, D. (2006). Snapshot of clinical supervision in counseling and counselor education: A five year review. *The Clinical Supervisor, 24*(1), 69–113.

Canfield, A., Clasen, C., Dobbins, J., Cauley, K., Hemphill, S., Rodney, M., & Walbroehl, G. (2000). Service-learning in health professions education: A multiprofessional example. *Academic Exchange Quarterly, 4,* 102–108.

Cummings, N. A. (1999). Managing a managed care organization. In W. O'Donohue & J. E. Fisher (Eds.), *Management and administration skills for the mental health professional* (pp. 133–153). San Diego, CA: Academic Press.

Dyer, R. L. (1999). Public policy administration and the psychologist. In W. O'Donohue & J. E. Fisher (Eds.), *Management and administration skills for the mental health professional* (pp. 261–274). San Diego, CA: Academic Press.

Falender, C. A., Cornish, J. A. E., Goodyear, R., Hatcher, R., Kalsow, N. J., Leventhal, G., Shafranske, E., & Sigman, S. T. (2004). Defining competencies in psychology supervision: A consensus statement. *Journal of Clinical Psychology, 60,* 771–785.

Fong, M. L., & Lease, S. H. (1997). Cross-cultural supervision: Issues for the White supervisor. In D. B. Pope-Davis & H. L. K. Coleman (Eds.), *Multicultural counseling competencies: Assessment, education and training, and supervision* (pp. 387–405). Thousand Oaks, CA: Sage.

Freeman, R. K. (1999). Information management in behavioral healthcare. In W. O'Donohue & J. E. Fisher (Eds.), *Management and administration skills for the mental health professional* (pp. 313–340). San Diego, CA: Academic Press.

Garrett, M. T., Borders, L. D., Crutchfield, L. B., Torres-Rivera, E., Brotherton, D., & Curtis, R. (2001). Multicultural supervision: A paradigm of cultural responsiveness for supervisors. *Journal of Multicultural Counseling and Development, 29,* 147–158. Alexandria, VA: American Counseling Association.

Hird, J. S., Tao, K. G., & Alberta, M. (2007). Examining supervisor' multicultural competence in racially similar and different supervision dyads. *The Clinical Supervisor, 23*(2), 107–122.

Kaslow, N. J., Borden, K. A., Collins, Jr., F. L., Forrest, L., Illfelder-Kaye, J., Nelson, P. D., & Rallo, J. S. (2004). Competencies Conference: Future directions in education and credentialing in professional psychology. *Journal of Clinical Psychology, 6,* 699–712.

Kaslow, N. J., Pate, W. E., & Thorn, B. (2005). Academic and internship directors' perspectives on practicum experiences: Implications. *Professional Psychology: Research and Practice, 36*, 307–317.

Kohout, J., & Wicherski, M. (1991). *1989 Doctorate employment survey.* Washington, DC: American Psychological Association.

Ladany, N., Constantine, M., Miller, K., Erickson, C. D., & Muse-Burke, J. L. (2000). Supervision countertransference: A qualitative investigation into its identification and description. *Journal of Counseling Psychology, 47*, 102–115.

Lewis, B. L., Hatcher, R. L., & Pate, W. E., II. (2005). The practicum experience: A survey of practicum site coordinators. *Professional Psychology: Research and Practice, 36*, 291–298.

Marwich DeMuth, N., Yates, B. T., & Coates, T. C. (1984). Psychologists as managers: Overcoming old guilt and accessing innovative pathways for enhanced skills. *Professional Psychology: Research and Practice, 15*, 758–768.

McHolland, J. D. (1992a). *Evaluating the management/supervision competencies in training in professional psychology.* Paper presented at the meeting of the Midwinter Conference of the National Council of Schools and Programs in Professional Psychology, Freeport, Bahamas.

McHolland, J. D. (1992b). National Council of Schools of Professional Psychology core curriculum conference resolutions. In R. L. Peterson, J. D. McHolland, R. J. Bent, E. Davis-Russell, G. E. Edwall, K. Polite, et al. (Eds.), *The core curriculum in professional psychology* (pp. 155–166). Washington, DC: American Psychological Association.

National Council of Schools and Programs in Professional Psychology. (2007). *NCSPP competency developmental achievement levels.* Retrieved December 1, 2007, from http://www.ncspp.info/pubs.htm

O'Donohue, W. & Fisher, J. E. (1999). *Management and administration skills for the mental health professional.* San Diego, CA: Academic Press.

Paszkiewicz, W. (2006). *2005 NCSPP self study with complementary data.* Paper presented at the meeting of the National Council of Schools of Professional Psychology Conference, Las Vegas, NV.

Peterson, R. L., McHolland, J. D., Bent, R. J., Davis-Russell, E., Edwall, G. E., Polite, K., et al. (Eds.). (1992). *The core curriculum in professional psychology.* Washington, DC: American Psychological Association.

Rau, D. R. (2002). Advanced trainees: Supervising junior trainees. *The Clinical Supervisor, 2*(1), 115–124.

Sales, B. D. (1984). The contexts of professional psychology. *Clinical Psychologist, 37*, 34–35.

Schindler, N. J., & Talen, M. R. (1996). Supervision 101: The basic elements for teaching beginning supervisors. *The Clinical Supervisor, 14*(2), 109–120.

Swift, M. (1996). *Clinical psychologists and the business of psychology: A training innovation.* Paper presented at the NCSPP Midwinter Conference on "Innovations in Professional Psychology Education and Practice: Preparing for the New Millennium," Clearwater, FL.

Watkins, C. E. (1997). Defining psychotherapy supervision and understanding supervisor functioning. In C. E. Watson (Ed.), *Handbook of psychotherapy supervision* (pp. 3–10). New York: Wiley.

Watkins, C. E. (1999). The beginning psychotherapy supervisor: How can we help? *The Clinical Supervisor, 18*(2), 63–72.

10

DIVERSITY COMPETENCE IN TRAINING AND CLINICAL PRACTICE

GARGI ROYSIRCAR, JAMES E. DOBBINS, AND KATHLEEN A. MALLOY

It has become increasingly accepted within professional psychology that psychologists must be able to competently serve diverse groups of people. Indicators of a commitment to services for diverse populations can be found in peer-reviewed journals designed to address issues unique to diverse populations as well as the establishment of ongoing conferences, for example, the biannual National Multicultural Conference and Summit, since 1999; the Cross-Cultural Roundtable of Teachers College, Columbia University, since 1978; and the National Council of Schools and Programs in Professional Psychology (NCSPP) conferences of 1989 and 2008. Further evidence of the field's commitment lies in the various guidelines endorsed by the American Psychological Association (APA): *Guidelines on Multicultural Education, Training, Research, Practice, and Organizational Change for Psychologists* (APA, 2003) and *The Professional Practice Guidelines for Psychotherapy With Lesbian, Gay, and Bisexual Clients* (APA, 2000). APA has recognized the need to provide competent care to diverse populations by also requiring that, to achieve APA accreditation, graduate programs must have a cogent plan in place for providing trainees with knowledge about the influence of diversity on human experience.

In this chapter, we provide an overview of issues of individual and cultural diversity (ICD) that are important to professional psychology. First, we briefly report outcome findings on practitioners' diversity competence and diversity training. This is followed with a larger emphasis on applications of theory and training models. Subsequently, we operationalize the requisite knowledge, skills, and attitudes (KSAs), substantiated by our personal experiences as diversity trainers, an integrative literature review, and the profession's developmental training focus, which is presented in a table. Because there is limited literature on diversity supervision, institutional climate and competence, and assessment of students' diversity competence, we fill such gaps by highlighting current practices (or lack thereof) and make suggestions for implications and future directions.

In framing this discussion on diversity competence, we rely on a commonly understood paradigm of functional professional training competencies, that is, KSAs. This generic graduate training paradigm has recently been elaborated by several training organizations into models that list criteria for graduated levels of training called *Benchmarks* (APA Board of Education Affairs [BEA] & Council of Chairs of Training Councils [CCTC], 2007) and *developmental achievement levels* (DALs; NCSPP, 2007). Table 10.1 describes the DALs for the diversity competency. The DALs describe the required KSAs in five domains across three stages of training: beginning practicum, beginning internship, and completion of degree.

OUTCOME EVIDENCE FOR DIVERSITY COMPETENCE

The belief that professional efforts in diversity competence are resulting in positive effects is empirically supported. For example, Griner and Smith (2006) conducted a meta-analysis of 76 studies that examined the efficacy of mental health interventions that were culturally adapted for use with racial and ethnic minority populations. They found that culturally adapted interventions "resulted in significant client improvement across a variety of conditions and outcome measures" (p. 541) and that cultural adaptations specific to a cultural group are more effective than general cultural adaptations, suggesting that clinicians need to be competent in their work with specific groups.

Diversity training increasingly has become acknowledged as intrinsic to training in professional psychology. Smith, Constantine, Dunn, Dinehart, and Montoya (2006) did a meta-analytic review of 45 published and unpublished studies conducted over a 30-year period (1973–2002) that examined the effectiveness of diversity education in professional psychology programs. Results indicated that participants who had received some form of multicultural education scored higher on various multicultural competence measures than those who had not. In addition, multicultural education in-

TABLE 10.1
Knowledge, Skills, and Attitudes and Domains
for the Diversity Competency

Begin practicum	Begin internship	Complete doctoral degree
Multiple identities domain		
K 1. Understanding of an individual's identity as an integration of multiple identities, including, but not limited to, race/ethnicity, gender, sexual orientation, etc. 2. Knowledge that everyone (including the student) has a perspective resulting from his/her unique identity that inherently creates bias 3. Understanding of how multiple identities impact his/her interactions with others	1. Knowledge of multiple identities and their impact on professional work 2. Understanding of how one's own identities and experiences create unique biases	1. Recognition that professional and institutional roles interact with personal identities and biases, which impact professional work 2. Understanding of how to continually monitor one's own biases throughout one's lifetime
S 1. Ability to articulate one's multiple identities, as well as those of others	1. Ability to appropriately use and apply the knowledge, perceptions, assumptions, values, and biases that result from own multiple identities to clinical, professional, and scholarly work	1. Ability to be self-reflective and articulate own attitudes, biases, and conflicts around individual and cultural diversity (ICD)
A 1. Demonstration of appreciation, curiosity, and respect for one's own multiple identities 2. Investment in understanding how own multiple identities impact clinical work 3. Appreciation that one's practice must incorporate an understanding of the impact of multiple identities.	1. Valuation of differences among diverse groups of people 2. Openness to feedback on issues related to ICD	1. Valuation of the need for ongoing examination of identities and biases throughout lifetime 2. Awareness of limits to one's own ability in the domain of ICD

continues

TABLE 10.1
Continued

Begin practicum	Begin internship	Complete doctoral degree
4. Acknowledgement of multiple identities and ICD as important in understanding human behavior		

Power, oppression, and privilege domain		
K 1. Knowledge that injustice exists and that it differentially affects diverse groups 2. Understanding of how oppression is often related to a history of colonization and trauma 3. Understanding of the constructs of power, oppression, and privilege, and their impact on the experiences of diverse individuals, including the self	1. Understanding of the complexity of power, oppression, and privilege, and their interaction with multiple identities of self and others 2. Knowledge of how professional psychology, even if inadvertently, may contribute to injustice 3. Understanding of the need to incorporate the history of marginalized groups, including the historical impact of oppression and trauma, into professional conceptualizations 4. Understanding of how power, a history of oppression, and privilege impact client experience, clinical presentation, and professional relationships	1. Understanding of how the impact of power, oppression, and privilege evolve over time 2. Understanding of why issues of power, oppression, and privilege require attention throughout one's professional lifetime and across all stages of professional services 3. Understanding of the need to impact systems that perpetuate oppression and privilege
S 1. Ability to recognize and discuss the impact of social injustice	1. Ability to recognize and discuss the impact of social injustice on an individual in case material 2. Ability to integrate the impact of the history of marginalized groups, including the historical impact of oppression and trauma, into with professional conceptualizations, assessments, and interventions	1. Ability to reflect on and responsibly use own experiences of power, oppression, and privilege in professional roles to promote social justice 2. Ability to seek out continuing education related to ICD through consultation, education, and exposure to a diversity of experiences and populations
A 1. Exhibition of curiosity and	1. Valuation of addressing power, oppression, and	1. Confident expression of, and consistent

openness regarding power, oppression, and privilege in self and others 2. Exhibition of openness and willingness to examine own biases and assumptions about differences	privilege in multiple professional roles (e.g., organizational consultant, supervisor, colleague, therapist) 2. Openness to discussing conflicts and/or personal impact of ICD issues with supervisors and colleagues 3. Willingness to discuss internal conflicts in supervision that arise in discussion of issues of ICD with clients	commitment to, the promotion of social justice in all professional roles 2. Courage and willingness to address power, oppression, and privilege in multiple professional roles (e.g., organizational consultant, supervisor, colleague, therapist)

ICD-specific knowledge domain		
K 1. Understanding of the socially constructed nature of identity 2. Knowledge of the scientific, theoretical, and application-based literature related to ICD (i.e., models of psychopathology, diagnosis, individual development, systems) 3. Familiarity with the existing knowledge base, including, but not limited to, evidence-based practice (EBP) and the importance of its application in the context of client characteristics, culture, and preferences 4. Knowledge of the APA Multicultural Guidelines (APA, 2003)	1. Understanding of the complexity and practice implications of the scientific, theoretical, and application-based literature related to ICD (i.e., models of intervention, psychopathology, diagnosis, individual development, systems) 2. Understanding of the complexity of the interaction between ICD and EBP 3. Understanding of the limitations of existing theories and how to apply those theories to diverse populations 4. Understanding of the limitations of exiting theories	1. Understanding of how the knowledge base related to ICD continues to evolve, requiring a commitment to lifelong learning
S 1. Ability to determine how ICD knowledge applies to one's identity and experiences as well as those of others	1. Ability to analyze, synthesize, critique, and apply major scientific theoretical and contextual bodies of knowledge related to ICD and professional work (e.g., models of psychopathology,	1. Ability to critique and modify traditional models of intervention and assessment to best fit diverse populations 2. Ability to review and critique the ICD literature, including

continues

TABLE 10.1
Continued

Begin practicum	Begin internship	Complete doctoral degree
	diagnosis, individual development, systems) under guidance and supervision 2. Ability to review and critique EBP to determine if they are appropriate for use with diverse populations	evidence-based scholarship on treatment, and to determine its appropriate application to diverse populations
A 1. Valuation of learning about issues related to ICD	1. Appreciation of the need to stay abreast of ICD-related scholarship that informs professional development	1. Commitment to remaining informed of and to contribute to ICD scholarship

Culturally competent service provision domain		
K 1. Beginning knowledge of alternative theories and models of healing 2. Knowledge that ICD should be integrated into case conceptualization 3. Understanding of the potential impact of variables related to ICD on the efficacy of intervention	1. Understanding of alternative theories and models of healing 2. Knowledge of culturally competent treatment approaches	1. Understanding of how to competently integrate knowledge of ICD into all professional services
S 1. Ability to establish rapport with individuals from diverse groups	1. Ability to conceptualize and articulate the psychological impact of injustice in multiple professional activities 2. Ability to discuss ICD-related internal conflicts that arise with clients and in supervision 3. Ability to synthesize cultural information and integrate it into case conceptualization and treatment planning 4. Ability to apply alternative theories and models of healing 5. Ability to articulate the impact of culturally specific variables on the	1. Ability to demonstrate the relevance of ICD knowledge in understanding self and others through analysis, synthesis, and application 2. Integration of alternative models of healing into interventions when indicated 3. Ability to integrate community healers and leaders and negotiate professional roles to include indigenous health practices 4. Ability to evaluate and

			of intervention and their applicability to diverse populations 5. Routine integration of ICD information in development of case conceptualization, treatment planning, assessment, and intervention 6. Ability to seek consultation regarding ICD when needed
A	1. Willingness to make active attempts to interact with persons of diverse backgrounds 2. Awareness that ICD issues should be considered in the provision of professional services	1. Openness to the integration of cultural information with development of case conceptualization, treatment planning, assessment, and intervention 2. Openness to integrating alternative models of healing into interventions when indicated	1. Commitment to the critique and modification of traditional models of intervention for use with diverse populations 2. Valuation of lifelong learning related to ICD

Ethics domain

K	1. Basic knowledge of ethical principles and guidelines that address professional relationships and issues of ICD	1. Understanding of how ICD issues play an important part in ethical decision making	1. Understanding of how ethical guidelines and their application are influenced and informed by ICD
S	1. Ability to discuss ethical guidelines and expectations pertinent to issues of ICD	1. Application of ethical guidelines and ICD knowledge in conceptualization, assessment, and intervention	1. Ability to integrate ICD issues into ethical decision making
A	1. Investment in behaving in an ethical and respectful manner with all people	1. Committed to understanding and incorporating ICD into personal ethical values and into ethical principles in all professional activities	1. Belief that one's practice is ethical only if it includes decision making that integrates ICD

Note. K = knowledge; S = skills; A = attitudes. From *Competency Developmental Achievement Levels (DALs) of the National Council of Schools and Programs in Professional Psychology (NCSPP),* (pp. 25–30), by the National Council of Schools and Programs in Professional Psychology, 2007. Available at http://www.ncspp.info/DALof%20NCSPP%209-21-07.pdf. Copyright 2007 by the National Council of Schools and Programs in Professional Psychology. Reprinted with permission.

terventions that were "explicitly based on theory and research" (p.132) were found to be nearly twice as beneficial as those that were not.

To be grounded in theory and research, we frame their discussion by how issues of power and privilege shape societal constructions that may be internalized or resisted by individuals as they define their identities (Dobbins & Malloy, 2008). Because clients have more than one aspect to their identities, clinicians should appreciate how various identity aspects interact within societal, social, and clinical contexts (Roysircar, 2008a).

DIVERSITY COMPETENCE: AN APPLIED UNDERSTANDING

Speaking primarily of ethnic and racial diversity competence, S. Sue (1998) put forth the argument that diversity competence is "the belief that people should not only appreciate and recognize other cultural groups, but also be able to effectively work with them" (p. 440). He viewed diversity competence as a workable professional compromise between a push for assimilation, which is the absence of diversity considerations in favor of the majority paradigm, and pluralism, which is a celebration of human diversity in the absence of a framework for the clinical enterprise. This recommendation for compromise is the integration of evidence-based practice with culturally sensitive treatment (Roysircar, 2009).

Psychologists who are diversity competent, according to S. Sue (1998), are, first, scientifically minded. *Scientific mindedness* is the practice of making cultural hypotheses about the status of a client and challenging the myth of sameness or the null hypothesis. Second, they have skills in *dynamic sizing*, which means that they know when to generalize and find client commonalities with others and when to individualize and exclude others from a client's experiences. Third, they have specific proficiencies to work with a particular group.

Psychologists with diversity competence have specific knowledge about the beliefs, behaviors, and perspectives of their clients and use this knowledge to assess those clients' unique standing within their reference group and contexts (Roysircar, 2005). They have the skills necessary to translate intervention models and constructs that make sense to their clients and that assist in the formation of a working structure that S. Sue (1998) called the *client–therapist cognitive match*. The skillful use of cognitive match, which belongs to no one theoretical perspective, is key to a working alliance owing to congruence between the therapist's worldview and the client's worldview. Psychologists are aware of social attitudes because they draw on their own experiences, including those of oppression and privilege (Fuertes, Mueller, Chauhan, Walker, & Ladany, 2002), and they use reflexive self-awareness to better sympathize with marginalized clients (Roysircar, 2004; Roysircar, Gard, Hubbell, & Ortega, 2005).

Competency-Based Models of Diversity Training

While S. Sue (1998) and D. W. Sue, Arredondo, and McDavis (1992) were working to delineate the competencies necessary to work with racial and ethnic minorities, the call for competency-based models of overall education, training, and assessment in professional psychology were building. In 2002, a Competencies Conference: Future Directions in Education and Credentialing in Professional Psychology organized under the leadership of the Association of Psychology Postdoctoral and Internship Centers (APPIC, 2002) was attended by representatives from clinical, counseling, and school psychology programs gathered to develop recommendations to advance competency-based education, training, and credentialing. The ICD competency work group (Daniel, Roysircar, Abeles, & Boyd, 2004) developed recommendations, with their primary conclusions focusing on two competency components: therapist cultural self-awareness and therapist knowledge of client contexts.

Subsequently, in 2007, the APA/BEA, in collaboration with the CCTC (2007) convened the Assessment of Competency Benchmarks Work Group. Similar to the APPIC Competencies Conference, the Benchmarks Work Group concluded that there are two essential components that ensure diversity competence: awareness of self as a cultural being and possession of skills to apply knowledge, sensitivity, and understanding regarding ICD. In addition, the Benchmarks Work Group and later NCSPP (2007) acknowledged the developmental nature of competency attainment and specified the proficiencies to be present at each level of training. In summary, the APPIC, APA/BEA and CCTC, and NCSPP models addressing competency-based training all noted that training to work with diverse groups must include a focus on both the provider and the client and that training should address KSAs.

Knowledge, Skills, and Attitudes

Diversity competence is characterized by three domains, namely, psychologists' (a) knowledge of the unique dimensions of clients' worldviews, the historical backgrounds of diverse groups, and current sociopolitical influences on these groups; (b) skills to devise and implement interventions that are relevant to clients' cultural values, beliefs, and expectations; and (c) awareness of their own attitudes of privilege, beliefs, and biases that might influence therapeutic perceptions and subsequent therapeutic dynamics. The language of the tripartite model uses an inclusive definition of *diverse*, such that differences and similarities across multiple social locations and cultural variables are considered (e.g., race, ethnicity, gender, sexual orientation, social class, power and privilege, religion and spirituality, age, ability status).

Knowledge

Fisher, Jome, and Atkinson (1998) asserted that "the skeleton of universal healing factors requires the flesh of cultural knowledge" (p. 525) in order for helping processes to be meaningful. Fisher et al.'s common factors model (e.g., the therapeutic relationship) underscores the importance of clinicians' competence to identify and attend to cultural considerations.

Knowledge competence requires that psychologists obtain accurate, useful information that addresses the general domains of content required of all graduate programs in professional psychology. This information includes the biological, social, and cognitive aspects of diversity behavior (see Leong & Lopez, 2006); history and systems that explain the interactive effects of individual identity and societal oppression (Helms & Cook, 1999); and research that explores the utility of developmental models and clinical issues (Roysircar, 2008b). We add diversity advocacy to this list (Speight & Vera, 2004).

Psychologists' general knowledge encompasses their investment in building their understanding of diverse experiences relevant to living in a multicultural society. Specific knowledge varies according to the populations under discussion (e.g., immigrants and U.S.-born children of immigrants) and the professional roles that operationalize relationships with such groups in prevention or remediation service (Atkinson, Thompson, & Grant, 1993). Psychologists possess an understanding of how unique client variables, such as personality, family of origin dynamics, and contextual factors, may interact to affect clients' self-presentations. This is not to say that model specificity (e.g., knowledge of immigrants) or breadth (e.g., general diversity knowledge) is more or less useful; instead, it can be argued that each knowledge base has specific explanatory use. The scope of knowledge is well represented in the DALs (NCSPP, 2007) and Benchmarks (APA/BEA & CCTC, 2007). The contents of multiple professional roles have been defined in the language of the DALs, but they are quite broad in scope so as to allow for application to various cultures and groups.

There are several handbooks for scholars interested in various focused aspects of knowledge about the values, customs, and physical attributes of diverse populations Clinchy & Norem, 1998; Cuellar & Paniagua, 2000; Gielen, Fish, & Draguns, 2004; Greene & Croom, 2000). These references may also include clinical case materials, research reviews, theoretical discussions, and personal narratives that provide examples of the ways that psychologists and students can become knowledgeable about diverse populations.

Core to the aspects of knowledge is the reality that diversity work is based on the ability of the psychologist to know how to process issues of identity and implications of their knowledge in the professional relationship (Malloy & Dobbins, 2007). One of the most important ways that professionals gain live knowledge is through affiliation with and immersion in societies

different from theirs (Roysircar, 2004; Roysircar et al., 2005). The application of diversity knowledge and its outcomes are considered next.

Skills

S. Sue (1998) recommended that cultural knowledge be made proximal to therapy when it is translated into clinical skills, such as case conceptualization, strategies for problem resolution, and the formulation of therapy goals. Skills include sensitivity in identifying culturally related contents and dynamics. The ability to coconstruct and maintain effective working alliances, which refer to clients and psychologists' agreement about the goals and tasks of treatment and their therapeutic bond, provides the foundation for culturally responsive care.

Skills stress the necessity of training students to take what they have learned in the classroom and translate it into actual interventions (CCTC, 2007; NCSPP, 2007). For example, while a student may be able to reflect on his or her own experiences with power, privilege, and oppression or may be able to discuss the cultural mores that affect a given ethnic population in a classroom setting, that student's training remains woefully inadequate if he or she cannot translate that insight or knowledge into interventions (Malloy & Dobbins, 2007). Students should be able to critique the ICD literature and apply that knowledge to all psychological practices, including traditional models of assessment, intervention, supervision, consultation, and research. They should routinely integrate ICD knowledge into case conceptualization, treatment planning, assessment, and intervention (Roysircar, 2008b). In addition, students should integrate ICD knowledge into their ethical decision making (Ridley, Liddle, Hill, & Li, 2001). Another important skill is to seek out consultation on ICD issues when needed (NCSPP, 2007). To master the skills necessary to become competent, classroom experiences are helpful, but education must also occur in work settings. In fact, most learning occurs in clinical settings, which leads to a discussion later in this chapter of diversity supervision.

Attitudes

In the diversity competence literature, limited reference is made to clients' experiences of their psychologists' attitudes and the interplay of clients' and psychologists' identities in therapy. An examination follows of the role of therapist awareness of attitudes within the therapy process.

As an example, Helms and Cook (1999) stated that psychologists need to be aware of the effect of their identity attitudes on the dyadic interaction process. They described therapy dyads in terms of the combination of the psychologists' and clients' racial-identity development (i.e., one's sense of collective identity with a given reference group, which informs cognitive and emotional processes about the self and differently identified others over

the course of time and in different circumstances). The interactional process relies on the degree to which there is convergence or divergence in the psychologist's and client's relative development toward a transcendent, nonoppressive identity and their attitudes toward people with power and people of marginalized status. Thus, interactional dyads (Helms & Cook, 1999) may be categorized as progressive (i.e., the psychologist exhibits greater levels of racial-cultural awareness and self- and other-awareness than the client); regressive (i.e., the psychologist exhibits less racial-cultural awareness than the client); parallel-high (i.e., both the psychologist and client are at comparable advanced levels of racial-cultural awareness); or parallel-low (i.e., both the psychologist and client are at similarly lower levels of racial-cultural awareness). Helms and Cook's interactional model can clarify therapeutic disconnections experienced by clients who are relatively more racially conscious than their therapists. On the other hand, psychologists with greater levels of racial-cultural awareness and self- and other-awareness may show *pseudo-independence* (i.e., intellectualized interest and acknowledgment of inequities without affective ownership of one's role in perpetuating oppression), *immersion* (i.e., search for a personal meaning of power and privilege that is informed by affective restructuring), *emersion* (i.e., feeling positive about associating with progressive and social justice-oriented people who have privilege), and *autonomy* (i.e., an adoption of a restructured definition of power and privilege that is committed to nonparticipation in oppressive systems). In summary, self-awareness of attitudes involves the degree to which psychologists can identify how their multiple identities and socialization experiences color the lenses through which they perceive, evaluate, conceptualize, and treat clients.

Psychologists are aware that culturally diverse clients react notably to avoidance of diversity content in therapy, such that the helping relationship may be negatively affected or experienced as ungenuine or harmful. Watkins and Terrell (1988) showed that Black clients with higher cultural mistrust attitudes toward Whites expected less from counseling regardless of the therapist's race; however, they also rated White therapists lower on immediacy and likeability. Constantine (2007) examined the relationships between African American clients' perceptions of racial microaggressions (i.e., subtle and commonplace racial slights or messages) by White therapists with various therapy processes. Some of the microaggressions of White therapists were characterized as colorblindness, overidentification with people of color, denial of personal or individual racism, minimization of racial-cultural issues, idealization, and patronization. Perceived microaggressions were negatively associated with client perceptions of the working alliance and perceptions of the therapist's credibility and multicultural competence. Because clients of color may be acutely aware of or sensitive to clinicians' behaviors with respect to race and culture, clinicians' awareness of the potential impact of their behaviors on clients is paramount. In an effort to develop cul-

tural self- and other-awareness, clinicians' commitment to examining the influences of their deliberate as well as unconscious interactions with diverse clients is inherent in providing effective care. Interviewees, who were European-American psychologists (Fuertes et al., 2002), provided lessons on self- and other-awareness. These psychologists revealed that they generally attended to differences in race between themselves and clients directly and openly within the first two sessions of counseling. This was done generally to acknowledge this difference and to convey to the client comfort and trust; psychologists also intended to engender client trust and participation in therapy. The psychologists saw race as a central component to be discussed and continually attended to establishing and maintaining a trusting and solid working relationship. They typically saw diversity-related issues as relevant to clients' concerns, regardless of particular presentations. In conclusion, clients' experiences of their psychologists' ability to attend to cultural concerns is likely to be enhanced through the psychologists' willingness to bring culture into the therapeutic space.

Within mainstream U.S. culture, differences in what individuals experience based on identity issues are not generally considered appropriate topics of conversation, resulting in a code of silence that reflects society's denial of the reality of the "isms" (e.g., sexism, racism, ableism, heterosexism) and of the privilege experienced by members of socially dominant groups (e.g., White privilege, male privilege, heterosexual privilege, middle class privilege; Roysircar, 2008a; Young, 2003). Thus, students generally approach such discussions with a range of reactions, including excitement, a sense of challenge, anger, incompetence, fear, feeling overwhelmed, intellectualization, withdrawal, and even dread. In response to the uncomfortable reactions that are triggered, students often develop forms of resistance that operate to create silence, passivity, avoidance, and anger as ways of maintaining social distance in the classroom (Jackson, 1999; Sanchez-Hucles & Jones, 2005). Such resistance, which results from the push to explore and challenge previously unexplored beliefs and values and to remain open to the differing experiences, beliefs, and values of others, should be interpreted as a normal part of the process of diversity training This resistance is especially acute when students are asked to become aware of ways in which their own privileged status has led them to, usually unwittingly, add to the pain experienced by others (Roysircar, 2008a).

Instructors must be prepared to deal skillfully with students' emotions and resistances that arise during class or supervision to be able to assess what is occurring in the learning process and to facilitate students' continuing movement toward diversity competence. Instructors and supervisors must first acknowledge that they have their own reactions and resistances to address before objectively addressing those of their students. One powerful tool is the instructor's ability to model the vulnerability and openness needed to challenge one's own worldview while considering that of another.

Other techniques include developing rules that will help to maintain a safe environment for discussion; consistently reminding students of the systemic nature of privilege and oppression to which every one falls a victim; defining the occurrence of painful emotions and resistances as opportunities for growth, not personal weaknesses; and noting that the majority of individuals experience both privilege and oppression based on the individual's various identities. This last point can help students to empathize with the impact of oppressions experienced by others who differ from them and to understand the often unintended impact of privilege (Greene et al., 2008; Roysircar, 2008a).

Diversity Supervision

Whereas diversity education in the classroom enhances trainees' knowledge of the historical and contemporary experiences of marginalized groups, effective diversity supervision can serve as a model for trainees to approach, address, and process diversity issues in therapeutic relationships. Moreover, whereas diversity education can foster cultural self-awareness, effective diversity supervision can foster therapeutic skill development as well as attention to diversity dynamics that influence the therapeutic relationship. In essence, diversity education and diversity supervision can complement each other over the course of trainees' development and beyond.

Diversity supervision can offer a unique training environment that serves as a primary means of diversity therapy skill development. Supervisors are to be charged with understanding and facilitating trainees' understanding of the interplay of diversity factors in interpersonal and therapeutic processes. However, currently one professional problem we are facing is that formal diversity training for supervisors is lacking.

Diversity supervision has several facilitative components. These include supervisors' awareness of their own racial, cultural, sexuality, class, and ability values; openness, vulnerability, and self-disclosure; sincere commitment to attending to and exploring cultural factors; and providing opportunities to their supervisees for diversity activities. In addition, qualitative studies (e.g., Hird, Tao, & Gloria, 2005; Inman, 2006) have suggested that supervisors initiate and address diversity and power-related concerns early and throughout supervisory relationships, inquire about supervisees' culture, and address cultural dynamics evidenced in the supervisory dyad.

Although fostering diversity discussions may contribute to trainees' diversity competence and responsive client care, it is also possible for supervisors to engage in behaviors that can influence supervisory experiences negatively. For example, some supervisors, because of their own fears of being perceived as insensitive or ignorant, may inhibit supervisees' emotional processing of concerns related to race, culture, or sexuality. In addition, supervisors may minimize the importance of addressing diversity con-

cerns within the client–trainee and trainee–supervisor dyads, thereby neglecting a potentially clarifying lens through which individuals may experience the world. Moreover, supervisors themselves who have not engaged in identity development activities (e.g., reflection, diversity self-awareness, building their theoretical knowledge of mental health concerns across multiple interfacing identities) may inhibit their supervisees' diversity competence.

Furthermore, the ways in which diversity concerns are discussed in supervision may affect the parties involved on deeply personal levels. For example, supervisors may discount the importance of race-related factors and experiences, hesitate to provide feedback for fear of being perceived racist, make stereotypic assumptions about supervisees and clients, focus on supervisees' weaknesses, or offer culturally insensitive treatment suggestions. These examples illustrate the power of supervisors' diversity competence, or limitations thereof, on supervisees' practical training experiences and, subsequently, clients' well-being.

Institutional Climate

For the training that has been described to occur, support must be present at all levels of the educational institution, including administrative, faculty, staff, and student levels. If students are going to feel safe to explore their own biases, privileges, oppressions, and beliefs, faculty and administrators must be willing to do the same. Faculty and administrators should engage in ongoing diversity training themselves to address their own attitudes and identities. In addition, faculty must obtain diversity training in the specific content and clinical areas in which they teach as well as develop skills in managing the diversity dialogue that will take place in their classrooms as a result of the diversity training that students are receiving.

In their institutions, psychologists are encouraged to use organizational change processes like strategic planning to support and inform new policies and practices that are culturally sensitive and equitable (see Multicultural Guideline 6, APA, 2003). In programs that have been successful in integrating diversity content, a great deal of effort over a long period of time was put into faculty development. Resources such as films and bibliographies were compiled and shared among programs and between faculties.

ORGANIZATIONAL DIVERSITY COMPETENCE: CONCLUSION AND RECOMMENDATIONS

Diversity competence thrives when it exists and interacts at various levels of role functioning: individual, professional, institutional, organizational, and societal. Because psychologists play multiple roles in a society

that is undergoing rapid changes, they need to become familiar with different frameworks, models, and methods for personal, professional and organizational development in diversity (APA, 2003). To accommodate the needs of a wide variety of clients, competent psychologists possess sophisticated and ongoing self-awareness and continuously evaluate their theories, cultural knowledge, clinical skills, and in-session behaviors to correctly apply culturally sensitive or culturally adapted interventions.

The student should be helped to see how the literature reflects two schools of thought about the relationship between assessment and diversity competence. One might be called a traditional approach, which assumes that scientific methods are objective (Garb, 1998) and that culture is only relevant as an individual difference. The second perspective is that scientific methods are located in socially constructed values and biases, and that assessment methods and the people who administer them are inherently biased (Hays, 2004; Roysircar, 2005).

A final consideration regarding diversity training is the assessment of students' diversity competence. Multiple measures of students' competence may be gathered through the use of self-reports, supervisor evaluations, peer reviews, and client feedback (Daniel et al., 2004). Another approach is the use of 360-degree evaluations "in which systematic input is gleaned by means of a comprehensive survey (often computerized), from one's supervisors, a diverse cadre of both peers and subordinates, and oneself . . . [which] can provide input" about diversity competence (Kaslow, 2004, p. 778). Coleman, Morris, and Norton (2006) suggested the use of portfolios as a way to collect a range of competence information. In this method, the reviewer tells trainees what data they are allowed to submit, which can range from papers to video and audio recordings of sessions. The student includes statements of why each piece was included and which competence dimension it demonstrates, as well as a statement of how the portfolio reflects his or her learning. The idea is to create a performance-based assessment that can assess the individual in a variety of contexts. The student then gets feedback on strengths and weaknesses that serve as a basis for the next review. In this way progress is tracked.

When faculty, supervisors, and organizations are aligned to provide diversity training, psychology graduates are prepared to provide effective treatment for diverse populations. However, diversity competence is not an end state, but a commitment to helping clients through ongoing enhancement of psychologists' KSAs specific to diversity.

REFERENCES

American Psychological Association. (2000). The professional practice guidelines for psychotherapy with lesbian, gay, and bisexual clients. *American Psychologist, 55*, 1440–1451.

American Psychological Association. (2003). Guidelines on multicultural education, training, research, practice, and organizational change for psychologists. *American Psychologist, 58,* 377–402.

Association of Psychology Postdoctoral and Internship Centers. (2002, November). *Competencies 2002: Future directions in education and credentialing in professional psychology.* Scottsdale, AZ: Author.

Atkinson, D. R., Thompson, C. E., & Grant, S. K. (1993). A three-dimensional model for counseling racial/ethnic minorities. *The Counseling Psychologist, 21,* 257–277.

Coleman, H. L. K., Morris, D., and Norton, R. A. (2006). Developing multicultural counseling competence through the use of portfolios. *Journal of Multicultural Counseling and Development, 34,* 27–37.

Constantine, M. G. (2007). Racial microaggressions against African American clients in cross-racial counseling relationships. *Journal of Counseling Psychology, 54,* 1–16.

Council of Chairs of Training Councils. (2007). *Assessment of competency benchmarks work group: A developmental model for the defining and measuring competence in professional psychology.* Proceedings of the Benchmark Conference. Retrieved June 6, 2008, from http://www.psychtrainingcouncils.org/pubs/ Comptency%20Benchmarks.pdf

Cuellar, J., & Paniagua, F. A. (Eds.). (2000). *Handbook of multicultural mental health: Assessment and treatment of diverse populations.* New York: Academic Press.

Daniel, J. H., Roysircar, G., Abeles, N., & Boyd, C. (2004). Individual and cultural diversity competence: Focus on the therapist. *Journal of Clinical Psychology, 25,* 255–267.

Dobbins, J. E., & Malloy, K. A. (2008, August). Integrative diversity: An emergent multicultural competency. In. B. Greene (Chair), *Teaching cultural diversity in mental health curricula: Matching syllabi to setting.* Symposium conducted at the Annual Convention of the American Psychological Association, Boston.

Fisher, A. R., Jome, L. M., & Atkinson, D. R. (1998). Reconceptualizing multicultural counseling: Universal healing conditions in a culturally specific context. *The Counseling Psychologist, 26,* 525–588.

Fuertes, J. N., Mueller, L. N., Chauhan, R. V., Walker, J. A., & Ladany, N. (2002). An investigation of Euro-American therapists' approach to counseling African-American clients. *The Counseling Psychologist, 30,* 763–789.

Garb, H. N. (1998). *Studying the clinician: Judgment, research, and psychological assessment.* Washington, DC: American Psychological Association.

Gielen, U. P., Fish, J. M., & Draguns, J. G. (Eds.). (2004). *Handbook of culture, therapy, and healing.* Mahwah, NJ: Erlbaum.

Griner, D., & Smith, T. (2006). Culturally adapted mental health interventions: A meta-analytic review. *Psychotherapy: Theory, Research, Practice, Training, 43,* 531–548.

Greene, B., & Croom, G. (Eds.). (2000). *Education, research and practice in lesbian, gay, bisexual and transgendered psychology: Psychological perspectives on lesbian and gay issues.* Thousand Oaks, CA: Sage.

Hays, P. A. (2004). *Addressing cultural complexities in practice*. Washington, DC: American Psychological Association.

Helms, J. E., & Cook, D. A. (1999). *Using race and culture in counseling and psychotherapy: Theory and process*. Needham Heights, MA: Allyn & Bacon.

Hird, J. S., Tao, K. W., & Gloria, A. M. (2005). Examining supervisors' multicultural competence in racially similar and different supervision dyads. *The Clinical Supervisor, 23*, 107–122.

Inman, A. G. (2006). Supervisor multicultural competence and its relation to supervisory process and outcome. *Journal of Marital and Family Therapy, 32*, 73–85.

Jackson, L. (1999). Ethnocultural resistance to multicultural training. *Cultural Diversity and Ethnic Minority Psychology, 5*, 27–36.

Kaslow, N. J. (2004). Competencies in professional psychology. *American Psychologist, 59*, 774–781.

Leong, F. T. L., & Lopez, S. R. (2006, Winter). Special issue: Culture, race, and ethnicity in psychotherapy. *Psychotherapy: Theory, Research, Practice, Training, 43*(4).

Malloy, K., & Dobbins, J. (2007, April). *Teaching integrative diversity*. Paper presented at the Quest Conference: A Call to Action, Wright State University, Dayton, OH.

National Council of Schools and Programs in Professional Psychology. (2007). *Developing our competencies in clinical training*. Mid-Winter Conference: Developing Our Competencies in Clinical Training, Fort Lauderdale, FL. Retrieved June 6, 2008, from http://ncspp.info/events.htm

National Council of Schools and Programs in Professional Psychology. (2008). *Advancing the NCSPP multicultural diversity agenda: From aspiration to actualization*. Mid-Winter Conference: Advancing the Multicultural Agenda From Aspiration to Actualization, Austin, TX. Retrieved June 6, 2008, from http://ncspp.info/events.htm

Ridley, C. R., Liddle, M. C., Hill, C. L., & Li, L. C. (2001). Ethical decision making in multicultural counseling. In J. G. Ponterotto, M. C. Cassas, L. A. Suzuki, & C. M. Alexander (Eds.), *Handbook of multicultural counseling* (2nd ed.; pp. 165–188). Thousand Oaks, CA: Sage.

Roysircar, G. (2004). Cultural self-awareness assessment: Practice examples from psychology training. *Professional Psychology: Research and Practice, 35*, 658–666.

Roysircar, G. (2005). Culturally sensitive assessment, diagnosis, and guidelines. In M. G. Constantine, & D. W. Sue (Eds.), *Strategies for building multicultural competence in mental health and educational settings* (pp. 19–38). Hoboken, NJ: Wiley.

Roysircar, G. (2008a). Social privilege: Counselors' competence with systemically determined inequalities. *Journal for Specialists in Group Work, 33*, 377–384.

Roysircar, G. (2008b, January). Lost in cross-cultural transition: Ecological practice in treating loss of an Asian Indian woman. In M. J. T. Vasquez & G. Roysircar, (Co-Chairs), *Interventions with people of color*. Symposium conducted at the Mid-Winter Conference of the National Council of Schools and Programs of Psychology, Austin, TX.

Roysircar, G. (2009). Evidence-based practice and its implications for culturally sensitive treatment. *Journal of Multicultural Counseling and Development, 37*(2), 66–82.

Roysircar, G., Gard, G., Hubbell, R., & Ortega, M. (2005). Development of counseling trainees' multicultural awareness through mentoring ESL students. *Journal of Multicultural Counseling and Development, 33,* 17–36.

Sanchez-Hucles, J., & Jones, N. (2005). Breaking the silence around race in training, practice, and research. *The Counseling Psychologist, 33,* 547–558.

Smith, T. B., Constantine, M. G., Dunn, T. W., Dinehart, J. M., & Montoya, J. A. (2006). Multicultural education in the mental health professions: A meta-analytic review. *Journal of Counseling Psychology, 53,* 132–145.

Speight, S. L., & Vera, E. M. (2004). A social justice agenda. *The Counseling Psychologist, 32,* 109–118.

Sue, D. W., Arredondo, P., & McDavis, R. J. (1992). Multicultural counseling competencies and standards: A call to the profession. *Journal of Multicultural Counseling and Development, 20,* 64–88.

Sue, S. (1998). In search of cultural competence in psychotherapy and counseling. *American Psychologist, 53,* 440–448.

Watkins, C. E., & Terrell, F. (1988). Mistrust level and its effects on counseling expectations in Black–White therapist relationships: An analogue study. *Journal of Counseling Psychology, 35,* 194–197.

Young, G. (2003). Dealing with difficult classroom dialogue. In P. Bronstein & K. Quina (Eds.), *Teaching gender and multicultural awareness: Resources for the psychology classroom* (pp. 347–360). Washington, DC: American Psychological Association.

III

KEY TRAINING ELEMENTS

11

CREATING A CULTURE OF ADVOCACY

JEFFREY M. LATING, JEFFREY E. BARNETT,
AND MICHAEL HOROWITZ

A variety of issues that impact the viability of the profession of psychology, psychologists' livelihoods, and the ability to provide essential services to those most in need are directly affected by legislative and regulatory decisions (Barnett, 2004). These include licensure laws and laws regulating who may provide psychological services, laws affecting our scope of practice, laws regulating insurance and managed care companies, parity legislation, and many others. Advocacy, which is considered a process of informing and assisting decision makers, entails developing active "citizen psychologists" who promote the interests of clients, health care systems, public health and welfare issues, and professional psychology (American Psychological Association [APA], n.d.). However, despite the need for psychologists to be active advocates at local, state, regional, and national levels, many remain either uninformed or indifferent with regard to public policy and political activities (DeLeon, Lofts, Ball, & Sullivan, 2006).

Unlike other American professions such as law, medicine, and social work, psychology has continued to separate its professional and educational agendas. More specifically, psychology is the only major health profession to

have its original professional training model based in PhD academic departments and to retain this model of training despite the creation of a professional training model. Therefore, because much of the profession was developed and socialized in academic departments largely isolated from the practice issues of psychology, this has likely contributed greatly to our discipline being less involved than other professions in terms of advocacy, politics, and legislation.

While a salient factor in the lack of advocacy proficiency is the field's failure until now to develop a united professional model of education linked with a practice agenda, other factors include (a) the historic draw of individuals to the field many of whom are most interested in interpersonal issues in nuanced ways as opposed to the larger socioeconomic and sociopolitical factors informing practice; (b) the lack of education on these topics in psychology graduate programs; and (c) psychologists' altruistic sense that guild issues are inappropriate agendas for advocacy. These reasons, however, have not prevented other professions from advocating both for guild issues and society at large. In the absence of any indication that organized psychology is adhering to a unified model, the National Council of Schools and Programs of Professional Psychology (NCSPP) has filled this void.

In many ways NCSPP is educating the first generation of psychologists as part of a profession of psychology, in educational settings that are more similar to the schools of the other professions (e.g., law, business, medicine) than to purely academic research departments. Whereas the other professions have benefited tremendously from aligning professional advocacy with their educational programs, psychology has suffered from the lack of a unified understanding of what it means to function as a true profession. NCSPP, which currently trains the majority of clinical psychologists in the United States (APA, 2007), now has a generation of alumni trained in its programs who are starting to create a coherent identity for professional psychology. This chapter begins with a review of some of the proposed knowledge, skills, and attitudes (KSAs) used to enhance advocacy awareness, acumen, and applied applications, followed by ways to recognize the need for and efforts to participate in legislative advocacy. Implications are then discussed.

ENHANCING ADVOCACY EFFORTS

Creating a culture of advocacy within psychology involves the development of a professional identity that incorporates participation in advocacy activities as one of its core elements. Practicing psychologists will need to lead by their active involvement and leadership roles in advocacy activities, and psychology faculty will need to instill within their students the premise that participation in advocacy efforts is a fundamental and essential role for all psychologists, including those in training.

Knowledge, Skills, and Attitudes

Many graduate students are not exposed to advocacy efforts and activities during their training and thus may not develop a focus on advocacy as a core aspect of their professional identity. Although some students may enter graduate school having already engaged in advocacy work, the vast majority will need to be exposed to it and to have it modeled, supported, and reinforced by faculty. It is through KSAs developed in graduate coursework and supervised clinical experiences that one's identity as a professional psychologist is cultivated. It is hoped that a wide range of advocacy activities will be integrated with all aspects of students' graduate training so that this important paradigm can be established and developed.

Becoming aware of the core beliefs, purposes, and objectives of advocacy, and infusing them into a programmatic philosophy should occur as early as orientation into a graduate program. Although a specific *skill set* may be taught, embarking in the realm of advocacy starts initially with establishing a mind-set or an attitude. Most students enter a clinical program with the primary goal of helping others through individual or group therapeutic interventions, not through advocating on behalf of health care systems or the profession. From their arrival into a graduate program, most students are encouraged to think critically and to question all aspects of psychology, including theoretical tenets, applied concepts, and research outcomes. However, from the beginning of their graduate careers, students should also be exposed to the basic tenets of advocacy, which develops an attitude that extends beyond helping others therapeutically to what may be conceptualized broadly as service to others. This service may be fostered in a variety of ways.

One way to develop this attitude is by encouraging students to accept that part of their responsibility in becoming a professional psychologist entails not only recognizing how their own thinking will affect their work with others but also being open to ways of thinking, perspectives, and ideas that are clearly divergent from their own. Another way to develop a core attitude of advocacy is by expanding upon an inherent part of most training programs that requires a willingness on the part of students to respond to the needs of others, including the underserved. From the perspective of advocacy, this means doing more than providing needed and valuable therapeutic interventions. It may also entail working to improve current living conditions for these clients, seeking to provide ways to increase access to care for them, or engaging actively in public policy issues to support initiatives to improve the quality of their lives. Fostering an attitude of advocacy is instilling the notion that as psychologists we may need to be the active voice for those who cannot speak for themselves. At other times, we may need to be the active voice that advances and protects our profession.

The specific KSAs necessary to advance advocacy efforts can be infused in a myriad of traditional graduate courses, including those that cover assess-

ment, ethics, psychopathology, pharmacology, and psychotherapy. Topics that allow for the development of the skill set include, but are certainly not limited to, understanding the structure of psychology's professional organizations, understanding policy issues relevant to psychology (e.g., prescription privileges, expanding scope of practice, health care reform), funding for research, funding for training, social justice and the need to help marginalized populations, access to care issues, and learning ways to understand the complexities of public policy issues and then effect change at local, state, and national levels.

The KSAs may also be infused into newer courses that are part of some doctoral programs' curricula. For example, several NCSPP schools now have a course covering business and organizational issues in professional practice. These courses' goals include having students construct and critique a business and marketing plan for work in private practice; identify, critique, and review current legislation relevant to the practice of psychology; and prepare an advocacy statement supporting or opposing current legislation relevant to psychology. An even more direct way to impart these concepts is through an entire course devoted to advocacy and public policy issues that include guest lecturers (e.g., legislators, local and state leaders) and direct lobbying efforts with psychologists (R. Newman, personal communication, January 2008).

Within an academic setting, it seems, however, that many faculty members, while endorsing advocacy at a conceptual level, remain unaware of its applications. One way to increase faculty awareness is to include advocacy as an ongoing agenda item for faculty meetings. This may foster discussions related to the topic as well as allow the faculty to explore, endorse, and actively participate in an advocacy issue. Also, because most doctoral programs include a series of colloquia throughout any given semester, it may be prudent to invite all faculty members to these talks and to have an aspect of advocacy as a central topic for one or more colloquia each semester. Moreover, considering the service learning perspective in many doctoral programs, and depending on the individual state and regional needs, there are clearly a myriad of topics for which advocacy may be relevant. Therefore, the choice of advocacy topics may be idiosyncratic to the particular concerns of a program. Advocacy may deal with legislative matters involving parity and insurance, or it may involve pursuing funding for community projects via the state or federal legislature, foundations, or corporate sponsors. Whereas a local agenda will be specific to a community or training program, the core skills of advocacy—political negotiation, public speaking, building coalitions, political giving, and persuasive writing—will be part of every advocacy effort. Advocacy for a community partnership may involve multiple and complex outreach efforts.

Applied Suggestions

Of course, advocacy, like most other key professional constructs, cannot be taught only in the classroom. One of the principal ways to enhance

student involvement in advocacy efforts is to foster its personal relevance through formal and informal applied experiences. By making the concept of advocacy less abstract, students are likely to feel more energized and empowered. For example, students who participate in service learning projects where they directly interact with individuals experiencing poverty, limited economic and educational opportunities, unsafe environments, and limited access to health care, will be able to directly see the importance of advocacy on behalf of these individuals at different levels of the political system.

Students may see how advocating for a client's access to subsidized housing in a safe environment may be essential in their clinical work to treat their client's anxiety and stress-related difficulties that are secondary to his or her present living situation. Some NCSPP programs have developed high-impact community partnerships that entail working with their largest training sites to develop a common social justice advocacy agenda, whether this is related to immigrant rights, development of exoffender programs, and many other issues critical to the larger community. In this way psychologists become part of the larger community fabric and part of broader societal agendas.

On a broader level, many students are becoming actively involved in advocacy efforts to alter the sequencing of supervised clinical experience required for licensure so that state laws will allow for licensure at the receipt of the doctoral degree. This is an example of an advocacy issue of direct relevance to graduate students and one that may motivate them to take action.

NCSPP programs have led the way in breaking down barriers between education and practice within state, provincial, and territorial psychological associations (SPTPAs), in many cases creating a graduate student division for the first time and creating a new vitality and opportunity for new members within the associations. SPTPAs annually send a delegation to Washington, DC, to attend workshops on advocacy, briefings on important issues before Congress, and then to visit legislators' offices to lobby on issues of great importance to our profession as part of the APA State Leadership Conference. Starting in the mid 1990s, many SPTPAs have brought student members with them to participate in this important experience. A number of SPTPAs engage in similar activities in their state legislatures as well. Some states, for example, host an annual legislative day when members visit the state capital to meet with legislators to discuss pending legislation and issues of importance to our profession. Members of SPTPA student organizations regularly attend and participate fully in this experience. It is hoped that such experiences on the state and national level will empower students and encourage them to continue these vital activities throughout their careers.

A suggested model is for students to work together to select an issue of importance for them to address over the course of a year or even several years. Students in each year of the graduate program will work collaboratively

with faculty advisors providing support and guidance. More experienced students in their 3rd or 4th year of advocacy involvement would take the lead and mentor less experienced students. Through collaboration with their SPTPA, efforts can be coordinated to ensure that they are not working at cross-purposes. Additionally, SPTPAs can provide valuable input and support.

These multiyear advocacy efforts can be integrated with colloquia, coursework, and ongoing discussions to help ensure the place of advocacy work in each student's professional identity and skill development. Seeing the results of their multiyear efforts will likely facilitate developing their professional identities as psychologists. Successful efforts can be recognized by SPTPAs and NCSPP and experiences can be shared with others through published articles authored by students in relevant newsletters and journals.

Students may also get involved directly in advocacy at a national level by becoming members of the American Psychological Association of Graduate Students (APAGS), which has existed since 1988 to develop and disseminate information about education and training, legislative issues, and future directions in the field (APA, 2008). APAGS has four specialized subcommittees, one of which is an advocacy coordinating team comprising students who engage in legislative advocacy work, including lobbying. For students more invested in being involved at a local level, many states have their own student associations. One way to promote these advocacy activities and to infuse students with the attitudinal mind set at a programmatic level is to have current graduate students, who are members of either APAGS or their state student association, speak to potential graduate students during the application and interview process for doctoral programs. Moreover, this type of exposure and encouragement may be actively guided by bringing legislators to campus and by taking students to legislative offices to cultivate a mutual awareness and build support for psychology.

ADVOCACY AND ESTABLISHING A PROFESSIONAL IDENTITY

Because the psychology profession is regulated by laws, political advocacy is essential; and because the psychology profession is driven by market forces, economic advocacy is critical. Teaching students to take responsibility for the future of the profession they are entering and demonstrating to them the impact they can have through active advocacy efforts is vital. Unfortunately, advocacy may frequently be seen (by both students and educators) as a self-serving endeavor focused solely on advancing the profession of psychology. Too many professionals may be turned off by what appear to be turf battles between different professions or groups.

Psychologists are often willing to devote time and energy to causes that provide very limited financial gain but that may positively affect the lives of

others, such as pro bono psychotherapy services, supervision of practica students, or giving lectures. However, most psychologists are reluctant to advance advocacy efforts by making financial contributions, which, in essence, are often the lifeblood of psychology's most productive advocacy endeavors. As noted by Ronald Fox (2003), a former APA president, past chair of the Association for the Advancement of Psychology (AAP), and vocal supporter of advocacy efforts, psychology's financial contributions to advocacy initiatives are among the lowest of all major professions. Data indicate that psychologists give on average $1.05 each year per professional to political causes, candidates, and advocacy activities. This places us far behind social workers at $4.42, physical therapists at $4.70, physicians at $7.75, and dieticians at $7.90 (AAP, 2002). For the health professions, psychologists come in last place in political giving. This cannot be merely an issue of limited financial resources because many psychologists earn more money than social workers and physical therapists, for example. Rather, it should be considered indicative of the absence of a professional identity that includes advocacy involvement as an important element. Moreover, only 2% to 3% of practitioners provide all of psychology's political contributions. As Fox (2003) noted, "if all special assessment payers gave just $45 per year, just 87 cents a week, psychology could raise $1.8 million per year, making it second in size only to medicine among all health care professions" (p. 3).

As noted throughout this chapter, most advocacy efforts do not involve political giving. However, considering psychology's minimal political contributions, it is a concern that needs to be addressed. An important initial step in addressing this issue is to foster open and honest dialogues with students and colleagues regarding their attitudes, concerns, and reluctance toward political giving. These dialogues will, the authors hope, lead to practical discussions on ways to alter this unfavorable pattern and may help infuse professional training with political giving as a requisite component.

IMPLICATIONS

Active involvement in ongoing advocacy activities has become essential for professional psychologists, for the profession of psychology, and perhaps most important, for those we serve. Failure to see ourselves as active agents of change on behalf of our profession represents a myopic view that such issues are simply not important to us. Those who are reticent to become involved in advocacy activities and the political process need to appreciate how others are actively working in this arena to advance their own interests, interests that may be inimical to our own.

Psychologists must see that their commitment to help those in need goes far beyond the provision of direct clinical services. We must educate those who make decisions about our ability to provide these services. Thus,

training programs in professional psychology must create a culture of involvement and a professional identity for all psychologists and psychologists-in-training that includes career-long involvement in advocacy activities. Such involvement must be fostered, and some would suggest ingrained, in all graduate students and trainees in all aspects of their professional training through the development and application of innovative education and training programs, mentoring activities, appropriate role modeling at all levels, and active communication among programs regarding methods used and lessons learned. Through experiential activities and actual immersion in ongoing advocacy efforts to include fundraising, lobbying, and grassroots political advocacy, students will experience firsthand the value and importance of advocacy work. Our hope as psychologists is that students will be inculcated with a sense of personal responsibility, a need for active and direct involvement in advocacy work, and a professional identity that has advocacy as its core.

REFERENCES

American Psychological Association. (2007). *Graduate study in psychology: 2008 edition*. Washington, DC: Author.

American Psychological Association. (2008). Frequently asked questions (FAQs). *APA Graduate Students*. Retrieved March 3, 2008, from http://apa.org/apags/faq.html

American Psychological Association. (n.d.). Legislative Advocacy. *APApractice.org*. Retrieved July 9, 2007, from http://apapractice.org/apo/pracorg/legislative.html

Association for the Advancement of Psychology. (2002, Spring). Comparison of health care professions political giving performance. *AAP Advance*, 6. Retrieved March 3, 2009, from http://www.aapnet.org/pdf/advance_archives/aap_spring_2002.pdf

Barnett, J. E. (2004). On being a psychologist and how to save our profession. *The Independent Practitioner*, 24(1), 45–46.

DeLeon, P. H., Loftis, C. W., Ball, V., & Sullivan, M. J. (2006). Navigating politics, policy, and procedure: A firsthand perspective of advocacy on behalf of the profession. *Professional Psychology: Research and Practice*, 37, 146–153.

Fox, R. (2003, Summer). From the desk of the chair *AAP Advance*, 3. Retrieve March 3, 2009, from http://aapnet.org/pdf/advance_archives/aap_summer_2003.pdf

12

CLINICAL TRAINING IN PROFESSIONAL PSYCHOLOGY PROGRAMS

KELLY DUCHENY

Since its inception, the National Council of Schools and Programs in Professional Psychology (NCSPP) has endorsed an "explicit and primary commitment to" the training of practitioners (Bourg, Bent, McHolland, & Stricker, 1989, p. 68). At the core of its educational model, NCSPP endorses a deep integration of intensive clinical activities, academic preparation, and educational mentorship (McHolland, 1991). This integration produces a sophisticated understanding and application of the knowledge, skills, and attitudes (KSAs) of professional psychology (Peterson et al., 1991) within NCSPP's educational competencies (Peterson, Peterson, Abrams, & Stricker, 1997). This chapter defines clinical training, practicum, and internship; discusses legitimate clinical training activities; explores the link between classroom learning and clinical training activities; and examines future directions in clinical training.

WHAT IS CLINICAL TRAINING?

Clinical training is an educational activity under the auspices of an academic program through which students obtain supervised experience provid-

ing psychological services to identified client populations. The supervised experience is of sufficient duration and intensity to adequately prepare students for the next level of clinical activity. Primary one-on-one supervision is provided by a licensed psychologist; additional supervision may be provided by other appropriately credentialed professionals. Client populations include individuals, families, couples, organizations, groups, and communities.

Clinical training includes practicum and internship activities. It does not include course embedded activities (e.g., practice test administrations, observation of a child for a course paper) or postdoctoral training. Clinical training experiences are sequenced by the academic program to provide students with increasingly complex exposure to clients and clinical issues and to prepare students for entry-level practice after completion of the degree (American Psychological Association Committee on Accreditation [CoA], n.d.).

Although including the same broad domain of clinical training activities, practica and internships have different developmental expectations of students, require different levels of mastery and independent functioning (Roberts, Borden, Christiansen, & Lopez, 2005), and are structured differently. Students are expected to achieve progressively greater proficiency and mastery of activities as they progress through the stages of clinical training. For example, whereas both a practicum student and an intern may conduct individual therapy, an intern would be expected to develop richer theoretical conceptualizations and craft effective plans for treatment with less supervisory assistance than a practicum student. In addition, the intern would be expected to identify strengths, weaknesses, and cultural issues more accurately in his or her work with the client and to take steps independently to improve his or her treatment effectiveness. Although similar activities occur on practicum and internship, research suggests that practicum students are less likely to be exposed to nontraditional roles and activities (e.g., supervision, administration, program evaluation) than interns (Lewis, Hatcher, & Pate, 2005).

Practicum

Practica are part-time clinical training experiences designed to develop basic- to intermediate-level KSAs in the provision of professional psychological services. Practica are typically categorized by their major focus of training, setting type, and duration. The most frequent and traditional types of practica are (a) an assessment or testing practicum, (b) a therapy or intervention practicum, (c) a practicum blending therapy and assessment, and (d) an advanced or elective practicum. Most professional psychology programs require 2 or 3 years of practicum, with an option to complete an additional practicum year. Practica can also be categorized by the settings in which they occur, such as hospitals, university-based training programs, social ser-

vice agencies, schools, and other settings (Lewis et al., 2005). Practica can range in duration from 10 weeks to 12 months and can require between 8 and 24 hours per week. Some short practica are designed to achieve specific, narrow learning objectives (e.g., interviewing skills, a very specific area of expertise). Longer practica allow students to develop a broader range of KSAs, in greater depth, across time.

Internship

Internship is the capstone clinical training experience designed to develop advanced-level KSAs in the provision of professional psychological services. Internships are categorized by four main variables: (a) full-time versus half-time status, (b) affiliated versus nonaffiliated, (c) internship placement in the academic program, and (d) organizational structure (Mangione et al., 2005). The majority of internships are full-time, requiring at least 40 hours per week for 12 months. Half-time internship slots approved by the American Psychological Association (APA) have decreased dramatically in the past decade and a half, dropping from almost 250 slots in the 1990s (Erickson Cornish, Roehlke, & Boggs, 2000) to 26 in 2002 (Erickson Cornish, Smith-Acuña, & Nadkarni, 2006) to 9 nonaffiliated slots in 2006 (Association of Psychology Postdoctoral and Internship Centers [APPIC], 2006b). To discuss barriers and encourage innovation in training, the California Psychology Internship Council sponsored a conference on half-time internships in 2005 (Mangione et al., 2005).

A second distinguishing variable is whether the internship is affiliated or nonaffiliated. Internships that are affiliated accept students only from the originating or affiliated academic program. Nonaffiliated internships do not restrict application to a single program, but, instead, allow all students to apply.

Placement in the academic program is a third distinguishing variable of internships. NCSPP academic programs endorse either an integrated or a capstone internship model. Integrated internships are woven into the final years of curriculum by the program (Mangione et al., 2005), are typically half-time, and require students to take concurrent coursework in their academic programs. Integrated internships may be affiliated or nonaffiliated. Several NCSPP programs endorse an integrated internship model (Erickson Cornish et al., 2006; Mangione et al., 2005). Programs that use a capstone internship model require students to complete their coursework prior to commencing internship. In this model, internship is viewed as a culminating experience that integrates previous practicum training and academic preparation (Erickson Cornish et al., 2006). Coursework is not taken concurrently, and interns often train at internships that are distinct from their academic programs. A large majority of professional psychology programs endorse a capstone internship model.

Internships are also categorized by their organizational and administrative structure. There are three main structures: allied, consortium, and independent. Allied internships are overseen by a single entity that takes responsibility for organizing and administrating the internship and that coordinates training with several outside entities. Allied internships act like a wagon wheel with the overseeing program at the center of the wheel and with spokes linked to a range of satellite organizations that provide training opportunities for their interns. Should a satellite organization decline to participate in future training, the overseeing program locates a new training satellite to replace it. The basic structure of the internship is not substantially altered by the loss of a satellite. A consortium internship is jointly overseen by several entities that endorse a shared responsibility for the internship. Consortium internships rest on a carefully crafted plan for shared governance established by multiple independent entities for the purposes of clinical training (Erickson Cornish et al., 2006; Mangione et al., 2005). Independent internships are those located primarily within a single entity that administrates and oversees training without significant use of satellite organizations. Independent internships can be located in a range of locations, such as Veterans Administration hospitals, college counseling centers, and community agencies.

WHAT ARE CLINICAL TRAINING ACTIVITIES?

Although many authors address issues of clinical training, an agreed-upon definition of what constitutes practicum and internship activities does not yet exist (Kaslow, Pate, & Thorn, 2005; Lewis et al., 2005; Roberts et al., 2005). Little research has been conducted on current practicum activities (Lewis et al., 2005), especially research that gathers data directly from practicum sites, supervisors, and students. Several surveys (Hecker, Fink, Levasseur, & Parker, 1995; Kaslow et al., 2005; Lewis et al., 2005) have demonstrated significant disagreement between academic programs and internships regarding what qualifies as legitimate practicum or internship activities as well as what amount of each activity a student should have accumulated before beginning internship. No authors have specifically investigated practicum or internship activities of professional psychology programs, and one study excluded all programs offering the PsyD degree from data collection (Hecker et al., 1995). On the basis of the number of students on practicum and internship in NCSPP programs and the minimum number of clinical training hours required by each program, I estimate that NCSPP students complete approximately 6.5 million clinical training hours each year. Given this, NCSPP should play a major role in the field's articulation of what constitutes legitimate clinical training activities. Based on the seven NCSPP competencies, NCSPP's educational model, the Council of Chairs of Training Councils Practicum Workgroup Recommendations for Practicum Poli-

cies (2007), and a review of the literature, the eight areas described next have been identified as clinical training activities.

Service Provision, Assessment, and Supervision

Service provision includes direct client contact, clinical and diagnostic interviewing, intervention, and therapy. *Assessment* includes test administration, scoring and interpretation, report writing, and needs assessment. *Supervision* activities include supervision received and supervision provided. Supervision received includes direct supervision and supervision-of-supervision received from appropriately credentialed professionals. Supervision provided includes direct supervision provided by students to supervisees. There is significant agreement among academic programs, internships, and accrediting bodies that direct service provision, assessment, and supervision should be counted towards practicum and internship hours (Hecker et al., 1995; Kaslow et al., 2005; Lewis et al., 2005). Although most surveyed sites offered training in assessment and intervention, only about 33% of practicum sites offered students the opportunity to provide supervision (Lewis et al., 2005).

Consultation and Liaison

Consultation includes "planned collaborative interactions" (Illback, Maher, & Kopplin, 1991, p. 116) with other professionals, peers, and staff regarding clients or clinical issues. It also includes short-term or extended liaison relationships with individuals, groups, organizations, or communities. Consultation and liaison activities have consistently been identified as components of practicum and internship training (Illback et al., 1991; Kaslow et al., 2005; Lewis et al., 2005).

Management

Management activities include case management (Sumerall, Lopez, & Oehlert, 2000), documentation and attendance at treatment team meetings or case conferences (Hecker et al., 1995), treatment planning, administrative and quality assurance activities, management of a treatment team, policy and procedure development, and coordination of a program, service delivery system, or grant (see chap. 9, this volume). These activities also include management of one's own clinical work and management and oversight of others. Most academic programs, internships, and practicum sites deem activities in this area as appropriate clinical training activities (Hecker et al., 1995). NCSPP's inclusion of management as a core competency and the high frequency with which psychologists' job responsibilities include management and administrative tasks (see chap. 9, this volume) provide strong support for its inclusion.

Program Development and Evaluation

Program development and evaluation activities stand out in the clinical training literature and in NCSPP's efforts to broaden the scope of psychology's intervention activities (Peterson et al., 1991). This area of activities includes the creation of programs that provide high-quality psychological services and the outcome evaluation of those programs. Program development and evaluation activities offer students opportunities to serve increasingly diverse communities and populations that might not otherwise be accessible. These activities are appearing more consistently in recent research as an accepted component of clinical training. Kaslow et al. (2005) found that 31% of academic programs and almost 39% of internships reported that program development was a legitimate practicum activity, although only 27.8% of practica offered training in program development (Lewis et al., 2005). In addition, research and program evaluation activities were rated as moderately to highly important by 82% of academic programs and 65% of internships (Kaslow et al., 2005).

Outreach and Education

Outreach and education includes outreach, community education programming, and in-service provision (Sears, Evans, & Perry, 1998); resource development, relationship development with organizational gatekeepers, and stakeholders (Humphreys, 2000); and provision of continuing education. This area does not include a student's participation in personal continuing education or in-service training. The literature offers a blurred picture of this area of practice. Survey research has typically blended aspects of outreach and education into other categories and has rarely defined the content of those categories. Given NCSPP's consultation and education competency and its focus on innovative applications of psychology, it is appropriate that professional services of this type would be included in approved clinical training activities.

Application of Scholarship

Application of scholarship includes the identification, review, and application of relevant scholarship to inform and improve the provision of services and supervision, management, outreach, and program development and evaluation activities. This area of clinical training directly echoes NCSPP's educational commitment to train local clinical scientists (McHolland, 1991; Peterson et al., 1991; Peterson et al., 1997). To ensure that all aspects of practice are informed by science and scholarship (Peterson et al., 1991), clinical training must overtly value and actively include these activities. Students must constantly be challenged to develop skills in disciplined inquiry

and hypothesis generation (Peterson et al., 1991; Stricker & Trierweiler, 1995), and to turn to the field's scholarly knowledge base and local data to inform their clinical work. Previous research on clinical training practices has not specifically addressed this area.

Advocacy

Advocacy includes local, regional, national, or international grassroots activism; lobbying efforts; public policy analysis or development; and participation in legislative or governmental activities to promote the interest of clients, "public health and welfare," and professional psychology (NCSPP, 2004, ¶ 2). Although advocacy is not one of the seven competencies, NCSPP (2004) has endorsed advocacy as an important professional value and attitude. Recent research offers some support for the inclusion of advocacy activities as legitimate clinical training activities. Approximately 56% of academic programs and 51% of internships included "community consultation, advocacy and training" as an appropriate practicum activity (Kaslow et al., 2005, p. 309), and 36.5% of training sites offered specific training activities in this area (Lewis et al., 2005).

Preparation and Observation

Preparation and observation activities include preparation for supervision, intervention, assessment, program development, consultation, and outreach; development of materials necessary for service provision (e.g., worksheet for use in therapy); and tape, transcript, or note review. In addition, this area includes observation or shadowing of other professionals and peers for the purposes of learning. The inclusion of preparation and observation in practicum activities emphasizes the developmental nature of clinical training, and supports "multiple ways of knowing" (McHolland, 1991, p. 156) and a diverse student body. In addition, an emphasis on self-care and the use of self in the provision of psychological services requires time for preparation and self-reflection. APPIC categorizes preparation activities as *support hours*, separating them from direct service and supervision hours (APPIC, 2006a). Most studies have not addressed the area of preparation, although the majority of academic programs and internships considered observation of others' clinical work as a legitimate practicum activity (Hecker et al., 1995).

HOW ARE CLINICAL TRAINING ACTIVITIES LINKED TO CLASSROOM LEARNING?

NCSPP strongly advocates the use of "integrative pedagogies" (Peterson et al., 1997, p. 380) through which clinical training and classroom learning

(McHolland, 1991; Peterson et al., 1991; Peterson et al., 1997) are integrated at every stage of student development. The APA CoA guidelines (n.d.) require that practicum activities be well integrated with other elements of an academic program. To catalyze student learning and achievement, clinical training activities should be carefully interwoven with classroom didactics (Kaslow et al., 2005) on a conceptual and a logistic level. On a conceptual level, students, faculty, and site supervisors must reinforce the reciprocal relationship between classroom or academic learning and clinical training. This reciprocal relationship should be a foundational component of each program's educational model. Faculty should constantly reinforce the use of theory in the conceptualization of actual clinical data that rarely fall perfectly onto a theoretical template. At the same time, practicum and internship supervisors should consistently encourage students to return to theory, local data, and their academic preparation when trying to conceptualize their clients' lives. This approach supports students' integration of academic learning and clinical training activities so that both are enriched.

Logistically, programs should craft a curriculum that constantly integrates applied examples into classroom learning activities (Peterson et al., 1997). Classroom learning, if possible, should occur just before students are required to apply that learning in their clinical training activities. Students should have multiple opportunities to bring their clinical cases into classroom environments and should, in turn, be taught by faculty who bring their own work samples into their classrooms. Professional psychology programs integrate clinical training and classroom learning in a range of different ways, including case-based practicum seminars, comprehensive examinations, courses that require direct application with clinical populations, integrated internships, focused practica linked to classroom learning (i.e., a course that requires a clinical training component), and curriculum sequencing (i.e., assessment practicum occurs after assessment courses).

HOW ARE CLINICAL TRAINING ACTIVITIES MEASURED?

The majority of academic programs, clinical training sites, licensure boards, and accreditation bodies in psychology have measured clinical training activities in accumulated hours in different activities (Hecker et al., 1995). To apply for internship, and later for licensure, students tally long lists of clinical training hours in various formats and derivations to document hours in minute detail. In 1995, Hecker et al. raised concerns regarding the utility of the current system of tracking and interpreting practicum hours given the lack of consensus regarding what constituted legitimate practicum activities. Because different students can develop significantly different levels of competence after completing the same number of practicum hours in the same

activities, the use of aggregate practicum hours as a means of determining proficiency has been called into question.

These concerns have led a range of authors and professional organizations to call for a shift away from using aggregate hours to estimate proficiency toward measuring competence and establishing agreed-upon criterion for different levels of clinical training (Erickson Cornish et al., 2006; Hecker et al., 1995; Kaslow, 2004; Ko & Rodolfa, 2005; Roberts et al., 2005). A move toward competency-based assessment will require students, academic programs, training sites, licensure boards, and professional organizations to reconceptualize the measurement of student learning. In addition, it will require a unified effort by all stakeholders to "set specific thresholds for expected competency at different developmental levels" (Kaslow, 2004, p. 775). Without a unified effort, each academic program could spend significant energy developing an idiosyncratic approach to assessment of competency (Erickson Cornish et al., 2006). This idiosyncratic approach, although matching the academic program well, would be unlikely to match the training models of practica and internships or the requirements of licensure boards.

To better assess competency to progress to the next level of clinical training and approach independent practice, NCSPP (2007) created developmental achievement levels (DALs) that list the KSAs expected at each clinical training stage (entry to practicum, entry to internship, completion of degree) across the seven NCSPP competencies. The DALs, in combination with the evolving literature and organizational work products, will help the profession develop a more unified vision of clinical training, allowing an increasingly accurate assessment of when and how students meet required levels of proficiency within each competency. It will be important to carefully balance the need to develop reliable, valid measurements of competency across clinical training stages (Hecker et al., 1995) while continuing to allow the innovation and creativity that has characterized NCSPP programs to date.

FUTURE DIRECTIONS IN CLINICAL TRAINING

Recent changes in the marketplace, service delivery systems, and reimbursement structures have affected clinical training opportunities and professional psychology as a field. To ensure a robust future for clinical training, professional psychology must continue to expand the scope of activities and the settings in which training occurs and creatively integrate technology to improve student learning and service provision. Although clinical training will continue to occur in traditional settings, the field must develop innovative partnerships that make psychology an indispensable component of interdisciplinary teams (Peterson et al., 1997) and that improve the quality and comprehensiveness of the services that professional psychologists provide (Humphreys, 2000).

To expand training opportunities and position professional psychology strategically, academic programs in psychology could partner with graduate programs in different disciplines to coordinate shared curriculum and training. Psychology programs could offer courses in medical schools, law schools, agriculture or architecture departments, and could coordinate shared practice opportunities. A practicum could be integrated into a law clinic. Psychology practicum students could work with law students to interview clients, address psychological issues that arise within the cases, and assist clients to participate fully with their legal counsel. As another example, Anderson and Lovejoy (2000) described a practicum that teamed psychology practicum students and family medicine residents. After completion of the 3-month rotation, family medicine residents increased their mental health referrals by over 1,260%. By ensuring productive, mutually beneficial relationships during formative training experiences, interdisciplinary practica could produce future psychologists who are adept at working in a range of settings and future lawyers and family physicians who see psychology as a natural component of their daily work (Anderson & Lovejoy, 2000).

Another expansion of clinical training settings will occur as programs increase international and public service training opportunities (Belar, Nelson, & Wasik, 2003; McMinn & Voytenko, 2004). Programs could internationalize their curriculum (Belar et al., 2003) and train students to work with international populations and issues (McMinn & Voytenko, 2004) through short 2- to 3-week service project trips, 3-month immersion practica, or year-long practica or internships. In addition, programs can become increasingly adept at mobilizing teams of trainees and professionals to address national disaster relief (Sears et al., 1998), community emergencies, and losses that require intense, short bursts of service. This could also allow students to complete immersion practica working with survivors of natural disasters, immigrant and refugee populations in the United States or Africa, or large-scale community losses like Columbine or the World Trade Center (NCSPP, 2006; Sears et al., 1998). Distributed learning models and technology will significantly affect clinical training in the future (Glueckauf & Ketterson, 2004; Rudestam, 2004). Distributed learning models emphasize structured learning opportunities that "can occur independent of time and place" (Rudestam, 2004, p. 427), often through utilizing technology. Technology will influence service delivery systems by providing means to conduct long-distance therapy, assessment, and consultation and supervision (Glueckauf & Ketterson, 2004). It will allow students in Minneapolis to work with clients in St. Paul, Fort Lauderdale, or Istanbul with similar ease. Likewise, it will allow the creation of virtual practica or internships. Virtual training sites could provide supervision through videoconferencing and could allow unobtrusive live supervision of student work through computer-based cameras. Interns, practicum students, and supervisors could access expert consultation from psychologists anywhere in the world to enhance the quality of services, enrich training

opportunities, and better meet local needs when local expertise in specialty areas is limited. Distributed and blended learning models will allow programs to reconceptualize how clinical training occurs, reducing the reliance on classrooms models if other more distributed models of education improve learning outcomes.

A recent APA policy change will also have a significant impact on the future of clinical training. In February 2006, APA revised its policy on recommended requirements for admission to licensure to allow both years of required experience to occur at the predoctoral level (Ducheny, 2006). In the near future, professional organizations, accrediting bodies, licensure boards, and academic programs will be determining what action will be taken as a result of this important change. The growing focus on predoctoral experience will push the entire field toward the creation of national standards for practicum and internship training (Roberts et al., 2005; Rodolfa, Ko, & Petersen, 2004) and could impact how programs construct, approve, and oversee their practica. The APA Council of Representatives' approval of this new policy included a commitment for improved methods of assessment and a continued development of clinical training competency goals (Bonecutter & Klehr, 2006). This will prove to be an especially challenging task given the variety of models of education, values, and foci of different professional organizations (e.g., Council of Graduate Departments of Psychology, NCSPP, APPIC) and the research that shows significant differences between the expectations and training emphases of academic programs and internships (Rodolfa et al., 2004).

REFERENCES

American Psychological Association Commission on Accreditation. (n.d.). *Guidelines & principles for accreditation of programs in professional psychology*. Retrieved November 20, 2008, from http://www.apa.org/ed/accreditation/G&P0522.pdf

Anderson, G. L., & Lovejoy, D. W. (2000). Predoctoral training in collaborative primary care: An exam room built for two. *Professional Psychology: Research and Practice, 31*, 692–697.

Association of Psychology Postdoctoral and Internship Centers. (2006a). *APPIC application for psychology internship 2006–2007 (AAPI)*. Retrieved July 29, 2006, from http://www.appic.org/downloads/AAPI2006-2007.doc

Association of Psychology Postdoctoral and Internship Centers. (2006b). *APPIC directory online*. Retrieved July 30, 2006, from http://www.appic.org/directory/4_1_directory_online.asp

Belar, C. D., Nelson, P. D., & Wasik, B. H. (2003). Rethinking education in psychology and psychology in education. *American Psychologist, 58*, 678–684.

Bonecutter, B., & Klehr, K. (2006, Spring). APA Council of Representatives (COR) report. *The Illinois Psychologist, 43*(4), 21, 31, 33.

Bourg, E. F., Bent, R. J., McHolland, J. D., & Stricker, G. (1989). Standards and evaluation in the education and training of professional psychologists: The National Council of Schools of Professional Psychology Mission Bay Conference. *American Psychologist, 44,* 66–72.

Council of Chairs of Training Councils Practicum Workgroup. (2007). *Recommendations for practicum policies.* Retrieved December 1, 2007, from http://www.psychtrainingcouncils.org/documents.html

Ducheny, K. (2006, Spring). Will the required postdoctoral year in Illinois go the way of the buggy whip? *The Illinois Psychologist, 43,* 32–33.

Erickson Cornish, J. A., Roehlke, H. J., & Boggs, K. R. (2000). Half-time doctoral psychology internship programs in university counseling centers: Advantages and disadvantages. *Professional Psychology: Research and Practice, 31,* 349–350.

Erickson Cornish, J. A., Smith-Acuòa, S., & Nadkarni, L. (2006). Developing an exclusively affiliated psychology internship consortium: A novel approach to internship training. *Professional Psychology: Research and Practice, 36,* 9–15.

Glueckauf, R. L., & Ketterson, T. U. (2004). Telehealth interventions for individuals with chronic illness: Research review and implications for practice. *Professional Psychology: Research, 35,* 615–627.

Hecker, J. E., Fink, C. M., Levasseur, J. B., & Parker, J. D. (1995). Perspectives on practicum: A survey of directors of accredited PhD programs and internships (Or, What is a practicum hour, and how many do I need?). *Professional Psychology: Research and Practice, 26,* 205–210.

Humphreys, K. (2000). Beyond the mental health clinic: New settings and activities for clinical psychology internships. *Professional Psychology: Research and Practice, 31,* 300–304.

Illback, R. J., Maher, C. A., & Kopplin, D. (1991). Consultation and education competency. In R. L. Peterson, J. D. McHolland, R. J. Bent, E. Davis-Russell, G. E. Edwall, K. Polite, et al. (Eds.), *The core curriculum in professional psychology* (pp. 115–120). Washington, DC: American Psychological Association.

Kaslow, N. J. (2004). Competencies in professional psychology. *American Psychologist, 59,* 774–781.

Kaslow, N. J., Pate, W. E., & Thorn, B. (2005). Academic and internship directors' perspectives on practicum experiences: Implications for training. *Professional Psychology: Research and Practice, 36,* 307–317.

Ko, S. F., & Rodolfa, E. (2005). Psychology training directors' views of number of practicum hours necessary prior to internship application. *Professional Psychology: Research and Practice, 36,* 318–322.

Lewis, B. L., Hatcher, R. L., & Pate, W. E. (2005). The practicum experience: A survey of practicum site coordinators. *Professional Psychology: Research and Practice, 36,* 291–298.

Mangione, L., VandeCreek, L., Nadkarni, L., Emmons, L., McIlvried, J., & Rodolfa, E. (2005, August). *Expanding internship models: Half-time, captive, consortia and others.* Paper presented at the annual convention of the American Psychological Association, Washington, DC.

McHolland, J. D. (1991). National Council of Schools of Professional Psychology core curriculum conference resolutions. In R. L. Peterson, J. D. McHolland, R. J. Bent, E. Davis-Russell, G. E. Edwall, K. Polite, et al. (Eds.), *The core curriculum in professional psychology* (pp. 155–166). Washington, DC: American Psychological Association.

McMinn, M. R., & Voytenko, V. L. (2004). Investing the wealth: Intentional strategies for psychology training in developing countries. *Professional Psychology: Research and Practice, 35*, 302–305.

National Council of Schools and Programs in Professional Psychology. (2004). *NCSPP resolution on advocacy as a professional value and attitude*. Retrieved August 15, 2006, from http://www.ncspp.info/Advocacyres.pdf

National Council of Schools and Programs in Professional Psychology. (2006). *News & awards*. Retrieved August 15, 2006, from http://www.ncspp.info/newsawards.htm

National Council of Schools and Programs in Professional Psychology. (2007). *NCSPP competency developmental achievement levels*. Retrieved November 17, 2007, from http://www.ncspp.info/pubs.htm

Peterson, R. L., McHolland, J. D., Bent, R. J., Davis-Russell, E., Edwall, G. E., Polite, K., et al. (1991). *The core curriculum in professional psychology*. Washington, DC: American Psychological Association.

Peterson, R. L., Peterson, D. R., Abrams, J. C., & Striker, G. (1997). The National Council of Schools and Programs of Professional Psychology educational model. *Professional Psychology: Research and Practice, 28*, 373–386.

Roberts, M. C., Borden, K. A., Christiansen, M. D., & Lopez, S. J. (2005). Fostering a culture shift: Assessment of competence in the education and careers of professional psychologists. *Professional Psychology: Research and Practice, 36*, 355–361.

Rodolfa, E., Ko, S. F., & Petersen, L. (2004). Psychology training directors' views of trainees' readiness to practice independently. *Professional Psychology: Research and Practice, 35*, 397–404.

Rudestam, K. E. (2004). Distributed education and the role of online learning in training professional psychologists. *Professional Psychology: Research and Practice, 35*, 427–432.

Sears, S. F., Evans, G. D., & Perry, N. W. (1998). Innovations in training: The University of Florida rural psychology program. *Professional Psychology: Research and Practice, 29*, 504–507.

Stricker, G., & Trierweiler, S. J. (1995). The local clinical scientist: A bridge between science and practice. *American Psychologist, 56*, 995–1002.

Sumerall, S. W., Lopez, S. J., & Oehlert, M. E. (2000). *Competency-based education and training in psychology: A primer*. Springfield, IL: Charles C. Thomas, Publisher.

13

PSYCHOLOGICAL SERVICE CENTERS: TRAINING INTEGRATION AND COMMUNITY SERVICE

ROBERT A. KING II, STEPHANIE C. WOOD, MARCIE KIRKUP,
CHRISTINE N. RUNYAN, AND MARK E. SKRADE

Beginning in 1896 with the first university-based clinic and reaffirmed by the 1965 Chicago Conference on the Professional Preparation of Clinical Psychologists, aspirations for university-based clinics have been rooted in the training of graduate students in clinical psychology (Serafica & Harway, 1980). Bent (1986) described the role of psychological service centers (PSCs) in the context of the professional psychology movement, asserting that PSCs were a major training source for graduate students and an advantage that the professional training model had over a more traditional model. PSCs continue to offer opportunities to transfer knowledge and competencies from the classroom to the therapy room. In 1986, Bent conducted a survey of PSCs in schools of professional psychology. Survey results indicated that of the 26 associate, affiliate, and member programs that responded, 18 (69.2%) had active PSCs. Of the 14 member programs evaluated, 13 (92.9%) had PSCs. The PSCs were found to have "considerable organizational development and support (in relation to limited available budgets) in the professional schools" (p. 155). Although the PSCs were shown to offer a broad

range of services, the small budgets and volume of services of the PSCs were found to limit the community impact of the clinics. Bent (1986) concluded that although PSCs were working toward being a major training resource for professional schools, more student involvement was needed. He further asserted that PSCs had the ability to affect the communities they serve and to provide an optimal training environment for applying knowledge and competencies learned in the classroom to clinical experience; however, this was not likely to occur "unless major changes and developments occur in center structure and operations" (p. 161).

Since 1986, work at several professional conferences has sought to develop a model for integrating the National Council of Schools and Programs of Professional Psychology (NCSPP) competencies in the training environment and structuring the transfer of knowledge from the classroom to the PSC. In 1997, NCSPP defined its education and training model, which included the core competencies for professional psychology (Peterson, Peterson, Abrams, & Stricker, 1997). In 2001, a working group at the American Psychological Association's (APA's) Education Leadership Conference identified nine principles to guide practica, graduate school education, and other training experiences. The summary of this work group specifically discussed the "importance of integration of field and classroom experience," noting that practica experiences "are exemplars of applying knowledge . . . and testing its application in the field" (APA, 2001, p. 2). The working group also identified areas and levels of competence in practica training analogous with the NCSPP core competencies. However, although identification and assessment of competencies in training programs is improving, there is limited research regarding the integration of training models in PSCs.

Jarmon and Halgin (1987) used a PSC case example to illustrate a philosophical and structural framework for integrating research and practice into psychological training clinics. The structural framework focused on multiple components including faculty roles, student involvement, use of graduate student supervisors, policies and procedures, economic considerations, and integration of research and practice. Sauer and Huber (2007) offered specific strategies for implementing the fundamental elements of the Boulder scientist–practitioner model within a psychological training clinic. The Boulder model is an educational and training approach that promotes adherence to scientific methods, procedures, and research in the day-to-day practice of clinical psychologists. In each of these instances, the authors offered a foundation for implementing the scientist–practitioner model into PSCs; however, there continues to be a significant need to evaluate the application of other training models within PSCs as well.

Additionally, PSC research has evaluated models of psychotherapy (Callahan & Hynan, 2005; Callahan, Swift, & Hynan, 2006), implementation of clinic-based research (Borkovec, 2004; Neufeldt & Nelson, 1998),

and implementation of empirically supported treatments (Cukrowicz et al., 2005). However, lesser emphasis to date has been placed on identifying the most viable organizational structure and economic strategies for PSCs. In the absence of current literature on issues affecting PSCs, it appears that the primary means of disseminating the most up-to-date information is through association listservs and PSC Web sites. To evaluate the current climate of PSCs in schools and programs of professional psychology, we conducted a survey of PSCs. The survey was modeled after Bent's 1986 survey of PSCs and meant to provide an update on the current status of NCSPP member PSCs. We constructed survey items to evaluate the key PSC characteristics that influence the PSCs' ability to meet the demands of training and service. In all, 11 characteristics of PSCs were evaluated. These were grouped into two categories: (a) operational and training characteristics that included competency model (descriptive), location (on-campus or off-campus), services provided (individual therapy, group therapy, counseling, and assessments), client volume (number of monthly appointments), and diversity of experiences (theoretical, diagnoses, ethnicity, and socioeconomic); and (b) structural and financial and service characteristics that included human resources (number of staff, faculty, students, interns, and residents), technology (information systems, client outcomes, and supervision), marketing and public relations (presence of personnel or funding), external partnerships and contracts (yes/no), faculty in practice (yes/no), and changes in clinical environment (descriptive).

A total of 51 NCSPP full members fell within the scope of the survey. Associates and affiliate programs of NCSPP were not contacted. Of the 51 member programs contacted, 35 programs (68.6%) had an affiliated PSC, whereas 16 programs (31.4%) did not. Of the 35 programs with an affiliated PSC, approximately one third of these PSCs were student counseling centers and the remaining two thirds were community-based clinics. Of these 35 programs, 18 (51.4%) agreed to participate in a more detailed telephone survey.[1] The remainder of this chapter addresses the current status of PSCs in NCSPP-member programs, the opportunities PSCs provide for transferring knowledge from the classroom to the PSC, and the challenges of balancing training program and community needs.

---

[1]Programs with PSCs (asterisks indicate those programs that completed the survey): Adelphi University, Adler School of Professional Psychology,* Antioch New England Graduate School,* Azusa Pacific, Biola University,* California Institute of Integral Studies, Carlos Abizu University, CSPP Alliant University–Fresno,* CSPP Alliant University–Los Angeles, University of Denver, Florida Institute of Technology, Forest Institute of Professional Psychology,* Fuller Theological Seminary,* University of Indianapolis,* James Madison University, John F. Kennedy University, La Salle University,* Loma Linda University, Long Island University, Loyola College in Maryland,* Nova Southeastern University,* Pace University,* Pacific Graduate School of Psychology,* Pacific University,* Pepperdine University,* Philadelphia College of Osteopathic Medicine,* Ponce School of Medicine, Regent University, Rutgers State University of New Jersey, Spalding University, University of St. Thomas,* Widener University, Wright Institute, Wright State University,* Xavier University.*

OPERATIONAL AND TRAINING CHARACTERISTICS OF PSCS

The NCSPP competencies have been identified as cross-cutting themes, critical to the success of both academic and training environments. Thus, given their connection to the doctoral program, PSCs have a unique opportunity to play a more active role in seamlessly integrating academic education and practitioner training. With regard to the competency model of individual training programs and its integration, all programs surveyed with affiliated PSCs indicated that the PSC was a vital part of student training; however, the degree of integration appeared to be dependent more on the efforts of the individual directors or supervisors and not the result of a systemic plan to integrate the competencies within the PSC. To provide meaningful feedback to the doctoral program regarding ways in which to improve the curriculum and training, systemic integration is necessary. Moreover, specific service activities and experiences in PSCs provide opportunities on which to build a foundation for systemic competency assessment. As doctoral programs continue to develop measures for NCSPP competency assessment, PSCs are currently in an ideal position to facilitate competency measurement and professional development as well as provide community services through the operational components of the clinic.

The location of a PSC influences accessibility, which is necessary to ensure adequate training and supervision opportunities for students. Of the participating PSCs in the recent survey, 67% were housed on-campus in close proximity to the doctoral program, whereas 33% resided in off-campus locations. Clinical psychology programs with on-campus centers were more likely to share their PSCs with counseling psychology or other programs. Location also seemed directly related to the community outreach of the center, and off-campus centers operated more as community mental health clinics rather than as student counseling centers. Two programs reported having three and four separate PSCs serving specific patient populations and settings. Other programs reported multiple satellite locations of a main clinic to service specific community-based agencies. These findings suggest that PSCs are attempting to reach out to the communities they serve.

Client service activities represent another characteristic with which to measure the degree to which a PSC is adequately providing experiential opportunities for students. Client volume varied across PSCs that responded to the survey, with an average number of client appointments of 470 per month and a range of 25 to 2,100 appointments. Most PSCs reported between 350 and 800 sessions monthly. Whereas service delivery constraints (e.g., limited numbers of eligible student/clinical trainees, appropriate supervisors, space) influenced the determination of client volume, so did variable methods of tracking and summarizing client volume (e.g., total number of patient sessions per patient, total number of sessions provided, sessions monthly/annually). Client volume is necessary for accumulation of practicum hours; how-

ever, although this measure is an important indicator of student experience, Kaslow, Pate, and Thorn (2005) supported the need to emphasize student attainment of competencies as opposed to practicum hours.

When evaluating the opportunities for student training, it is also helpful to consider the breadth of services provided, diagnoses evaluated, and theoretical orientations used at PSCs. All PSCs surveyed offered individual therapy, while 94% offered group therapy, 89% offered psychological evaluations, 39% offered family and couples therapy, and 28% offered career counseling. In addition, PSCs reported providing "other therapy" services that were often tailored to meet demands of specific programs or external contracts (e.g., neuropsychological evaluations, trauma, drug abuse, biofeedback, geriatric, learning disabilities, forensic evaluations). Of the programs surveyed, 17% specifically noted regular use of empirically supported treatments. Although 11% of PSCs indicated they screen at-risk populations and subsequently refer those patients with more intensive psychotherapy needs (e.g., hospitalization, medication, specialized services) to other community agencies and resources, 89% reported experiences with very broad disorders, including patients with persistent mental illness. All PSCs described a high level of theoretical diversity; however, the primary orientations reported were cognitive–behavioral and psychodynamic. Overall, the variability of services provided, theoretical diversity, and diagnostic breadth enhance the opportunities to evaluate NCSPP competencies within PSCs.

The diversity competency of the NCSPP clinical training model emphasizes the need for programs to provide psychological trainees with the knowledge, skills, and attitudes (KSAs) necessary to understand, respect, and value cultural and individual differences. The survey assessed the degree to which PSCs provide students exposure to and training opportunities consistent with NCSPP's diversity competency. Specifically, respondents reported a notable difference in ethnic diversity of clients based on the geographic location of the PSC. Of the PSCs surveyed, 70% reported their patient population to be high in ethnic diversity. Limited ethnic diversity was reported by 22% of PSCs located in primarily rural areas, and the remaining 8% of PSCs were unsure of how to categorize the ethnic diversity of their patients because of a lack of reliable data collected on this parameter. PSCs appear to be well positioned to offer services to a socioeconomically disadvantaged population, and 94% surveyed indicated they operate with an income-based, sliding fee scale.

Supervision is the primary means by which competencies are evaluated in PSCs. As a result, core and adjunct supervisors are an integral part of any PSC environment. Survey findings indicated that on average, 5.7 ($SD = 2.068$) core program faculty provided supervision to practicum students in the PSCs and often functioned in an administrative role or in developing specialty centers for patient services (e.g. neuropsychology, child/adolescent, geriatric, trauma). Adjunct supervisors were used in 78% of the centers. Although

most of the PSCs indicated a desire for all students in their doctoral program to rotate through the PSC to achieve continuity in training, only two programs reported that a PSC rotation is a required component of practicum training. It appears that the primary limitation to implementing this requirement is the lack of available supervisors and/or lack of available clients to support such a training model; however, physical and financial resources at some of the PSCs also appear to prevent this implementation from routinely occurring.

STRUCTURAL, FINANCIAL, AND SERVICE CHARACTERISTICS OF PSCS

Clinic operations are carried out in PSCs through nonprofessional and professional staff as well as through students in various levels of training. All clinics in the survey reported that nonprofessional staff is responsible for maintaining daily operations of the centers (e.g., reception, billing, patient records). The number of nonprofessional personnel reported ranged from 1 to 25 persons and an average of 5 persons. Approximately half of respondents also reported the use of part-time graduate assistants (GAs) or work–study students serving in nonprofessional capacities. An informal observation noted the use of GAs to support the internal research function of the center; two clinics specifically noting the use of part-time GAs to compile research on clinical outcomes and coordinate data requests from faculty and students. Provision of services was primarily accomplished through the participation of practicum students with variable student volume in the PSC ranging from 4 to 80 students. On average, 30 students-in-training were available at any given time to provide supervised patient services. Fifty percent of respondents also had predoctoral interns in the PSC, with an average of eight interns in the training setting. Only four PSCs employed postdoctoral residents in the PSC, and of these, each PSC had two residents.

Information technology provides the ability to capture, transmit, and record targeted clinic activities. The survey assessed management and clinical outcome applications and supervision technology use at PSCs. Management applications support the finance, accounting, and service activities at the PSCs and were reported in 78% of responding PSCs. Examples of reported management application software included Quick Books/Excel (3 clinics), SOS (Synergistic Operating Systems; 2 clinics), QRS, Shrink Wrapped, and Titanium, and one clinic reported a custom-designed software program to support their daily operations. Although 22% of PSCs had no active management application to support their clinic operations, this was not found to be due to a lack of desire but to limited financial resources. Approximately 61% of PSCs reported evaluating and tracking client outcome information through the use of the following: Outcome Questionnaire (OQ) measures,

OQ45 (5 clinics); SPSS software (3 clinics); Beck Depression Inventory; Patient-Oriented Evidence that Matters; Targeting Outcomes of Programs; Microsoft Access; and Vertigo Handicap Questionnaire. Audiovisual technology was the most common supervision technology used, with 78% of PSCs reporting its use. Live observation as the only mode of supervision observation was reported by approximately 10% of the PSCs. One PSC reported the use of digital audiovisual technology to aid supervision, and three additional programs reported being in the process of converting analog to digital recording technology.

To the extent that PSCs build and manage relationships to strategically promote their program's mission, 61.1% of those surveyed reported a lack of planned, purposeful marketing strategies to increase client volume. Among the remaining 38.9% of PSCs that reported some marketing attempts, one responding PSC had invested in a professional firm to develop a marketing campaign for services. Others used their university marketing department resources, whereas two others had a part-time staff person dedicated to developing community relationships and marketing services. Half of PSCs relied on student presentations to community agencies. The larger PSCs reported reasonable success as well as a great deal of satisfaction with these patient-related marketing efforts. Such presentations reinforce the consultation and education competencies of NCSPP for students as well as foster referral sources for the PSC with minimal financial investment. These presentations are usually overseen by a faculty supervisor and are included in practicum requirements to ensure quality and continuity.

Moreover, it appears that agency-to-agency marketing occurs through collaborative community partnerships for many PSCs surveyed. Both formal and informal relationships with community agencies existed among 78% of PSCs that responded to the survey. The majority of these relationships fulfilled specific needs for the partnering agency as well as initiatives of individual faculty, or the PSC, or both. Examples included work with hospitals, homeless shelters, probation/parole/corrections/court/police, children/juveniles, diversity centers, and schools/universities/colleges. Programs who reported a lack of structured marketing or a strategic public relations plan often indicated receiving direct marketing benefits from contacts or referrals established through services offered at external practicum site placements.

The current survey revealed that as a whole, NCSPP-member PSCs consistently aim to serve the underserved population in their respective communities through the use of an income-based sliding fee schedule. Sliding scale fee structures undeniably offer PSCs a unique advantage to serve a socioeconomically disadvantaged population and can be considered a training and community-service strength. However, serving a low-revenue-generating population can place unrealistic fiscal demands on the centers. Many PSCs reported substantial pressure to generate revenues for universities and academic programs; however, most were struggling to financially break even.

To broaden PSC revenue streams, external partnerships and formal and informal contracts with community agencies were reported by 61% of PSCs. Unfortunately, not all of the partnerships result in significant reimbursement, if any at all. Contracts and agreements with insurance networks and employee assistance programs (EAPs) have not been successfully negotiated: 79% of the PSCs surveyed reporting no involvement with insurance networks or EAPs. Inherent challenges found within the PSC structure contribute to difficulty securing EAP and commercial insurance contracts. A primary challenge is that a student-centered workforce, as found in PSCs, contributes to greater difficulty negotiating contracts when there are available licensed masters- and doctoral-level mental health providers from the community at the same negotiating table.

Another way that PSCs potentially offset training costs is through development of practice plans in which faculty offer services through the PSC. One PSC reported annual revenues of approximately $50,000 derived directly from faculty practice in the center. The current survey revealed that 47% of PSCs had faculty who provided direct services through the clinic, and of those, only 44% operated from a formal practice plan arrangement. All faculty practice plans included a sharing of revenues with the center to varying degrees, including revenue splits of 20/80 or 30/70 and, in one instance, a flat rental expense based on square footage used by the individual faculty member. In addition to the monetary benefits of PSCs, practice plans also provide the added benefit that faculty are able to keep clinical skills sharpened through ongoing clinical practice.

When PSCs offer practice plans for faculty, the opportunity exists to use revenues in other creative means for faculty benefits. One example would be to place revenues generated from the practice plan into a faculty professional development fund. Or practice plans could be used to strategically diversify services, develop new business, meet community needs, or obtain EAP contracts. Regardless of the specific structure of the plan, these plans need to work in coordination with the academic demands of the program. Despite the potential for financial and professional benefit that practice plans may offer PSCs and faculty, 50% did not have a formal practice plan for faculty in the center.

PSCs appear to be increasingly relied on for affordable mental health care for a variety of reasons, including cuts to state and federal programs that have traditionally provided such services, changes in managed care, decreases in health insurance benefits for mental health services, and decreases in access to health insurance. In fact, 78% of PSC respondents were not authorized as network providers for private insurance companies or EAPs. A lack of significant reimbursement dollars to cover provision of service and training costs at PSCs challenges the delicate balance between training and service that PSCs are tasked to maintain.

DISCUSSION

PSCs and clinical training programs are complex entities with multifunctioning individuals; both have common goals, yet competing demands, for resources. This complexity is further complicated by the diffuse boundary between the goals of the PSC, academic and training department, and supporting institution. For example, PSCs often adapt services to meet community needs. The resulting services may or may not be perfectly congruent with the training needs of the students. This incongruence between PSC community services and the academic department's training needs in addition to the limited literature regarding the integration of training models in PSCs exacerbates a general uncertainty with how the core competencies become integrated in the PSC environment.

Moreover, the uncertainty in the training role of the PSC is understandable given the varying, and at times, divergent interests of many stakeholders. Indeed, the PSC serves many masters: the needs and demands of the community, the academic program, students, staff, supervisors, and the active client population. Given the uncertainty and multiple stakeholders in PSCs, a snapshot of the PSC structure and operations can inform the training program as to how successfully it is fulfilling the training role. The survey discussed in this chapter was developed to ascertain this structure and operations of PSCs in schools and programs of professional psychology and to evaluate the opportunities that PSCs provide to assess the NCSPP competencies.

We identified five key characteristics of PSCs that provide opportunities to evaluate competencies. First, location, marketing, and external partnerships of PSCs influence accessibility for clients, which in turn have the ability to affect client volume and clinical experiences. Second, breadth of services provided, range of diagnoses treated, and theoretical orientations used by PSCs also expand the opportunities to evaluate competencies. Third, information technology provides the mechanism by which clinical activities are captured, transmitted, and recorded. Fourth, with the diversity competency, students are able to be evaluated also on their KSAs associated with diverse populations. Finally, supervision and faculty resources provide the cornerstone by which competencies are evaluated in PSCs, and these resources are required to determine whether competencies have been met or not. In addition to providing opportunities to evaluate competencies, PSCs also provide psychological services to the community.

A working model for practicum competency assessment identified by the Association of Directors of Psychological Training Clinics (ADPTC; Hatcher & Lassiter, 2005, 2007) as well as the recent approval of the development achievement levels (DALs) by NCSPP (2007) has propelled competency evaluation and assessment in professional psychology training programs. However, while the ADPTC working model and the NCSPP DALs provide

greater definition to the KSAs for competency-specific domains, doctoral programs continue to focus energies on ways to measure these competencies.

According to Kaslow et al. (2007), a primary component for evaluation of competencies is that methods be developmentally appropriate. Inherent in a comprehensive, developmentally based evaluation system are the practical challenges of programmatic costs and burdens. For those programs in professional psychology that have PSCs, these centers provide a unique environment in which to facilitate efficient and effective competency measurement and professional development. PSCs allow for direct observation in actual situations, which is viewed as key for assessing KSAs of emerging professionals (Kaslow et al., 2007). Faculty supervision at PSCs provides observation over time of multiple samples of behavior in both classroom and clinical practice settings. Greater control over the clinical training environment is also provided by PSCs, which allows for operational modifications in training and service as needed. Furthermore, PSCs positioned to focus primarily on training can optimize real-time, systematic feedback that identifies competency problems early in practicum training and provides continual programmatic and curriculum improvement. In addition to promoting competency measurement, programs in professional psychology that have PSCs also provide community services through the operational components of the clinic.

The survey suggests that the majority of PSCs do, in fact, fulfill the mission of providing psychological services to the community quite well, especially those PSCs designated as off-campus locations. This is evidenced by the average number of reported client sessions per month (470), which is a significant contribution to the communities they serve. PSCs are meeting considerable and increasing mental health needs through the provision of affordable services to a growing number of underserved, uninsured, and underinsured Americans, either by proxy or by intent.

The National Association of State Mental Health Program Directors Medical Directors Council (Parks, Pollack, Bartels, & Mauer, 2005) reported that many states focus their public mental health systems on the seriously mentally ill (SMI) Medicaid population, with minimal levels of support for non-SMI or uninsured populations. Consequently, there exists a disparity between target populations by community health centers and state public mental health. Sered and Fernandopulle (2005) extrapolated four factors that contribute to the gaps in health care services: (a) high number of low-income need exceeds the country's safety net resources, (b) scarcity of affordable specialty care services, (c) lack of a systematic process to finance prescription drugs for those without the means to pay, and (d) difficulty in and complications with coordination of care within and outside the safety net. Of the PSCs surveyed, 94% operate based on a sliding fee scale to attract those in the community who cannot afford mental health services due to high costs, high deductibles, high copayments, or lack of insurance coverage.

PSCs appear to fill the gaping holes in care that formal community safety nets are not addressing and serve an expanding community need for accessible and affordable mental health care to the non-SMI and uninsured. Successfully meeting community needs for affordable and accessible mental health services comes with a substantial cost to NCSPP member programs through their PSCs.

In addition, PSCs are in a taxing position of balancing training program needs and the fiscal realities of operating a clinic. A majority of PSCs (78%) reported formal and informal partnerships and contracts with community agencies; however, most of the arrangements target the same low-revenue-generating population. Targeting the same low-revenue clientele that a majority of clinics report to serve is likely one reason 61% of PSCs surveyed reported a lack of planned, purposeful strategies to increase client volume. Increasing the volume of the same clientele only adds to the disproportional cost of training and supervising for services that lack commensurate revenue. Additionally, 79% of PSCs reported no involvement with potentially higher revenue sources such as insurance networks or EAPs. In effect, NCSPP member programs are subsidizing the shortfall of clinical service revenues through practicum student tuition and fees assessed for clinical experiences at PSCs, which subsequently places the students in the position of subsidizing the inadequacies of local mental health care access. In essence, it is the educational debt that students incur through their education and training that finances the inadequate public and private financing for mental health services. The result is an often overwhelming dependence and financial burden on PSCs to provide a greater number of accessible and low-revenue-generating services to a segment of the population that is increasingly omitted from adequate government-sponsored or private insurance coverage. Though an exchange of practicum experience for low-cost mental health service to the community may seem to be a reasonable swap, for many programs it is too ambitious of a training and service model to be fiscally sustainable. It would appear that PSCs have fallen short of Bent's (1986) assertion that PSCs should support the major share of their functions through affiliations, contracts, and income generation.

The survey data and discussion with PSC personnel following the survey illuminated the fiscal constraints under which many PSCs continue to operate. Most PSCs surveyed reported pressure to generate service revenue while struggling to financially break even. To maintain financial viability, PSCs will have to begin to create service opportunities that yield higher rates of reimbursement and broaden revenue streams. One area that should be explored and developed is the use of faculty practice plans. If used strategically, the participation in practice plans at a PSC could offset a portion of the shortfall in revenue. As mentioned previously, slightly less than half of PSCs operate with formal faculty practice plans. Those programs that use practice plans reported varying arrangements ranging from revenue sharing

to a specific faculty-use contribution fund. Considering both the revenue needs of the PSC and identifying unique faculty expertise within the program can lead to a cooperative strategic initiative that can benefit both the faculty and the PSC. Identifying faculty expertise and the source(s) and level of service revenue, developing lines of service around the identified expertise, and marketing and promoting the service provide the potential for new service development, higher reimbursement rates, and increasing direct and indirect referrals to the PSC. Having personnel to manage or coordinate the efforts of practice plan participants at the PSC will ensure follow-through and adherence to the PSC strategic use of practice plans. Additionally, a PSC more populated with licensed professionals through such practice plan arrangements has a greater potential to attract third-party arrangements and contracts such as insurance panels and EAP programs.

As a result of the acceleration of health insurance premiums and high costs of health care services, the value of health professional services will continue to be scrutinized. Industry-wide consideration of cost and quality in health care has led to the systematic focus on continuous quality health care management. Students must be aware that health care services for the next generation will be delivered in an environment that focuses on the evidence of both cost and clinical effectiveness. PSCs have the opportunity to create training environments that are as close to the current landscape of health care that is fiscally possible. A PSC that is sensitive to continuous quality improvement can also position itself as a community resource for outcome data that contributes to local, evidence-based consensus on mental health care.

Health maintenance, prevention, and advocacy efforts are services that PSCs could provide more of to their communities. What may be required is a modification in professional training focus and a change in the lens through which PSCs see their role in community mental health care; specifically, a focus more on improving health care in the community rather than providing health care to the community places PSCs in a more proactive service position. Faculty practice plans could be used to leverage faculty time in the academic setting with time in the applied setting to achieve such purposes. For example, efforts in secondary prevention through early screening in schools and businesses in conjunction with affordable services, community education, and advocacy will enhance the visibility of the PSC and offer solutions to a national need for early detection and prevention. PSC revenue can be generated through consulting fees and offering topic-related continuing education courses to local educational, health and wellness, and human resource professionals.

Opening the PSC to local practitioners to practice on a full-time or part-time basis may help cover some overhead costs at the PSC as well as diversify the payer mix. Financial arrangements could consider supervision responsibilities at the PSC in addition to provision of direct services. Addi-

tionally, hiring administrative staff at the PSC who have the experience, knowledge, and skill set to effectively manage cash flow, billing, and collections will ensure effective service revenue management.

The fiscal weakness of the PSC is also the center's social strength. An argument made previously is that the fractured health care system as well as underfunded state social systems has left PSCs holding the net for the safety nets. An opportunity exists to aggregate the efforts of all NCSPP member PSCs into one national database. An organized effort to capture the individual and the overall economic impact that PSCs have in their respective communities could be used by NCSPP member programs with PSCs to promote the clinics' functions and advocate for mental health service and educational training dollars on local, state, and federal levels. What is clear from the current status of PSCs is that their ability to meet training program and community needs while maintaining financial viability will require planning, cooperation, and innovation among NCSPP programs.

REFERENCES

American Psychological Association (2001). *Educational leadership conference question working group #5: Practicum*. Retrieved July 19, 2006, from http://www.apa.org/ed/elc/group5.pdf

Bent, R. J. (1986). Psychological service centers. In J. E.Callan, D. R. Peterson, & G. Stricker (Eds.), *Quality in professional psychology training: A national conference and self-study* (pp.149–183). Washington, DC: American Psychological Association.

Borkovec, T. D. (2004). Research in training clinics and practice research networks: A route to the integration of science and practice. *Clinical Psychology: Science and Practice, 11*, 211–215.

Callahan, J. L., & Hynan, M. T. (2005). Models of psychotherapy outcome: Are they applicable in training clinics? *Psychological Services, 2*, 65–69.

Callahan, J. L., Swift, J. K., & Hynan, M. T. (2006). Test of the phase model of psychotherapy in a training clinic. *Psychological Services, 3*, 129–136.

Cukrowicz, K. C., White, B. A., Reitzel, L. R., Burns, A. B., Driscoll, K. A., Kemper, T. S., et al. (2005). Improved treatment outcome associated with the shift to empirically supported treatments in a graduate training clinic. *Professional Psychology: Research and Practice, 36*, 330–337.

Hatcher, R. L., & Lassiter, K. D. (2005). *Report on practicum competencies. Association of Directors of Psychology Training Clinics (ADPTC) Practicum Competencies Workgroup*. Retrieved January 11, 2008, from http://www.adptc.org/public_files/CCTCPracticumCompetenciesChartRevFeb2005.doc

Hatcher, R. L., & Lassiter, K. D. (2007). Initial training in professional psychology: The practicum competencies outline. *Training and Education in Professional Psychology, 1*, 49–63.

Jarmon, H., & Halgin, R. P. (1987). The role of the psychology department clinic in training scientist–professionals. *Professional Psychology: Research and Practice, 18,* 509–514.

Kaslow, N. J., Pate, W. E., II, & Thorn, B. (2005). Academic and internship directors' perspectives on practicum experiences: Implications for training. *Professional Psychology: Research and Practice, 36,* 307–317.

Kaslow, N. J., Rubin, N. J., Forrest, L., Elman, N., Van Horne, B., Jacobs, S., et al. (2007). Recognizing, assessing, and intervening with problems of professional competence. *Professional Psychology: Research and Practice, 38,* 479–492.

National Council of Schools and Programs of Professional Psychology (2007, August). *Competency developmental achievement levels (DALs) of the National Council of Schools and Programs in Professional Psychology (NCSPP).* Retrieved January 2, 2008, from http://www.ncspp.info/DALof%20NCSPP%209-21-07.pdf

Neufeldt, S. A., & Nelson, M. L. (1998). Research in training clinics: A bridge between science and practice. *Journal of Clinical Psychology, 54,* 315–327.

Parks, J., Pollack, D., Bartels, S., & Mauer, B. (2005). *Integrating behavioral health and primary care services: Opportunities and challenges for state mental health authorities.* Retrieved July 17, 2007, from the from the National Association of State Mental Health Program Directors, Medical Directors Council Web site: http://www.nasmhpd.org

Peterson, R. L., Peterson, D. R., Abrams, J. C., & Stricker, G. (1997). The National Council of Schools and Programs of Professional Psychology educational model. *Professional Psychology: Research and Practice, 28,* 373–386.

Sauer, E. M., & Huber, D. M. (2007). Implementing the Boulder model of training in a psychological training clinic [Electronic version]. *Journal of Contemporary Psychotherapy,* DOI 10.1007/s10879-007-9057-x.

Serafica, F. C., & Harway, N. I. (1980). The psychology department clinic: Its organization and development. *Professional Psychology: Research and Practice, 11,* 741–748.

Sered, S. S., & Fernandopulle, R. (2005). *Uninsured in America: Life and death in the land of opportunity.* Berkeley: University of California Press.

14

MENTORING IN PROFESSIONAL PSYCHOLOGY

CLARK D. CAMPBELL AND TAMARA L. ANDERSON

The practice of faculty members mentoring students in educational settings appears to be pervasive at both the undergraduate and graduate levels. Whereas undergraduate student mentoring may focus on student retention, career entry, and advancement of students to graduate programs, mentoring in graduate schools appears to focus on developing professional attitudes and skills as well as preparation for professional success. In traditional graduate programs in the natural and social sciences, this success has been defined in terms of graduates obtaining research and teaching positions in other universities. As described next, mentoring in professional psychology has expanded this approach to better meet the needs of students and the profession.

In this chapter, mentoring is discussed in broad terms as it relates to graduate education, but specific attention is given to the National Council of Schools and Programs of Professional Psychology (NCSPP) educational model and the ways in which mentoring is developed within this model. Also consistent with the NCSPP model, gender issues in mentoring are discussed.

MENTORING GRADUATE STUDENTS

Mentoring graduate students usually involves the development of a significant relationship between a mentor and protégé, and there are important aspects to the initiation and sustenance of the relationship.

Definitions

One of the difficulties in describing *mentoring* lies in the various definitions found in the literature. Jacobi (1991) described six different definitions of mentoring in academic settings, whereas Johnson (2002) provided a broad and traditional definition of mentoring.

> Mentoring is a personal relationship in which a more experienced (usually older) faculty member or professional acts as a guide, role model, teacher, and sponsor of a less experienced (usually younger) graduate student or junior professional. A mentor provides the protégé with knowledge, advice, challenge, counsel, and support in the protégé's pursuit of becoming a full member of a particular profession. (Johnson, 2002, p. 88)

Kram (1988) defined the mentoring role as facilitating both the development and forward movement of the protégé and stressed the need for role modeling (based on the mentor's experience) as a necessary part of the psychosocial function of mentoring.

Functions

Kram's (1985) conceptualization of mentoring involves both career-related and psychosocial functions. Career functions involve activities such as coaching and visibility within the profession. Psychosocial functions involve activities like friendship, role modeling, and counseling. Both career and psychosocial functions are seen as essential to a healthy mentoring relationship and a successful outcome for the protégé.

Benefits

There seems to be little doubt about the benefits of mentoring for both students and faculty. The benefits for students include enhanced networking, dissertation success, publication productivity, and professional skill development and confidence (Johnson & Huwe, 2003). Surveys of graduate students and professionals revealed that mentored students were more likely to have published their research in engineering (Reskin, 1979) and psychology (Cronan-Hillix, Gensheimer, Cronan-Hillix, & Davidson, 1986). Graduate students in psychology also reported greater satisfaction with their doctoral program when they received mentoring (Clark, Hardin, & Johnson, 2000; Cronan-Hillix et al., 1986; Johnson, Koch, Fallow, & Huwe, 2000).

The benefits of mentoring extend beyond graduation to include more collaboration with colleagues, more involvement in professional organizations, higher rates of publication, and increased grant funding (Cameron & Blackburn, 1981). Career satisfaction and achievement, early employment,

and increased income were some of the benefits reported by Johnson and Huwe (2003). Furthermore, having a published and respected mentor was the strongest predictor of postdoctoral employment in a survey reported by Sanders and Wong (1985). Mentors appear to benefit most by enriched relationships with students and enhanced research productivity.

Frequency

Surveys of mentoring in psychology indicated that approximately 50% of graduate students are mentored overall (Cronan-Hillix et al., 1986; Mintz, Bartels, & Rideout, 1995) and 51% of ethnic minority students are mentored (Atkinson, Casas, & Neville, 1994). A more recent survey (Clark et al., 2000) indicated that approximately 66% of clinical psychology students were mentored and identified a difference in frequency of mentoring between PhD clinical students (73%) and PsyD clinical students (56%). Groody (2004) challenged this finding with a survey employing a broader definition of mentoring. Johnson et al. (2000) reported less mentoring for graduate students in clinical (53%) than in experimental psychology (69%). Campbell (2007) summarized the literature review provided by Johnson and Huwe (2003), stating that not all graduate students get mentored, that protégés often initiate the mentoring relationship, and that university-based graduate programs (as compared with independent schools) with small student–faculty ratios appear to place greater emphasis on mentoring.

DEMOGRAPHICS CALL FOR GENDER DIFFERENCES IN MENTORING

A traditional model of mentoring clinical psychology graduate students involves a faculty member working with a few graduate students on a focused area of scholarship, typically centered on the professor's research interests. Often this research is funded by grants, and the professor may select specific students to admit to the doctoral program to enhance the research (Groody, 2004). In addition to enhancing the likelihood of publication of studies on the professor's research, the graduate student is able to complete his or her dissertation and learn important research skills in the process. The successful outcome of mentoring is usually described in terms of graduate students securing additional grant-funded research or obtaining an assistant professorship in a college or university. Clinical activities such as assessment, psychotherapy, supervision, and consultation tend not to be the focus of mentoring in these traditional mentoring programs.

As more and more women enter professional fields, there has been increasing interest in gender differences in mentoring. Although male and fe-

male graduate students are mentored at about the same rate (Johnson & Huwe, 2003), there are gender-specific issues related to mentoring.

Gender-Specific Issues

According to Fassinger and Hensler-McGinnis (2005), women are likely to experience the psychosocial functions of mentoring, whereas men are more likely to experience the career functions of mentoring. The researchers reported further that women tended to experience difficult mentoring relationships with men that involve sexual harassment and exclusion from the mentor's professional network.

If modeling and experience base are germane to mentoring, what role does gender play in how this takes place in the mentoring relationship? A female student can certainly learn from a male mentor's field experience but will not be able to align with this experience in terms of gender. In fact, female professionals and students experience many situations that their male counterparts do not. Some authors have addressed these areas, which range from sexual harassment issues to a failure on the part of male mentors to understand the life and career concerns of female protégées (Gilbert, 1985; Gilbert & Rossman, 1992; Gutek, 1989; Kitchener, 1989; Ragins, 1997; Ragins & Cotton, 1999).

Ragins and Cotton (1999) examined mentor functions and outcomes and compared men and women in formal and informal mentoring relationships. These authors found that same gender relationships allowed women to become more involved in social activities with their mentors. This is important because the role modeling for women is not strictly for the purpose of career advancement and to gain field expertise, but is also about how to integrate family and work life for maximum productivity and satisfaction in both areas. Traditionally, this is not something that male students have articulated as a felt need in their mentoring relationships.

The unique concerns of female students call for a thoughtful and tailored approach by the mentor. However, despite the origin of the word *mentor* as defined in Greek mythology (Athene, the daughter of Zeus who becomes Mentes the warrior and advises Telemachus), contemporary models of mentoring are based on a male mentor and male protégé relationship. Furthermore, the research tools and methods employed to study the mentoring relationship "were developed by men, for men . . . in honour of men's ways of knowing" (DeMarco, 1993, p. 1247). Therefore, it is not surprising that women may not have had their mentoring needs properly assessed, let alone met in the traditional mentoring relationship model. Several authors have noted that the traditional mentoring relationship may not meet the needs of women as well as it has met the needs of men (Chandler, 1996; Gilbert, 1985; Johnson, 2003; McGowen & Hart, 1990). In fact, Johnson (2003) pointed out that

women prefer a more relational style of mentoring with attention given to issues not usually addressed in the traditional model, such as how to weave together professional and personal roles.

There are limitations with traditional models of mentoring when applied to women. The field of psychology has made a marked demographic shift in regard to a higher percentage of women seeking graduate degrees in psychology. The doctoral degrees in psychology awarded to women rose from 32% in 1975 to 71% in 2005 (American Psychological Association [APA] Education Directorate, Board of Educational Affairs, 2007), yet those female faculty in a position to mentor are typically not in the higher academic ranks, nor available because of other professional responsibilities. It is still the case that women are required to conform to the traditional male model in academia regardless of their personal roles. This model originated from a family-free culture (monastery) and is still today organized around a non-primary care–giving male lifestyle.

There is heightened awareness that traditional models of mentoring are not adequate to meet the personal and professional needs of female students. Mentoring women who now account for more than two thirds of graduate students in clinical programs is a specific interest of professional schools.

Meeting the Needs of Female Students

The female student population in professional psychology (in which more female professors are represented than in traditional programs) has experienced the benefits of the NCSPP legacy and, the authors hope, will in turn train and mentor their students in like ways. In addition, male students in NCSPP programs have also been exposed to a different way of interacting with women, both within their own student bodies and with faculty. As with the female students, this interaction creates a new schema for how women can function effectively as coprofessionals with these men.

Gilbert and Rossman (1992) suggested that when men mentor women, they should strive to create a relationship in which the woman feels empowered and has a sense of being sponsored and that helps the woman create a professional identity. Given that most mentors in the academic setting (especially those of higher rank) are men, these findings are helpful in facilitating successful mentoring relationships between male mentors and female students. Unfortunately, and as mentioned earlier, it is impossible for a male mentor to model for female students what it looks like to be a professional woman. Therefore, the need for female mentors to provide the context for what it means to be a female professional still exists.

Female mentors willing to open their lives and homes to female students as an in vivo modeling of the interweaving of different roles (e.g., mother, wife, professor, scholar) is invaluable. As female students witness the blending of roles by their female professors they are then able to envision

such realities for themselves. This demonstration serves to instill the belief that "competent, achieving women can have successful personal lives" (Deweese, 2004, p. 19).

Another important role of the successful female mentor is to allow the female student a window into the difficulties that may arise in the weaving of different roles. It is helpful to model that there is no perfect balance that is sought after and attained. It is more accurate to convey that balance is an elusive and defeating mind-set. Although most duties in academia allow for women to be flexible with their schedules in order to meet family needs, on any given day the balance can be upset. This type of role conflict is typically unique to women, for example, when a female professor is scheduled to chair a final oral defense for a student and is suddenly presented that morning with her young child's earache and need for her (mom's) care. This dilemma does not typically arise for men in the academy. Even if their wives work, it is typically the expectation (and heartfelt desire) of the mother to rearrange her schedule to nurse a sick child.

As discussed earlier, the fact that women are typically primary caregivers for both children and aging parents necessitates a blending of roles that is unique to women (Hall, Anderson, & Willingham, 2004). Research supports the idea that if women have both practical and emotional support, they will experience greater levels of self-esteem and a decrease in anxiety and depression (Klein, Hyde, Essex, & Clark, 1998).

Mental labor is another concept that has been identified with how women experience the management of multiple roles. Walzer (1996) investigated divisions of infant care between mother and father and found that the mother did the majority of worrying, preparing intellectually, and managing in order to meet the infant's needs. She termed this intellectual tasking *mental labor*. Extrapolating from Walzer's work, it is reasonable to assume that by providing mentors who are familiar with the realities and pressures the new female professional might encounter as she weaves together her roles, a graduate program or work environment will help alleviate some of her mental labor and anxiety. Not all places of employment are aware of the difficulties in weaving roles together, nor do they rise to the occasion when given the opportunity.

Discussing these types of situations with female graduate students and including the decisions that in retrospect were not the most helpful is valuable in communicating to the student that there is no right decision, just the next best decision given the current circumstances. Women faculty who model these experiences of internal tensions (guilt, sense of duty) and external tensions (faculty responsibilities) provide female students with a more realistic picture of what the weaving of roles entails. By watching and learning from female mentors these female students are also able to project themselves into similar situations and mentally experiment with how they would respond.

MENTORING AND THE NCSPP MODEL

Ward, Johnson, and Campbell (2004) noted several differences between traditional PhD scientist–practitioner clinical programs and professional school programs that typically award the PsyD degree. For one, traditional programs often exist in large university systems that continue to reward faculty with promotion and tenure on the basis of research productivity rather than on that of clinical supervision or mentoring professional development in clinical activities. Another difference is that professional program graduates see themselves as practitioners (Hershey, Kopplin, & Cornell, 1991), whereas scientist–practitioner program faculty often express little interest in clinical practice (Himelein & Putnam, 2001). Furthermore, students in PsyD programs may have to deal with economic pressures, including high tuition, outside work, and escalating student loans, that interfere with the development of traditional mentoring relationships. The economic pressure is obvious in that PsyD graduates have nearly twice the debt load related to doctoral training compared with PhD graduates (APA Education Directorate, Board of Educational Affairs, 2007).

The NCSPP model of training has implications for mentoring. Unlike the traditional mentoring model that emphasizes one long-term relationship with a professor who initiated the protégé into the profession by individual research supervision and networking with other colleagues, the NCSPP model requires a breadth of personal, interpersonal, and professional skills. It is unlikely that all of these skills will be found within one significant relationship. Mentoring within the NCSPP model calls for mentoring relationships with multiple faculty members and supervisors. Since the goal is not focused on research, writing, or teaching, the roles of the mentors are expanded. Groody (2004) described the relevance of mini-mentors in professional training for PsyD students. Her research indicates that mentor–student relationships may not be monolithic in the traditional sense, but rather may involve multiple, intense, and shorter relationships designed to enhance the professional skill of the protégé. Even with the existence of mini-mentors, it is likely that one faculty member will have the primary responsibility for a student's progress through the program as well as his or her overall professional development.

Two significant mentoring relationships in professional psychology training programs are research mentors and clinical mentors (usually practicum and internship supervisors). Some programs use advisors separately from the research mentor role, but often the advisor and research mentor roles are combined as they are in more traditional mentoring model programs. Whereas the research in traditional programs is likely to be experimental or nomothetic in nature, the research projects of professional programs are likely to involve case studies, program evaluations, or qualitative research (Peterson, Peterson, Abrams, & Stricker, 1997).

Clinical mentors may be practicum and internship supervisors. Relationships with supervisors often go beyond assurance that appropriate inter-

ventions are provided to clients in clinical settings. These relationships may become significant modeling relationships that promote personal as well as professional growth. Since clinical work involves interpersonal skill as well as personal qualities such as patience, tolerance of perspectives, and appreciation of diversity, professional development under the direction of a supervisor has significant meaning for personal growth.

Primary goals of professional psychology training programs are to produce graduates who function clinically with broad applied skills, so the focus on research mentoring is obviously attenuated when compared with more traditional scientist–practitioner programs. Elman, Illfelder-Kaye, and Robiner (2005) described *professional development* as a key process in developing professionalism in graduate psychology programs. Professional development, they asserted, is based on two fundamental components—interpersonal functioning and thinking like a psychologist (critical thinking). Mentoring in professional school programs likely has professional development as the overarching goal of mentoring relationships rather than research productivity, which seems to be a primary goal of scientist–practitioner programs.

As part of its mission, NCSPP has identified nontraditional students (e.g., women, minorities, older students) as valuable and important contributors to the field of psychology. Those in NCSPP have worked to create graduate programs that allow these groups to achieve graduate training without requiring them to sacrifice their identities and multiple roles. Schools adhering to the NCSPP model of training typically display a sensitivity to the role conflicts that arise and have been proactive in proposing and implementing solutions that allow students to succeed (e.g., half-time internships for women or men with child care or elder care responsibilities).

MATCHING MENTORS AND PROTÉGÉS

One of the most important issues in mentoring is the match between mentor and protégé (Jackson et al., 2003). The intentional structuring of mentoring relationships is one of the best practices in faculty–student mentoring (Campbell, 2007). Like any interpersonal relationship, the match of personality variables and personal interests is important in forming and maintaining the relationship. Huwe and Johnson (2003) provided a list of personality characteristics and behavioral patterns that facilitate mentoring relationships. Qualities such as emotional stability, coachability, emotional intelligence, and commitment to the profession are seen as important elements to consider in mentor matches.

Race and gender also play a significant role in mentor–protégé matches. Race and gender are just two of the many cultural identities that interact with relationship factors to create complexity in the mentoring process (Fassinger & Hensler-McGinnis, 2005). When possible, matching mentors

and protégés on similarity of race, gender, and cultural identity is important in successful mentoring relationships.

CONCLUSION

Mentoring is a significant aspect of education and training in psychology, yet only in the past couple of decades has the role of mentoring been described as such a prominent part of professional development. Professional psychology programs, with the direction and leadership of NCSPP, have advanced and broadened the meaning of mentoring beyond that typically seen in research-oriented training programs. Particular attention has been given to including those who otherwise may be excluded from training, such as women and minorities. An emphasis on mentoring women has been a focus of professional psychology programs. Because NCSPP has a strong record of advocating for the needs of students in training, it is likely that this organization will continue to enhance the mentoring focus in professional education.

REFERENCES

American Psychological Association Education Directorate, Board of Educational Affairs. (2007). *A report on the professional psychology internship match imbalance.* Washington, DC: Author.

Atkinson, D. R., Casas, A., & Neville, H. (1994). Ethnic minority psychologists: Whom they mentor and benefits they derive from the process. *Journal of Multicultural Counseling and Development, 22,* 37–48.

Cameron, S. W. & Blackburn, R. T. (1981). Sponsorship and academic career success. *Journal of Higher Education, 52,* 369–377.

Campbell, C. D. (2007). Best practices for student–faculty mentoring programs. In T. D. Allen & L. T. Eby (Eds.), *The handbook of mentoring: A multiple perspective approach* (pp. 325–343. Malden, MA: Blackwell Publishing.

Chandler, C. (1996). Mentoring and women in academia: Reevaluating the traditional model. *NWSA Journal, 8,* 79–100.

Clark, R. A., Harden, S. L., & Johnson, W. B. (2000). Mentor relationships in clinical psychology doctoral training: Results of a national survey. *Teaching of Psychology, 27,* 262–268.

Cronan-Hillix, T., Gensheimer, L. K., Cronan-Hillix, W. A., & Davidson, W. S. (1986). Student's views of mentors in psychology graduate training. *Teaching of Psychology, 13,* 123–127.

DeMarco, R. (1993). Mentorship: A feminist critique of current research. *Journal of Advanced Nursing, 18,* 1242–1250.

Deweese, E. J. (2004). *A qualitative study of the mentoring relationships of Christian women in academia.* Unpublished doctoral dissertation, Rosemead School of Psychology, Biola University, La Mirada, CA.

Elman, N. S., Illfelder-Kaye, J., & Robiner, W. N. (2005). Professional development: Training for professionalism as a foundation for competent practice in psychology. *Professional Psychology: Research and Practice, 36,* 367–375.

Fassinger, R. E. & Hensler-McGinnis, N. F. (2005). Multicultural feminist mentoring as individual and small-group pedagogy. In C. Z. Enns & A. L. Sinacore (Eds.), *Teaching and social justice: Integrating multicultural and feminist theories in the classroom* (pp. 143–161). Washington, DC: American Psychological Association.

Gilbert, L. A. (1985). Dimensions of same-gender student-faculty role-model relationships. *Sex Roles, 12,* 111–123.

Gilbert, L. A., & Rossman, K. M. (1992). Gender and the mentoring process for women: Implications for professional development. *Professional Psychology: Research and Practice, 23,* 233–238.

Groody, A. (2004). Mini-mentors: Differences in mentoring between PsyD and PhD psychology doctoral students. *Dissertation Abstracts International: Section B: The Sciences and Engineering, 64*(10-B), 5199.

Gutek, B. A. (1989, March). *Sexual harassment: A source of stress for employed women.* Paper presented at the Radcliffe Conference on Women in the 21st Century, Cambridge, MA.

Hall, M. E. L., Anderson, T. L., & Willingham, M. M. (2004). Diapers, dissertations, and other holy things: The experiences of mothers working in Christian colleges and universities. *Christian Higher Education, 3,* 41–60.

Hershey, J. M., Kopplin, D. A., & Cornell, J. E. (1991). Doctors of psychology: Their career experiences and attitudes toward degree and training. *Professional Psychology: Research and Practice, 22,* 351–356.

Himelein, M. J., & Putnam, E. A. (2001). Work activities of academic clinical psychologists: Do they practice what they teach? *Professional Psychology: Research and Practice, 32,* 537–542.

Huwe, J. M., & Johnson, W. B. (2003). On being an excellent protégé: What graduate students need to know. *Journal of College Student Psychotherapy, 17,* 41–57.

Jackson, V. A., Palepu, A., Szalacha, L., Caswell, C., Carr, P. L., & Inui, T. (2003). Having the right chemistry: A qualitative study of mentoring in academic medicine. *Academic Medicine, 78,* 328–334.

Jacobi, M. (1991). Mentoring and undergraduate academic success: A literature review. *Review of Educational Research, 61,* 505–532.

Johnson, W. B. (2002). The intentional mentor: Strategies and guidelines for the practice of mentoring. *Professional Psychology: Research and Practice, 33,* 88–96.

Johnson, W. B. (2003). A framework for conceptualizing competence to mentor. *Ethics & Behavior, 13,* 127–151.

Johnson, W. B., & Huwe, J. M. (2003). *Getting mentored in graduate school.* Washington, DC: American Psychological Association.

Johnson, W. B., Koch, C., Fallow, G. O., & Huwe, J. M. (2000). Prevalence of mentoring in clinical versus experimental doctoral programs: Survey findings, implications and recommendations. *Psychotherapy, 37,* 325–334.

Kitchener, K. S. (1989, August). *Unethical practices with students: Destroying the myths.* Paper presented at the annual meeting of the American Psychological Association, New Orleans, LA.

Klein, M. H., Hyde, J. S., Essex, M. J., & Clark, R. (1998). Maternity leave, role quality, work involvement, and mental health one year after delivery. *Psychology of Women Quarterly, 22,* 239–266.

Kram, K. E. (1985). *Mentoring at work: Developmental relationships in organizational life.* Glenview, IL: Scott Foresman.

Kram, K. E. (1988). *Mentoring at work: Developmental relationships in organizational life.* Lanham, MD: University Press of America.

McGowen, K. R., & Hart, L. E. (1990). Still different after all these years: Gender differences in professional identity formation. *Professional Psychology: Research and Practice, 21,* 118–123.

Mintz, L. B., Bartels, K. M., & Rideout, C. A. (1995). Training in counseling ethnic minorities and race-based availability of graduate school resources. *Professional Psychology: Research and Practice, 26,* 316–321.

Peterson, R. L., Peterson, D. R., Abrams, J. C., & Stricker, G. (1997). The National Council of School and Programs of Professional Psychology educational model. *Professional Psychology: Research and Practice, 28,* 373–386.

Ragins, B. R. (1997). Diversified mentoring relationships in organizations: A power perspective. *Academy of Management Review, 22,* 482–521.

Ragins, B. R., & Cotton, J. L. (1999). Mentor functions and outcomes: A comparison of men and women in formal and informal mentoring relationships. *Journal of Applied Psychology, 84,* 529–550.

Reskin, B. F. (1979). Academic sponsorship and scientists' careers. *Sociology of Education, 52,* 129–146.

Sanders, J. M., & Wong, H. Y. (1985). Graduate training and initial job placement. *Sociological Inquiry, 55,* 154–169.

Walzer, S. (1996). Thinking about the baby: Gender and divisions of infant care. *Social Problems, 43*(2), 219–234.

Ward, Y. L., Johnson, W. B., & Campbell, C. D. (2004). Practitioner research vertical teams: A model for mentoring in practitioner-focused doctoral programs. *The Clinical Supervisor, 23,* 179–190.

15

FACULTY AND ADMINISTRATORS IN PROFESSIONAL PSYCHOLOGY PROGRAMS: CHARACTERISTICS, ROLES, AND CHALLENGES

MARY BETH KENKEL AND RAYMOND E. CROSSMAN

The model of professional psychology education, as described in this volume, is a comprehensive guide for those involved in professional training. But it takes much effort to make that guiding model a reality. Faculty and administrators of professional programs have the hard, yet rewarding, work of implementing the model. To do so effectively, they must understand and espouse the model, be vocal champions for it, and navigate the considerable challenges that arise in implementing it. This chapter describes the characteristics and roles of faculty and administrators in professional programs and the challenges they face as educators of future professional psychologists.

ROLE OF FACULTY IN PROFESSIONAL
PSYCHOLOGY PROGRAMS

Although faculty in professional programs have many of the same characteristics and responsibilities as other psychology graduate faculty, they evi-

dence some differences. In a 2006 National Council of Schools and Programs of Professional Psychology (NCSPP) self-study of its members, NCSPP programs, as compared with American Psychological Association (APA)–accredited PhD programs not in NCSPP, have more female faculty (44% vs. 38%) and also more female faculty at the rank of professor (33% vs. 25%). In addition, non-Caucasians constitute a greater percentage of faculty at NCSPP programs compared with APA-accredited (non-NCSPP) PhD programs (14% vs. 10%) and a greater percentage at each rank (for more information about this NCSPP self-study, see the NCSPP Web site at http://www.ncspp.info/resources.htm#self). Norcross, Castle, Sayette, and Mayne (2004) found PsyD faculty had theoretical orientations that were primarily cognitive–behavioral (33%), psychodynamic (29%), or systems-oriented (19%), and lesser percentages held humanistic/phenomenological (11%) or applied behavioral/radical behavioral (8%) perspectives. PsyD programs and those PhD programs with an equal emphasis on research and practice differed from research-oriented PhD programs in having lesser percentages of cognitive–behavioral faculty and greater percentages of psychodynamic and humanistic faculty. These findings suggest a greater diversity in composition and orientation among professional program faculty and reflect a correspondence with the educational model's emphasis on a broad and inclusive education for students.

Like most faculty in higher education, professional program faculty have three major roles: teaching, scholarship, and service. However, in contrast to the primary emphasis on faculty research in most traditional doctoral programs, professional programs typically stress the primacy of faculty's teaching role and the duties associated with it, such as clinical supervision, supervision of doctoral research projects, evaluating clinical qualifying exams, advising, and mentoring. Professional program faculty are very aware of the heavy responsibility they have to ensure that their graduates are prepared to deliver psychological services in a knowledgeable, skilled, and ethical manner. Great good will come from skilled practitioners; great harm from the incompetent ones. This certainty is ever present in the minds of faculty in professional programs. Why? Because most faculty in professional programs are themselves clinical or counseling psychologists and many continue to be engaged in the real world of practice. In doing so, they see firsthand the good and the bad, the competent and incompetent; these experiences and their cautions inform and energize their teaching.

Faculty of professional programs are typically there because they have great respect for the work of practicing psychologists and a strong commitment to prepare students well for it. The preceding chapters in this book describe the pedagogies and innovative methods used in professional education. Faculty not only demonstrate currency in the science and practice of psychology but also demonstrate attention to, and excitement about, future trends in the practice. In doing so, faculty serve as excellent models and mentors for students.

One defining role for faculty in professional education in psychology is ensuring that students attain the professional competencies outlined in the educational model (see Part II, this volume). Competency-based education requires a coordinated and deliberate approach among faculty to determine how each competency will be learned and evaluated in the curriculum (e.g. through a course, practicum, project). Doing so requires significant interdependence among faculty to ensure the planned and sequential acquisition of knowledge and skills. New learning must be built upon groundwork laid by others. Faculty must be willing to curtail some of their individual preferences in course material and in evaluative procedures (e.g., clinical comprehensives) to ensure that students receive a coherent, comprehensive, and developmental preparation for professional practice.

Faculty scholarship has some unique aspects in professional psychology programs. Although there is considerable diversity among scholarship goals and activities among professional schools, many professional programs, especially those housed within schools of psychology, define *scholarship* broadly, similar to the dimensions outlined by the Boyer (1990) report on Scholarship Reconsidered. Boyer, challenging higher education to move beyond a narrow meaning of scholarship, proposed four interrelated dimensions of scholarship: discovery, integration, application, and teaching. Later, Boyer (1996) expanded the definition to include the scholarship of engagement that regards service as scholarship when it requires the use of one's disciplinary knowledge. R. L. Peterson and Trierweiler (1999) likewise called for a broader, more flexible vision of scholarship in psychology that emphasizes the study of pedagogy, applied research that benefits psychological practice and/or the larger community (D. R. Peterson, 1996), and integrative scholarship involving creative review and synthesis of knowledge and linking it to practice. These definitions of scholarship fit well with the mission and goals of professional programs. This type of research would go far to bridging the gap between research and practice so often described in our psychological literature. Who better to do so than professional program faculty who have a foot in each setting? Even though professional school students clearly are more interested in clinical, rather than research, activities, they do become engaged and excited about applied research that answers pertinent clinical practice questions and are eager to join research teams investigating clinical issues. Some of the more productive scholars in professional programs coalesce their teaching, supervision, research, and outside practice around particular clinical topics. Others have correctly realized that there is much interest in the study of teaching and learning in professional psychology, as exemplified by the establishment of the new journal *Training and Education in Professional Psychology*. Professional program faculty should be filling that journal with ideas and examples of their teaching and training methods and their views on professional education and practice issues. The chapters in this volume provide ample evidence that they have much to share.

ROLE OF ADMINISTRATORS IN PROFESSIONAL PSYCHOLOGY PROGRAMS

Professional psychology programs vary in size and scale and reside in a number of different organizational settings. Most professional programs are within universities, either comprehensive universities or multicampus universities focused mostly on professional education. Within the university setting, many programs are housed in separate schools of psychology. Fewer programs are in independent schools of psychology. A few programs are located in traditional psychology departments, mainly within small liberal arts colleges. Because of this variety in organizational setting, the head administrator of a professional psychology program may be variously called a director of clinical training, a program chair, a department head, or a dean. Along with the head administrator may be others with major administrative functions, for example, overseeing practicum placement and evaluation or directing the psychological services center. In some educational settings, the upper administration is fully aware of, and completely dedicated to, professional psychology education, whereas in other settings, the professional psychology program is just one of several graduate programs, each vying for resources. Because this diversity makes it difficult for professional programs to have clear referents for organizational issues, the head administrator in each case assumes a number of important roles. These include the internal roles of leading and managing the program and negotiating program issues within the university (or organizational system) and the external roles, which are shared with faculty, of representing and advocating for the program with local communities and with national associations and bodies.

The most important role of the academic head of a professional psychology program is to be the leader of the program. What does this entail? Most critical, the leader must develop and articulate a clear vision and mission for the program and ensure that faculty, staff, students, curriculum, and resources are aligned with that vision. The power of that vision to motivate action and produce high morale cannot be overstated. A strong vision is needed to counteract the greatly independent stance and highly valued autonomy of the academician. Professional programs require significant interdependence among faculty. The program's leader must guide them into working together.

In addition, a strong vision and mission are needed to propel faculty to continuously make curriculum changes that incorporate new issues and practices within the behavioral health field. Administrators must keep a constant eye on the outside world of psychology services as well as on the research literature on best practices in psychology to keep programs current and responsible in their efforts to prepare students for professional careers. Then, administrators must create the appropriate organizational structures and climates (Durlak & Dupre, 2008) to promote the adoption of new edu-

cational practices and promote inclusion and cultural sensitivity (see chap. 10, this volume). Therefore, first and foremost, the administrator must articulate the common goals and actions needed to reach the program's vision and mission and the benefits that all (students, faculty, the program, society) will derive from attaining that vision.

Within the program, the administrator must be not only a leader but also a manager. Managing requires deploying resources and putting the structures in place to reach the program's goals. Administrators might find that traditional policies, procedures, and practices of psychology departments or universities do not quite fit the needs of the professional psychology program. The differences may be due to the singular mission of the professional program, the size of the program, or the particular and desired qualities of the faculty (e.g., part-time practitioner faculty) or students (e.g., post-masters) within the program. These differences require the crafting of new policies or practices as opposed to contorting the program to fit into traditional categories. One example referred to earlier is the broadened view of scholarship that fits so well with some professional programs' missions. Not all universities value or adopt this expanded definition. The administrator may need to lead the charge for a change in the definition of scholarship. As another example, the value and contributions of part-time practitioner faculty are widely acknowledged within professional programs, but these individuals often are relegated to adjunct faculty by universities and accrediting bodies. However, several programs began to distinguish these faculty who had ongoing and substantial contributions to the program by the designation *core faculty* and to provide them with rights and responsibilities of full-time faculty. Subsequently, APA's Committee on Accreditation adopted definitions of core faculty and *associated program faculty* to distinguish them from adjunct faculty and to acknowledge their substantial and important participation in professional programs (APA Commission on Accreditation, 2007, IR C-18).

Determining faculty workload is another place where differences between professional and traditional programs may become apparent. Compared with faculty in research-oriented programs, professional program faculty may be more involved in the clinical supervision of students, intensive evaluation of clinical competence through such procedures as clinical qualifying exams and visiting and evaluating external practicum sites. These activities, which are at the crux of the education in professional programs, need to be acknowledged and compensated in workload assignments and not relegated to a catchall (and largely unrecognized) designation of "other" departmental service duties.

Professional program administrators also must represent and advocate for the program within the larger organizational system, typically the university. Administrators must forcefully describe the key characteristics of professional education and how the training might require new or different types of resources and accommodations. The distinguishing characteristic, of course,

is the increased emphasis on clinical training and the resources required to provide high-quality training, such as close faculty supervision (that should be appropriately recognized in workload assignments), an on-campus training clinic (which requires space, a director, supervisors, and clients), or off-campus practicum sites with doctoral-level supervision and faculty oversight. Along with this comes the potential for different sources of graduate student funding—through the delivery of clinical services. This can augment funding that comes from teaching and research assistantships for students and can lead the program to seek contracts using faculty and students to deliver these services.

In summary, the administrator of a professional program needs to ensure that the program's resources and policies, including those governing faculty selection, retention, promotion, and assignment, are aligned with, and support, the program's mission and goals. In carrying out their roles, faculty and administrators must deal with a number of challenges. These are discussed next.

CHALLENGES FOR FACULTY AND ADMINISTRATORS

Faculty and administrators of professional programs take on the weighty responsibility of preparing the next generation of psychology practitioners. In carrying out this responsibility, faculty and administrators strive to model professional psychology at its best. However, in doing so, faculty and administrators are challenged to reflect on their own attitudes, behavior, and impact on the training program. Some of the key challenges are presented next.

Walking the Talk

Professional psychology faculty are foremost excellent teachers and skilled practitioners who draw on their own professional practice to mentor and model for a changing profession. Compared with PhD programs, PsyD programs are more likely to require faculty candidates to be licensed prior to employment or soon after hiring. Professional programs require and encourage licensure so faculty can serve as better role models for students, maintain their professional identity and credibility, and engage in the clinical work, such as supervision, associated with the training program (DiLillo, DeGue, Cohen, & Morgan, 2006).

However, until recently, when more PsyDs have joined professional schools' faculties, most faculty have not come from professional psychology programs. Their clinical education most likely has not been as comprehensive as that described in the professional model. In addition, over time, ideas about the required knowledge, attitudes, and skills needed for competent practice have evolved. The challenge is, Have individual faculty, adminis-

trators, and programs grown and evolved as well? One of the model's core competencies is on diversity issues, requiring an understanding of individual and cultural differences and the ability to provide culturally competent services. With all the recent knowledge in this area, have all faculty and administrators advanced their understanding of diversity issues and has the program provided opportunities for them to do so? The model calls for lifelong learning and responsiveness to social issues. Is that reflected in course syllabi? Are new practice developments and clinical and social issues reflected in the program's curriculum? The importance of social responsibility and advocacy on behalf of marginalized groups are also emphasized. Are faculty, administrators, and the program active in community and national social issues? The model stresses a number of attitudes that are hallmarks of professional psychologists—disciplined inquiry, reflective practice, intellectual curiosity and flexibility, and personal integrity. Are these attitudes apparent in classroom discussions, as well as in faculty meeting deliberations, administrators' communications, and hallway conversations?

The professional psychology educational model sets out a tall order not only for students but also for the faculty and administrators. As role models, faculty and administrators must be ever vigilant to walk the talk.

When Advising Isn't Fun

One of the most rewarding aspects of academic life is the contact with students—teaching, supervising, advising, and mentoring. That is, until you encounter a student who is not progressing or is showing behaviors or attitudes vastly discrepant with desired professional behavior. An extremely important, but almost universally dreaded, responsibility of faculty members and administrators is to provide feedback and correction to students who are performing poorly. An important aspect of professional training is developing professional skills and attitudes through the feedback process. However, many faculty and administrators are reluctant to deliver feedback to students about poor clinical suitability and performance. This becomes even more difficult when there are concerns about a student's character and fitness for the field (Johnson & Campbell, 2004), that is, questions about a student's honesty, integrity, judgment, emotional stability, or substance use. Although clinical training directors believe that it is a responsibility of graduate program to ensure graduates' fitness and soundness for the field (Johnson & Campbell, 2004), few protocols have been developed for dealing with such student issues (Forrest, Elman, Gizara, & Vacha-Haase, 1999). Moreover, faculty and administrators might ignore, minimize, or excuse problematic behaviors in a misguided attempt to be supportive of students or because of their own discomfort with giving negative feedback, because they are concerned about being seen as the bad guy, or because they have confused a therapeutic role with an educational role.

Clearly, students' professional behavior, conduct, and integrity are areas of central concern in the education of professional psychologists. Therefore, faculty and administrators need to deal with the issues early on in students' training. Annual evaluations, if done thoroughly, are one way to address the concerns, but nothing can replace immediate feedback from a firm yet supportive faculty advisor once an issue is raised. Faculty and students alike will be aided by clear policies and procedures defining the program's values, standards for professional behavior, and the necessity for adherence to APA Ethical Standards and Principles. In that way, students understand what is expected, and faculty can refer to policies when identifying problematic behavior. In addition, there should be clear policies and procedures for handling alleged ethical violations, professional misbehaviors, impairment, grievances, and interpersonal conflicts. At the same time, supports and guides for students should be built into the program. These include ways for students to access personal therapy, to request medical or family leave, to deal with classmates' problematic behavior, and to resolve conflicts with faculty or staff.

Beyond the Ivory Tower

With all the internal demands on program faculty and administrators, it may seem foolhardy to suggest additional external duties. However, the necessity for these external roles is both pragmatic and principled. Pragmatically, a quality professional program cannot exist without strong ties to the local community. The community is a rich source of practicum sites, practitioner adjunct faculty, guest speakers, contracts for clinical services, applied research projects, consultation contracts, collaborative clinical and educational ventures, continuing education participants, and potential clients for the on-campus clinic. However, to tap into these resources, the faculty and administrators need to know who and where they are, and the community needs to know the capabilities and personnel of the academic program. Nothing supplants just getting to know the community and the many individuals committed to improving it. Although it is not uncommon for the faculty and administrators to have ongoing contact with other psychology and mental health professionals in the area, they should expand that network to include those in the social service, health, educational, and law and criminal justice fields as well as state and federal legislators. All have needs that can be effectively addressed by an expanded application of psychological interventions, but often they do not know it yet. And they, in turn, have resources that could benefit our students and programs. Our role is to educate them on how we can work together to better the community.

The external roles of faculties and administrators extend beyond the local community to the broader profession of psychology. Representing one's own program and professional programs in general to national psychological associations is critical to ensuring greater knowledge and regard for profes-

sional education. Professional programs were at the forefront in employing a competence training model, in developing training collaborations with physicians and nurses, in offering joint programs with business and law, in developing comprehensive training clinics, in using multiple means for assessing clinical competence, and in developing innovative internships. The NCSPP has facilitated the sharing of these ideas and best practices with member schools, and the broader psychology community could benefit from these ideas as well. Faculty and administrators of professional programs too long have been content to speak to our own kind—those with common views and activities—and neglect participation with psychology groups with more diverse or contentious opinions about professional training. However, the reality is that if the faculty and administrators do not let people know what they are doing, then ignorance and misinformation persist. To garner recognition and respect for professional psychology programs, students, and graduates, the faculty and administrators need to educate others about the professional training model, about programs' innovations and achievements, and about faculty's and students' talents and accomplishments. Therefore, greater numbers of professional program faculty and administrators must participate and seek leadership positions in APA committees and divisions, journal editorial boards, accreditation teams, state psychological associations, and licensing boards. Such participation will help to eradicate myths about professional schools (Norcross et al., 2004), to educate others about professional training, and to advance a psychology profession consistent with the professional training model's values and aspirations.

CONCLUSION: ONE LAST ROLE

One last role remains for the faculty and administrators of professional psychology programs. As designers and leaders of the program, they need to have a vision of professional psychology's future and to develop the contacts and resources for educating students for that future. Just one of the major directions for professional psychology is a fuller realization of its role as a health profession. It seems likely that over time, psychological care will become integrated with other health care services in a seamless and collaborative arrangement (Kenkel, DeLeon, Mantell, & Steep, 2005). Close working relationships will develop among psychologists, physicians, nurses, and other allied health professions, and behavioral and physical health care will be seen as inseparable. For this future, psychology program faculty and administrators should be well aware of the trends and issues facing health care and health professional training and be prepared to incorporate relevant material into the curriculum. Staying abreast of developments in medicine and nursing and making contacts with those professional associations distinguish the visionary programs from the rest.

Beyond these pragmatic concerns are principled reasons for professional program educators to make external contacts and collaborations both locally and nationally. Social responsibility is a central tenet of the professional psychology educational model (Kenkel, DeLeon, Albino, & Porter, 2003). D. R. Peterson (1996) spoke compellingly of professional psychology's central responsibility to deal with the fundamental needs of society. We believe that professional psychology programs also bear that responsibility. Speaking about Canadian medical colleges, Dr. Jean Parboosingh stated that

> the medical schools of the future will need to formally address not only their roles in education and research but also their social roles in the community . . . [For students] to understand their broader social roles, they need to see them demonstrated by their medical schools and deans and by their universities. Medical schools need to be socially accountable. The World Health Organization has defined the social accountability of medical schools as the obligation to direct their education, research, and service activities towards addressing the priority health concerns of the community, region, and/or nation they have a mandate to serve. (Hawkins, 2003, p. 852)

The authors' belief is that professional programs of psychology have similar social contracts to fulfill. The mission statement of each professional psychology program should include such aims. Only through active involvement with the community will programs discover priority needs and know how to design education, research, and service programs that address them. We have much to learn and share.

REFERENCES

American Psychological Association Commission on Accreditation (2007). *Policy statements and implementing regulations*. Washington, DC: American Psychological Association.

Boyer, E. (1990). *Scholarship reconsidered: Priorities of the professoriate*. Princeton, NJ: The Carnegie Foundation for the Advancement of Teaching.

Boyer, E. (1996). The scholarship of engagement. *Journal of Public Outreach, 1*, 11–20.

DiLillo, D., DeGue, S., Cohen, L. M., & Morgan, R. D. (2006). The path to licensure for academic psychologists: How tough is the road? *Professional Psychology: Research and Practice, 37*, 567–586.

Durlak, J. A. & DuPre, E. P. (2008). Implementation matters: A review of research on the influence of implementation on program outcomes and the factors affecting implementation. *American Journal of Community Psychology, 41*, 327–350.

Forrest, L., Elman, N., Gizara, S., & Vacha-Haase, T. (1999). Trainee impairment: A review of identification, remediation, dismissal, and legal issues. *The Counseling Psychologist, 27*, 627–686.

Hawkins, D. (2003). Medical schools' social contract: More than just education and research. *Canadian Medical Association Journal, 168,* 852.

Johnson, W. B., & Campbell, C. D. (2004). Character and fitness requirements for professional psychologists: Training directors' perspectives. *Professional Psychology: Research and Practice, 35,* 405–411.

Kenkel, M. B., DeLeon, P. H., Albino, J. E., & Porter, N. (2003). Challenges to professional education in the 21st century: Response to Peterson. *American Psychologist, 58,* 801–805.

Kenkel, M. B., DeLeon, P. H., Mantell, E. O., & Steep, A. E. (2005). Divided no more: Psychology's role in integrated health care. *Canadian Psychology/Psychologie Canadienne, 46,* 189–202.

Norcross, J. C., Castle, P. H., Sayette, M. A., & Mayne, T. J. (2004). The PsyD: Heterogeneity in practitioner training. *Professional Psychology: Research and Practice, 35,* 412–419.

Peterson, D. R. (1996). Making psychology indispensable. *Applied and Preventive Psychology, 5,* 1–8.

Peterson, R. L., & Trierweiler, S. J. (1999). Scholarship in psychology: The advantages of an expanded vision. *American Psychologist, 54,* 350–55.

IV

CONCLUSION

16

THE FUTURE OF THE PROFESSIONAL PSYCHOLOGY EDUCATIONAL MODEL

MARY BETH KENKEL

This is the final chapter in this book on the educational model for professional psychology, yet it is simply a high point on the road toward further development of the model itself. No model of education can remain static and still be relevant to new challenges and advancements. Here is what the future looks like from here.

First, current components of the model need to be further developed. As described in preceding chapters, some aspects of the model, such as consultation and education and supervision and management, still get short shrift in most programs even though those activities constitute a large portion of graduates' careers. Ways to incorporate these missing elements into the curriculum need to be explored. For the research and evaluation competency, the aim, scope, and evaluation of the culminating research project (i.e., the dissertation, clinical dissertation, doctoral research project) still show considerable variation across programs, though this variety may in fact be positive. A reexamination of the process and outcomes of the research project and its connection with future practice is overdue. In addition, although progress has been made, much more work is needed to prepare students for the diverse clients whom they will serve. Given the changing client demo-

graphics in this country and abroad and psychologists' outreach to new populations, this competency will need constant updating. Furthermore, we need more measures and improved ways to assess students' competencies and to evaluate academic programs' overall effectiveness. With new knowledge, institutional innovations, and the dissemination of best practices, these aspects of the model will evolve over time.

Some aspects of the model need more intentional and intensive development. As illustrated in the preceding chapters, each competency is composed of knowledge, skills, and attitudes (KSAs). At the same time methods for teaching knowledge and skills are becoming more defined, more energy should be directed to finding ways to foster desired attitudes in students. Training programs have been most explicit in targeting the attitudes associated with the diversity competency. For example, Finkel, Storaasli, Bandele, and Schaefer (2003) assessed attitudes toward lesbian, gay, bisexual, and transgender populations as a result of their diversity training. A major part of diversity training is a critical assessment of one's own attitudes toward members of minority and disenfranchised groups and the creation of learning experiences aimed at fostering attitudes associated with positive and facilitative interactions with these individuals.

For attitudes associated with other competencies, the training is not as intentional or direct as it might be. Instead of creating learning experiences that target student attitudes, training programs typically expect attitudinal shifts through the less designed process of *professional socialization*, that is, modeling and reinforcement by professors and supervisors, mentoring, peer interaction, or students' personal psychotherapy. However, because training programs so seldom measure students' attitudes, training directors and faculty really do not know whether attitudes change as a result of these experiences. In fact, in contrast to other aspects of the model, attitudes are the most poorly assessed component. Therefore, training programs continue to rely on the traditional, but unproven, ways of fostering desired attitudes. Unfortunately, this results in a lack of experimentation with new ways of fostering professional attitudes and oftentimes a denouncement of nontraditional means of professional education, such as distance education, part-time education, multiple mentors, or large class sizes, which may include different forms of professional socialization. Therefore, important next steps in the development of the professional psychology educational model are to design educational experiences intentionally focused on attitude change and to incorporate measures of attitudes associated with the different competencies.

Certainly, challenges exist for doing this. For example, self-report measures of professional attitudes are likely to be highly associated with social desirability, as was found with multicultural competence measures (Constantine & Ladany, 2000). Furthermore, while ongoing assessments of students' attitudes are important both to support their professional development and to determine the programs' effectiveness, it is less clear how to

handle students who do not show the desired attitudes by the end of their training (Johnson & Campbell, 2004). However as training programs become more explicit and intentional about fostering attitudes needed for professional practice, best practices for developing and measuring those attitudes will evolve.

Even as these modifications will further the development of the professional psychology education model, they will not be enough. The world does not stand still. The issues and needs of society change; demands for new and different types of education and services emerge; technology brings new advances; government enacts new regulations; and funding sources and levels fluctuate over time. These types of changes will require a constant reevaluation of the model. Over time, what is covered in each competency might expand or be modified. Competencies might be added, combined, or (much less likely) eliminated. There may be a need to change the "typical" curriculum or modify the standard means and methods of teaching, supervising, or evaluation. In this chapter, I describe some of the changes already taking place and point out the potential future areas of change.

The two major forces that will affect the professional psychology educational model and processes are the changing scope and practice of professional psychology and the general trends and changes in U.S. higher education.

Changes in the practice of professional psychology must have an impact on the educational model. Professional programs must be training the psychologist of the future, not the psychologist of the past generation. There is no crystal ball to predict the future, yet professional programs educators must do their best to determine the societal, political, and professional forces affecting behavioral health care and psychology practice. Periodically, an *environmental scan* of the practice of psychology is needed to ensure psychology training is keeping apace with practice innovations.

What is an environmental scan? An environmental scan identifies issues, situations, and trends in the external environment that might pose opportunities, challenges, or changes to an organization or profession. The information gathered from such a scan is useful in guiding the plans and decisions of the organization (Albright, 2004). By using core and adjunct faculty who are active in practice activities, professional psychology programs have a readily available source for quick scans of practice issues. However, on a periodic basis, broader scans are needed.

Fortunately, several resources exist to provide information for these scans. The Association of State and Provincial Psychology Boards, in an effort to keep their licensing exams current, periodically surveys a sample of licensed practitioners about the main activities of their practices and the knowledge areas and responsibilities that they deem of high importance, frequency, and criticality. In the most recent practice analysis (Greenberg & Jesuitus, 2003), respondents rated ethical behaviors very highly on all di-

mensions and also identified knowledge and skills needed in the future. Most frequently cited were

> knowledge regarding the interplay between the mind and body; neurology/biology/genetic determinants; brain functions; affect; and interventions for traumatic care situations; professional skills associated with procedures to integrate medicine into psychology, including working with primary care physicians; procedures to combine aspects of spirituality into therapy; and generic skills, such as obtaining business training in order to run a practice. (p. 2)

These findings are helpful in determining the KSAs that should be added or emphasized more in each competency.

Another resource in conducting environmental scans will be the newly established Center for Psychology Workforce Analysis and Research of the American Psychological Association (APA). The Center will research where psychologists currently work and where they will be needed in the future. The Center plans to conduct environmental scans every 5 years (with annual updates) to determine "the scientific, technical, economic, social, and political trends important to psychology that will provide the context for decisions about need, demand and supply" of psychologists (APA, 2007, p. 15).

Important parts of an environmental scan are surveys of alumni of professional programs. These should be done regularly and aggregated across programs to not only inform educators of the adequacy and quality of their existing programs but also to suggest new practice developments that should be incorporated into the professional training model. For example, graduate surveys are showing that alumni are more frequently assuming management and supervisory roles in clinical settings. Yet, the National Council of Schools and Programs of Professional Psychology's (NCSPP) Self Study (2006; see http://www.ncspp.info/resources.htm#self) showed that while supervision is getting greater attention in programs, most training programs still provide little coverage of management and supervision. Follow-up surveys with alumni about the KSAs needed from them as they entered these management roles would be extremely useful.

Too often, psychologists do not extend their scans beyond psychology or mental health practice. If psychology truly is a health profession, then the scan also must view the trends and issues affecting health care more generally and the training of health care professionals. It is somewhat ironic that when professional psychology was born, the professional school model of the health professions was adopted, but then little else. Part of that divorce was the longtime dichotomy in funding and thinking between services for the body versus the mind. However, that split is healing, and integrated health care is becoming a common part of psychology's lexicon (Kenkel, DeLeon, Mantell, & Steep, 2005).

What would such a scan of health care reveal today? The most pressing forces include issues of cost, access, accountability, changing patient demographics, informed health care consumers, treatment of chronic conditions, heavy reliance on pharmacology, and increased technology use. We must prepare students for practice environments affected by these issues.

Cost and access issues are prompting experimentation with integrated health care, experiments in which physical and behavioral health care are delivered in a highly coordinated manner in the same setting. Some professional psychology programs already are incorporating new aspects into their curriculum to prepare students for this field of practice (Talen, Fraser, & Cauley, 2005). In doing so, the elements of several competencies in the model are being expanded. For example, for the relationship competency, students will need to expand their working relationships beyond the traditional mental health professionals (psychiatrist, social worker, LPC) to developing ones with primary care physicians, nurses and nurse practitioners, and other allied health professionals. They will need to establish rapport quickly with patients seeking medical care, rather than behavioral health care. Assessments may be very brief and targeted as opposed to detailed and comprehensive. The typical intervention with patients may be brief (15–30 minutes) and have a more focused assessment or treatment goal. Competence in consultation and education are very important in this setting. A major part of the psychologist's job will be to consult with the physician and other medical staff on a coordinated treatment plan. The psychologist's skill in doing this is crucial to making the integrated care model work. In addition, the psychologist will often be sought out by the medical staff to provide education on behavioral health issues to both patients and staff, so competence in providing education is essential. Last, in accord with the calls for greater accountability in the health care arena, psychologists must be able to demonstrate the effectiveness of their treatment in improving patients' behavioral health. Therefore, as integrated health care expands and provides more career opportunities for psychologists, several competencies (relationship, assessment, intervention, research, and consultation) in the professional education model also should be expanded. Coursework and/or practicum experiences should incorporate these newer competency elements to prepare students for practice in these settings.

The baby boomers will have an impact on health care in the near future, just as they have had an impact on so many other societal issues and institutions as they have traversed the life span. Already alarms are sounding about the insufficiency of health care providers to deal with the aging baby boomers (Institute of Medicine, 2008). Geriatric health care costs are expected to increase dramatically, as will the demands for extending life. The baby boomer generation was the first generation to be familiar with, use, and have positive attitudes toward mental health care. Therefore, the model's competencies need to be expanded to better prepare students for working

with this aging population; some programs already are doing so (Zweig, Siegel, & Snyder, 2006).

What is evident in the above examples is that while the components of the different competencies might be changed or emphasized more in response to a changing practice environment, that is, the integrated health care setting, the basic seven competencies, and their definitions, remained the same. That is because these competencies define the current scope of practice for clinical psychologists.

However, the time may come when the scope of psychological practice changes so significantly that a new competency must be added to the model or the definition of the current ones substantially changed. The most likely candidate for dramatically changing the scope of practice is the growing efforts to attain prescriptive authority for psychologists. The states that now allow prescriptive authority for psychologists mandate that the training occur postdoctorally. However, some leaders in the field (Tulkin & Stock, 2004) have called for a predoctoral preparation and have prepared a curriculum for doing so. There is considerable opposition to requiring training predoctorally due to concerns about changing the professional identity of psychologists to a more biomedical as opposed to psychosocial orientation and realistic concerns about "not enough room in the curriculum." However, if such a change were adopted and became a part of all training programs, one or more additional competencies would need to be added to the professional model.

While changes in the practice of psychology and health care have an impact on the competencies and their associated KSAs, trends in higher education in the United States will have a bearing on the standards and processes of the professional psychology educational model. What are these trends and issues in higher education? Some key ones are (a) issues of affordability and access, (b) the increasing pressure for accountability throughout the entire educational system (U.S. Department of Education, 2006), (c) the increasing use of technology, particularly distance education, in higher education (Society for College and University Planning, 2007, July), and (d) the internationalization of higher education (Altbach, 2002). These trends will affect the teaching and assessment of professional competencies and the type of students in professional psychology programs.

Within higher education, income disparities are the most significant barrier to access and graduation for all students, although minority students are most affected (Walpole, 2007). "Students are graduating with debts that would astonish the previous generation" (Society for College and University Planning, 2006, p. 1), and students' and parents' concerns about debt affect whether and where students go to college (National Association for College Admission Counseling, 2007). These are ominous trends for professional psychology programs, which, when contrasted with clinical PhD programs, provide less financial aid for students and have students graduating with higher debt loads (Norcross, Castle, Sayette, & Mayne, 2004; Wicherski & Kohout,

2007). The high costs might cause students whose background, values, and educational and career goals make them best suited for professional psychology programs to seek other types of degrees/training or no further education at all. In addition, graduates with huge loans to repay might feel forced to take the best paying employment even though their initial professional goals were infused with social justice and were to work with underserved populations or in other settings that provide less remuneration. There is no easy answer for this problem as the general economic downturn, cuts in state and federal funding, and rising costs are affecting tuition and student financial assistance at all but the most richly endowed universities. However, training programs and professional psychology organizations must do all they can to seek out and advocate for additional sources of funding, for example, through federal initiatives like the Graduate Psychology Education program, Graduate Medical Education program, or the National Health Services Corps, or through community service contracts and grants. The emphasis on advocacy in the educational model (chap. 11, this volume) shows the importance of, and dedication to, these activities.

Whereas many are concerned about costs reducing access to professional psychology training, others (Robiner & Crew, 2000) worry about there being too much access and too many professional psychology students and graduates. Supply and demand issues are raised periodically in connection with internship imbalances, employment opportunities, and psychologists' salaries. As the national economic situation becomes bleaker, with tighter markets, increased unemployment, and budget cutbacks at the federal, state, and local levels, these concerns about psychologist oversupply become more pronounced and evidence of it becomes all too real, for example, too few internships for the students who are seeking them. Recently, there have been calls to examine the larger context of this issue through workforce analysis and to seek multiple solutions (Rozensky, Grus, Belar, Nelson, & Kohout, 2007). Professional psychology programs must be centrally involved in these discussions and problem-solving sessions. For one, they must do their part to develop and foster resources for training their students, such as developing new practica and internships. Innovative ways of doing this are described in chapter 12, this volume, on clinical training and chapter 13, this volume, on psychological service centers. In addition, programs have an obligation to set admission and graduation standards such that only the truly qualified enter and graduate. Finally, they must instill in their students the responsibility to advocate for the profession to preserve and enhance its standing.

Accountability is another burning issue in higher education. Professional psychology education has a head start on this one. The model of professional psychology training described in this book is a major achievement in making the goals and processes of professional psychology education highly visible and accountable. This is no "black box" of education. Professional programs hold themselves out as preparing students in a set of competencies

that are defined and measured. This is a highly accountable educational model. In addition, because of the APA-accreditation process and its emphasis on self-study and the assessment of programmatic and learning outcomes, professional psychology programs have a long record of demonstrating accountability to the profession. Furthermore, the more recent requirement for programs to publicize certain process and outcome measures, including licensure rates, contributes to greater accountability to the public. In this model, the next steps in demonstrating accountability are increased methods for assessing competencies, both for student in the program as well as graduates in the field.

The use of technology in professional psychology training is slowly expanding beyond supervisors' viewing of videotapes of practicum students and PowerPoint presentations in the classroom. Some programs are better preparing students for the future technology-enhanced life of a practitioner by introducing such things as electronic clinical records, automated systems to track clients' progress and treatment outcomes, Web-based treatment and psychoeducational programs, teleconferencing/supervision, and other forms of telehealth.

Online education is growing exponentially, expanding at nearly three times the rate of overall higher education enrollments (Allen & Seaman, 2007), and although it has been embraced by certain academic fields, professional psychology education has been slow to warm to the idea of distance education, particularly to fully online programs. There is a concern that although knowledge can be assessed via online education, attitudes and skills for professional practice cannot be easily taught, acquired, or assessed via online education. However, even with these concerns, the future is certain to bring major changes in the use of technology in professional psychology education (Rudestam & Schoenholtz-Read, 2002). The new wave of students grew up with technology, and they incorporate it into all aspects of life. While psychology educators may still be searching for how to "build community" online, college-age and younger students are doing it through text messaging and through Facebook and other social networking sites. At the other end of the age span, established practitioners have been successful in lobbying and getting approval to do required continuing education courses through online or other distance education means. So the press is on. Although face-to-face instruction will continue to be the norm in the foreseeable future, programs will be experimenting with more hybrid forms of education, that is, those that incorporate some aspects of distance education with the traditional face-to-face format (Rudestam, 2004). In higher education, learning management systems, such as Blackboard or Angel, are almost uniformly being adopted as a way for students to access coursework, participate in online discussions, take exams, and receive feedback, and 82% of students report having taken at least one class using such a course management system (Salaway, Caruso, & Nelson, 2007). Using video technology to connect stu-

dents to off-campus instructors or supervisors or to a group of students in a distant site is becoming more commonplace. Classes that include some face-to-face time as well as some online instruction are also becoming more common. The challenge for professional psychology programs is to evaluate whether and how the emerging technologies can be effectively incorporated into professional psychology training (Murphy, Levant, Hall, & Glueckauf, 2007). The goal is to ensure that such distance and online education technologies maintain or increase the quality and availability of instruction, enhance learning of the competencies, and ensure an emphasis not only on the knowledge part of competencies but also on the skill and attitude components.

In contrast to many other disciplines, particularly engineering, business, and the physical sciences, U.S. psychology programs have attracted fewer international students (Institute of International Education, 2007). Moreover, until recently, there were few opportunities for professional psychology students to study overseas or do practica and little interest on their part in doing so. However, things are changing. Recently, a number of professional programs have launched international initiatives by establishing academic programs, research programs, or clinical service practica overseas. Some of these were described at NCSPP's 2008 conference, Advancing the Multicultural Agenda: From Aspiration to Actualization, promoting an expansion of the diversity competency to include a focus on international issues. As the profession of psychology gains heightened stature and relevance in other countries, more international students will be interested in professional psychology programs. Training programs' international graduates as well as their international research and service initiatives will be the means for exporting the professional psychology education model, or parts of it, to other countries. In doing so, U.S. psychology must be sensitive to the degree to which the model is relevant to the professional, educational, and cultural practices in the different countries. Certainly, modifications to the model will be necessary to incorporate indigenous practices and cultural variables (Stevens & Wedding, 2004). However, these changes will benefit not only the international students but also U.S. students who need to be better prepared for the globalization of all facets of our society (see Leong & Leach, 2007, who discuss internationalizing counseling psychology in the United States). Future graduates will be practicing in a global society and, in contrast to earlier generations of psychologists, will have more opportunity and need to treat newly arrived immigrants to the United States, consult or do clinical practice abroad, access international populations for clinical research, and be involved with international societies and initiatives. Therefore, it will be important to incorporate training for the new international contexts, clients, and practices into the professional model.

The professional psychology educational model has guided the training of many psychologists over the past 3 decades. Not only has the training of

the graduates of professional psychology programs been defined by the model but also other clinical psychology programs, internships, and the profession at large have been shaped by various elements of the model, including its emphasis on clinical training and practica during graduate school (i.e., preinternship), competency-based education, multicultural training, and the explication of the local clinical scientist. Recent aspects of the model, such as advocacy training, and novel ways of implementing the model, such as through innovative types of internships (Emmons, Kenkel, Newman, Perl, & Mangione, 2006; Mangione et al., 2006), most assuredly will have similar impacts.

As the number of professional psychology programs in NCSPP has grown from 17 to 83, there has been greater differentiation in the institutional settings of the programs (Norcross et al., 2004) and in the application of the model. This differentiation has allowed potential students to find programs that best fit with their backgrounds (e.g., post-master's, mid-career, international, rural, religion-affiliated) and interests (e.g., child psychology, geropsychology, health psychology, forensic psychology). However, even with this differentiation, the core components and competencies of the model remain similar across programs. Because of the model's clarity, common adoption, and continuing development, the profession and the public can be assured that graduates from professional psychology programs possess the competencies needed for today's practice realities and tomorrow's clinical challenges.

REFERENCES

Albright, K. S. (2004). Environmental scanning: Radar for success. *The Information Management Journal, 38,* 38–45.

Allen, I. E., & Seaman, J. (2007). *Online nation: Five years growth in online learning.* Needham, MA: The Sloan Consortium. Retrieved February 28, 2009, from http://www.sloan-c.org/publications/survey/pdf/online_nation.pdf

Altbach, P. G. (2002, May/June). Perspectives on international higher education. *Change, 34,* 29–31.

American Psychological Association. (2007, February). New APA center analyzes psychology employment and training trends. *Monitor on Psychology, 38,* 15.

Constantine, M. G., & Ladany, N. (2000). Self-report multicultural counseling competence scales: Their relation to social desirability attitudes and multicultural case conceptualization ability. *Journal of Counseling Psychology, 47,* 155–164.

Emmons, L., Kenkel, M. B., Newman, G. H., Perl, R., & Mangione, L. (2006). A framework for half-time internship training in psychology. *Professional Psychology: Research and Practice, 37,* 643–650.

Finkel, M. J., Storaasli, R. D., Bandele, A., & Schaefer, V. (2003). Diversity training in graduate school: An exploratory evaluation of the Safe Zone project. *Professional Psychology: Research and Practice, 34,* 555–561.

Greenberg, S., & Jesuitus, L. (2003). *Study of the practice of licensed psychologists in the United States and Canada prepared for the Association of State and Provincial Psychology Boards.* New York: Professional Examination Service Department of Research and Development.

Institute of International Education. (2007). *Open Doors 2007.* Retrieved May 31, 2008, from http://www.opendoors.iienetwork.org

Institute of Medicine. (2008). *Retooling for an aging America.* Washington, DC: National Academies Press.

Johnson, W. B., & Campbell, C. D. (2004). Character and fitness requirements for professional psychologists: Training directors' perspectives. *Professional Psychology: Research and Practice, 35,* 405–411.

Kenkel, M. B., Deleon, P. H., Mantell, E. O., & Steep, A. E. (2005). Divided no more: Psychology's role in integrated health care. *Canadian Psychology/Psychologie Canadienne, 46,* 189–202.

Leong, F. T. L., & Leach, M. M. (2007). Internationalising counseling psychology in the United States: A SWOT analysis. *Applied Psychology: An International Review, 56,* 165–181.

Mangione, L., VandeCreek, L., Emmons, L., McIlvried, J., Carpenter, D.W., & Nadkarni, L. (2006). Unique internship structures that expand training opportunities. *Professional Psychology: Research and Practice, 37,* 416–422.

Murphy, M. J., Levant, R. F., Hall, J. E., & Glueckauf, R. L. (2007). Distance education in professional education in psychology. *Professional Psychology: Research and Practice, 38,* 97–103.

National Association for College Admission Counseling. (2007). *Balancing acts: How high school counselors view risks and opportunities of student loans.* Retrieved June 6, 2008, from http://projectonstudentdebt.org/files/pub/Balancing_Acts.pdf

National Council for Schools and Programs for Professional Psychology. (2006). *2005 NCSPP Self-Study with complementary data.* Retrieved March 3, 2009, from http://www.ncspp.info/resources.htm#self

Norcross, J. C., Castle, P. H., Sayette, M. A., & Mayne, T. J. (2004). The PsyD: Heterogeneity in practitioner training. *Professional Psychology: Research and Practice, 35,* 412–419.

Robiner, W. N., & Crew, D. (2000). Rightsizing the workforce of psychologists in health care: Trends from licensing boards, training programs, and managed care. *Professional Psychology: Research and Practice, 31,* 245–263.

Rozensky, R. H., Grus, C. L., Belar, C. D., Nelson, P. D., & Kohout, J. L. (2007). The psychology internship match: Changing the paradigm to move beyond the status quo. *Training and Education in Professional Psychology, 1,* 238–248.

Rudestam, K. E. (2004). Distributed education and the role of online learning in training professional psychologists. *Professional Psychology: Research and Practice, 35,* 427–432.

Rudestam, K. E., & Schoenholtz-Read, J. (Eds.). (2002). *Handbook of online learning: Innovations in higher education and corporate training.* Thousand Oaks, CA: Sage.

Salaway, G., Caruso, J. B., & Nelson, M. R. (2007). *The ECAR study of undergraduate students and information technology, 2007 (Research Study, Vol. 6)*. Boulder, CO: EDUCAUSE Center for Applied Research. Retrieved February 28, 2009, from http://www.educause.edu/ecar

Society for College and University Planning. (2006, December). *SCUP trends in higher education*. Retrieved May 31, 2008, from http://www.scup.org/pdf/SCUP_Trends_12-2006.pdf

Society for College and University Planning. (2007, July). *SCUP trends in higher education*. Retrieved May 31, 2008, from http://www.scup.org/pdf/SCUP_Trends_7-2007.pdf

Stevens, M. J., & Wedding, D. (2004). *The handbook of international psychology*. New York: Brunner-Routledge.

Talen, M. R., Fraser, J. S., & Cauley, K. (2005). Training primary care psychologists: A model for predoctoral programs. *Professional Psychology: Research and Practice, 36,* 136–143.

Tulkin, S. R., & Stock, W. (2004). A model for predoctoral psychopharmacology training: Shaping a new frontier in clinical psychology. *Professional Psychology: Research and Practice, 35,* 151–157.

U.S. Department of Education. (2006). *A test of leadership: Charting the future of U.S. higher education*. Washington, DC: Author.

Walpole. M. (2007). Economically and educationally challenged students in higher education: Access to outcomes. *ASHE Higher Education Reports, 33,* 1–144.

Wicherski, M., & Kohout, J. (2007, November). *2005 Doctorate Employment Survey*. Washington, DC: APA Center for Psychology Workforce Analysis and Research. Retrieved May 30, 2008, from http://research.apa.org/des05.html

Zweig, R. A., Siegel, L., & Snyder, R. (2006). Doctoral gero-psychology training in primary care: Preliminary findings from a clinical training project. *Journal of Clinical Psychology in Medical Settings, 13,* 21–29.

INDEX

ABOUT THE EDITORS

Mary Beth Kenkel, PhD, has been involved with the education and training of professional psychologists for the past 30 years, first at the California School of Professional Psychology (CSPP), where she started as faculty and then held many senior administrative positions, including chancellor of the Fresno campus, and then, since 2001, as dean of the College of Psychology and Liberal Arts at the Florida Institute of Technology.

Dr. Kenkel received a PhD in clinical psychology from Miami University (Ohio) after completing a clinical–community psychology internship at the Community Mental Health Center of Rutgers Medical School. Dr. Kenkel is a licensed psychologist and a Distinguished Practitioner and Member of the National Academies of Practice. Much of her research and writing has focused on finding effective ways of bringing mental health services to underserved populations, including rural areas, through innovative programs and community participation. She is a leader in the professional training area, having served as president of the National Council of Schools and Programs of Professional Psychology (1995–1996) and chairperson of two national NCSPP conferences (1995, 2003). As editor (2000–2006) of *Professional Psychology: Research and Practice*, she concentrated on publishing articles that presented current research findings or clinical knowledge and drew out the implications of that work to inform practicing psychologists, helping to close the gap between research and practice.

Dr. Kenkel is a fellow of the American Psychological Association (APA; Divisions 12, 27, 42) and has served on numerous committees within APA. She has been most involved in determining the societal and broader human resources issues affecting psychology and therefore has served on the APA Committee on Employment and Human Resources, the Committee on Rural Health, the Task Force on the Changing Gender Composition in Psychology, and the Task Force on Training Issues in the Emerging Market-

place, and she cochaired the Task Force on Women in Society and Technology. She was the recipient of the APA Presidential Citation in 2000 for her work and commitment to the education of current and future leaders in professional psychology.

Roger L. Peterson, PhD, is professor and chair of the Department of Clinical Psychology, Antioch University New England. He received a BA from Harvard University in 1966 and a PhD from Purdue University in 1971, after an internship at Duke University Medical Center. He is a Diplomate in Clinical Psychology, American Board of Professional Psychology (1999). Dr. Peterson is a past president of the National Council of Schools and Programs of Professional Psychology (1994–1995) and past co-chair of two national NCSPP conferences (1990, 1994). He has been a member of the Committee on Accreditation of the American Psychological Association (1999–2004) and is now a member of the Commission on Accreditation (2008–2009). He was editor of *The Core Curriculum in Professional Psychology* and senior author of "The National Council of Schools and Programs of Professional Psychology Educational Model" (1997) and is an associate editor of *Training and Education in Professional Psychology*. In 2008, Dr. Peterson received the National Council of Schools and Programs of Professional Psychology Distinguished Professional Psychologist Award for Exemplary Contributions to Professional Psychology Education. He is licensed in New Hampshire.